Filming the Modern Middle East

Filming the Modern Middle East

Politics in the Cinemas of Hollywood and the Arab World

Lina Khatib

Published in 2006 by I.B.Tauris & Co. Ltd
6 Salem Road, London W2 4BU
175 Fifth Avenue, New York NY 10010
www.ibtauris.com

In the United States and Canada distributed by Palgrave Macmillan
a division of St Martin's Press
175 Fifth Avenue, New York NY 10010

Library of Modern Middle East Studies 57

PB ISBN 10: 1 84511 191 5
PB ISBN 13: 978 1 84511 191 5
HB ISBN 10: 1 84511 192 3
HB ISBN 13: 978 1 84511 192 2

A full CIP record for this book is available from the British Library
A full CIP record for this book is available from the Library of Congress

Library of Congress catalog card: available

Typeset in Amasis by Keystroke, 28 High Street, Tettenhall, Wolverhampton
Printed and bound by TJ International, Padstow, Cornwall

To Fady
For the sun will eventually shine

Contents

List of Figures   ix

Acknowledgments   xi

Introduction: Orientalism and the Cinematic Middle East   1

Chapter I: The Politicized Landscape   15

Why space matters   15

Hollywood's spatial political stage   18

The spatial contradictions of Arab cinemas   33

Conclusion   60

Chapter II: Gendered Tools of Nationalism   63

The changing face of the American male/nation   64

The female nations of Arab cinemas   80

Conclusion   101

Chapter III: Conflicts Within and Without:
The Arab–Israeli Conflict (and the Gulf War)   105

Hollywood's America: world police   108

Arab cinemas: nostalgia and resistance   120

Conclusion   157

Chapter IV: From the Other Outside to the Other Within:
Representing Islamic Fundamentalism   165

Why fundamentalism matters   165

Hollywood's fundamentalist terrorists   173

Islamic fundamentalism in Egyptian and Algerian cinemas:
the Other within 183
Conclusion 197

Epilogue: On Difference, Resistance, and Nationalism **201**
On difference 201
On resistance 203
On nationalism 207
Beyond the East/West divide 209

Bibliography 211
Filmography 229
General Index 233
Index of Films 241

List of Figures

1. American helicopters descend on Yemen—*Rules of Engagement*   20
2. Arab-Americans forced into camps in *The Siege*   30
3. Ali in his barren space—*The Terrorist*   35
4. Said and his fundamentalist men—*Bab el-Oued City*   38
5. Fat'hallah chatting to Margaret on the internet—*The Other*   40
6. Graffiti in *Canticle of the Stones*   51
7. Um Ibrahim in her courtyard—*Ticket to Jerusalem*   53
8. The three men on their boat trip—*A Summer in la Goulette*   59
9. *Spy Game*'s larger-than-life American hero in Beirut   66
10. Iraqi women walk on milk-soaked ground—*Three Kings*   75
11. Sahar: the liberated nation as liberated woman—
    The Fertile Memory   93
12. Rana awaits her wedding—*Rana's Wedding*   94
13. Rachida after being attacked by Islamic fundamentalists—
    Rachida   96
14. The jewels turn to blood drops—*Tale of Three Jewels*   128
15. The Arafat balloon—*Divine Intervention*   133
16. *Divine Intervention*'s ninja fighter   133
17. Ahmad Zaki as Nasser—*Nasser*   137
18. The father's anger at his powerlessness—*Nights of the Jackal*   145
19. An Arab terrorist about to blow himself up in *Executive Decision*   176
20. *Iron Eagle*'s materialist Arab leader in gold-embroidered
    uniform   181
21. Hamada peering at female students through a hole in
    the classroom wall—*The Closed Doors*   189

Acknowledgments

I would like to thank Paula Saukko for her valuable advice that resonates throughout this book; my editor at I.B.Tauris, Philippa Brewster, without whose belief this book would not have been written; Naomi Sakr for her ongoing encouragement; John Ellis for his help in making this book happen; Annabelle Sreberny and Ziauddin Sardar for opening up this space for me; and my supportive family in the UK and Lebanon, especially my father Hekmat El-Khatib, who never objected to being summoned to selflessly help me research this book throughout the six years it took to materialize. I would also like to thank Yabous Productions, Rashid Masharawi, Neil Smith, and Zahera Harb for their assistance.

Finally, I would like to thank the British Academy for a grant to present the Introduction, "Orientalism and the Cinematic Middle East", at the MESA conference in 2005.

Part of Chapter I appeared as "The Politics of Space: The Spatial Manifestations of Representing Middle Eastern Politics in American and Egyptian Films." In *Visual Communication*, February 2004, Vol. 3, issue 1, pp. 69–90.

Part of Chapter II appeared as "The Orient and its Others: Women as Tools of Nationalism in Political Egyptian Cinema." In *Women and Media in the Middle East*, edited by Naomi Sakr, pp. 72–88 (London: I.B.Tauris, 2004).

Part of Chapter IV appeared as "Nationalism and Otherness: The Representation of Islamic Fundamentalism in Egyptian Cinema." In *European Journal of Cultural Studies*, January 2006, Vol. 9, issue 1, pp. 63–80.

Introduction: Orientalism and the Cinematic Middle East

The Middle East is at the heart of political debate today. With the events of September 11, 2001, the war on Iraq and shifting American interests in the on-going Palestinian–Israeli conflict, the Middle East has been perceived globally as a place of conflict that is no longer confined to its geographical setting. So while until recently intrinsic details about political matters in the Middle East were largely confined to a place outside the immediate Western imagination, today the media across the globe are granting the Middle East a central position. This applies not only to news coverage, but also to fiction.

Cinema, as a powerful tool of cultural production, stands at the heart of representation of the modern Middle East. One of the most salient angles of this representation is cinema's engagement with the depiction of politics in the region. This cinematic representation is not confined to Western cinema industries, like Hollywood. The Arab world has also engaged in the creation of such cinematic images. Over the last 25 years, both Hollywood and Arab cinemas have been prolific in producing films revolving around this theme. While those cinema industries often differ in the stance they present on various aspects of Middle Eastern politics, there are several connections that can be established between them. So while it is important to examine Hollywood's representation of the Middle East, with Hollywood being the most powerful film industry in the world, and with its representation of the politics of the Middle East forming at least part of people's imagination of the region, it is necessary to compare this with how Arabs represent themselves and Others through cinema. Egyptian cinema, for instance, is the biggest film industry in the Middle East. Egyptian films are distributed across the Arab world and are also watched by Arab expatriates globally. Palestinian cinema has recently emerged as a strong contender in the Arab world. It has produced a significant number of films that have been distributed globally and have given Palestine a new voice. Other Arab countries have also contributed to this cinematic representation, though to a lesser degree. Syria, Algeria, Lebanon, Morocco, and Tunisia have created films commenting on various aspects of Middle Eastern politics, from pan-Arab nationalism to Islamic fundamentalism to the Arab–Israeli conflict and the Gulf War.

The films made by all those industries, as texts, are therefore produced by history. Some authors like Conrad have stressed fiction's salience in history, by presenting fiction as a closer account of "events" than formal historical accounts. As he puts it,

> Fiction is history, or it is nothing. But it is also more than that; it stands on firmer ground, being based on the reality of forms and the observation of social phenomena, whereas history is based on documents, and the reading of print and handwriting—on second-hand impression. Thus fiction is nearer truth.
>
> (Conrad 1925, p. 17)

The position taken by this book, however, does not follow Conrad's distinction between formal history and history as fiction; it is not concerned with whether the films represent historical Truth or not. It thus diverges from ideas on the scientific determinism of history (as "oppressively exterior to human activity" [Lentricchia 1989, p. 231]) and into examining the complicated principle of causality. This principle is examined in terms of not only how the past affects the present, but also how the present affects the past. The films' linking of the past and the present then is examined as a form of knowledge, ideology, and power relations (Williams and Chrisman 1994). As Lehtonen (2000) puts it, "*Context does not exist before . . . the text, neither does it exist outside of* [it]" (p. 111). Moreover, the films do not constitute a kind of "representation" or "reflection" that is detached from a non-signifying "reality" or "historical background." This means that the films, the cinema industries, and political events all form part of a reality characterized by power/knowledge relations (Pecora 1989). The book thus follows Edward Said's (1993) contention in *Culture and Imperialism*, where he argues that narrative is the site in which struggle takes place, where people assert their identity and the existence of their history.

The films analyzed in this book cover the last 25 years—from 1980 till 2005—a period marked by several salient events in the political history of the modern Middle East. The 1980s are bounded by the Iranian Islamic Revolution in 1979, and are punctuated with events like the Israeli invasion of Lebanon in 1982, and the attacks against a group of American marines in Beirut in 1983. The decade saw divisions among Arabs, triggered by Egyptian president Anwar Sadat's signing of the Camp David Accords in 1978. The 1980s also saw an increase in PLO engagement in various anti-Israeli activities, including the hijacking of airplanes. Plane hijacking was also practiced by Lebanese Islamist groups (Hizbullah and Amal), such as the hijacking of the TWA flight in 1985. The Palestinian *intifada* started in 1987, and with it Hamas and other Islamic fundamentalist groups inside and outside Palestine started or took advantage of the situation to intensify their activities. The eruption of the Gulf War in 1989 re-established the United States' control in the region. In 1993, Islamic fundamentalists planted a bomb in the World Trade Center, and their increasing influence in the Middle East and beyond has made them a force not to be ignored by the United States, which saw Islamic fundamentalism as a direct threat. This has reached its peak with the events of September 11, 2001. Finally, throughout the past two and a half decades, the Arab–Israeli conflict has continued, in various forms, with efforts towards peace being put in place and not quite realized.

More often than not, the films analyzed have concerned themselves with the salient political issues of the time, and therefore cannot be discussed in isolation from this historical framework. As Foucault argues, "[a]ny discourse, whatever it be, is constituted by a set of utterances which are produced each in its place and time" (1979, p. 19). The films' relationship with history is subjective. This means that the same historical event is given different, often contradictory, interpretations in Hollywood and Arab cinemas. Perhaps the most salient example is the Arab–Israeli conflict, with Palestinian resistance interpreted as mere terrorism (or, at best, a "revolution") in Hollywood, while it is portrayed sympathetically in Arab cinemas. A similar point can be made about Hollywood's representation of Islamic fundamentalism, where fundamentalism is conflated with terrorism on one hand and with Islam on the other hand. This is contrasted with how Egyptian and Algerian cinemas portray fundamentalism from other angles (social, personal) ignored by Hollywood, and their distinction between Islam and the extremism of Islamic fundamentalism. The 1973 October War is represented as a threat to American oil interests in Hollywood, but as a celebrated victory in Egyptian cinema. The analysis thus pays attention to the various Truths constructed in the context of history by the films. The book's highlighting of the different ways historical events are represented destabilizes fixed interpretations of those events. This denaturalizes the various binaries the films present (East versus West, barbaric versus civilized), and shows how the Truths constructed by each side about the Self and Others are produced by specific historical contexts (Saukko 2003). Therefore, the book highlights not only how history can be read differently from different angles, but also how history can be written differently from different angles. The films are thus shown to present alternative histories that are rooted in the political agendas of each side, and that aim at the construction of alternative futures for the United States and the Arab world respectively (Clifford 1997b).

In this context, it is important to go beyond familiar discourse on the representation of the Middle East in cinema. This familiar discourse has often located this representation within the framework of Orientalism. While it is important to study how the West represents the East, it is even more crucial to see how the "Orient" represents itself. Comparing Hollywood's and Arab cinemas' engagement in filming the modern Middle East both affirms and disturbs the focus on Western dominance often witnessed in discourses on the East. Moreover, juxtaposing Hollywood with Arab cinemas establishes a link between discourses of the "West" and those of the "East." This breaks away from the more common frameworks of victimization or celebration of the "East" as well as from the analysis of regional cinemas in isolation.

It is impossible to ignore the contribution of Edward Said's 1978 book *Orientalism* to current discourse on the cinematic Middle East. Said's work shows how Orientalism implies that there exists a primordial difference between the West and the East. This constructed difference has been implanted in relations of power between the West and the East, whereby the first dominates the second, and where the East is constructed as the West's Other and the source of its identity. Thus the West uses the East, perceived in terms of lack and inferiority, to form its superior identity. Orientalist discourse uses this argument to justify the West's control over the East, portraying the East as in need of Western dominance and definition as it is incapable of defining itself.

Said (1978) looks at Orientalism as a multifaceted discourse charac- terized by four major ideas which he calls "dogmas of Orientalism." First, there is an absolute and systematic difference between the Orient (irrational, undeveloped, inferior) and the West (rational, developed, superior). Thus, the West defines itself as the opposite of the Orient. In the 1999 American film *The Mummy*, for example, Egyptian Arabs are comically portrayed as ignorant, cowardly, and barbaric (for instance, being referred to as "smelly like camels"), while American characters in contrast are portrayed as "civilized" (being composed, acting logically and bravely in the face of a mummy that accidentally comes back to life). The West is portrayed not only as the diametrical opposite of the East, but also as its protector and its carer. This can be seen in the film *Three Kings*, for instance, where American soldiers rescue Iraqi civilians from their Iraqi suppressors. Moreover, the Orient is constructed in terms of lack (of power, morals). This is portrayed in several Hollywood films depicting Arab terrorism, such as *Hostage*, in which we see an Arab plane hijacker not only raping an American female flight attendant, but also killing a mother on board the plane who is trying to shield her son from the terrorist's violence. At the end of the film the Arab terrorists are eventually captured by an American hero, suggesting the terrorists' ultimate lack of power. In this way Orientalism fetishizes the Other, reducing him/her to a set of essentialist variables that are often contradictory.

Second, abstractions about the Orient are preferable to direct evidence (Said 1978). Orientalism has lumped the non-West into one large entity, disregarding the vast differences among non-Western cultures, in terms of religion, social structure, and values, thereby creating a fictional monolithic Orient. Edward Said sees this phenomenon as a way of maintaining the superiority of the West over the East. Said argues that the mere fact of using the terminology "Orient versus Occident," presenting the two as being endpoints on the pole of analysis, results in widening the gap between them: "the Oriental becomes more Oriental, the Westerner more Western" (Said 1978, p. 46). He argues that such terminology does not "correspond to . . . [a] stable reality that exists as a natural fact" (Said 1978, p. 331). One example of the monolithic Orient is the concept of Arabia—that all Arab countries are uniform and poised against the West. This is reflected in a number of Hollywood films depicting the Middle East, whereby Arab characters are not assigned a particular nationality or even a particular Arabic accent or dialect, as seen in *True Lies* for example.

Said presents the third dogma as the idea that the Orient is eternal, uniform, and incapable of defining itself, and that therefore a generalized Western vocabulary to describe the Orient is "scientifically objective" (Said 1978, p. 301). This is another way by which the West tries to justify its hegemony over the East. By giving something the status of scientific truth, one is actually making it unchallengeable. This denies any kind of resistance to such a notion. This is again seen in films like *The Mummy* (1999), where the cinema of mystery (mummies coming back to life) is mixed with "realism" (casting one of the leading characters—a British woman—as an expert on Egyptology; using authentic-looking scenery). This use of authenticity corresponds with Lant's argument on photographs of the East; he argues that images "taken outside Europe and exhibited within Europe [the West, generally] functioned as symbols for taking possession and could thereby assuage the 'irresistible desire for spaces to conquer'" (1997, p. 77).

Finally, the Orient is something to be feared or controlled. This is perhaps best presented in the American film *The Siege* (1998), where the Orient is both feared (through the association of Arabs with American-threatening Islamic fundamentalist terrorism) and controlled (the American army declaring martial law in New York and placing all Arabs in camps until terrorists are found). Thus, Said states that the relationship between the Orient and the Occident is that of domination and hegemony, and it "is hegemony . . . that gives Orientalism . . . durability and strength" (Said 1978, p. 7).

Said further argues that Orientalism is characterized by how "the . . . [Orientalist] *writes* about, whereas the [Oriental] is *written* about" (1978, p. 308). "Writing" refers to how it is the West that creates discourse about the East, and not vice versa. The Orient is thus constructed as a silent Other, an object that is incapable of defining or representing itself, and that is therefore in need of Western subjectivity. This objectification is also seen in how the Orient is presented as "a metaphor for sexuality," namely through the portrayal of Oriental women. These women are often shown to be veiled and yet exposed, such as the scene in the 1995 movie *Don Juan de Marco* where all 1,500 wives of the sultan gather naked in a Turkish bath. Ella Shohat argues that "this process of exposing the female Other . . . [allegorizes] the Western masculinist power of possession, that she, as a metaphor for her land, becomes available for Western penetration and knowledge" (Shohat 1997b, pp. 32–33).

This brings us to the issue of representation. According to Said, Orientalism has created a representation of the Orient which serves to justify the *actions* of the Occident. Applying that to cinema, one may argue that the representation of Arabs in Hollywood films is a creation aimed at preserving the status quo of the United States as a world policeman controlling, among others, Arabs and Arab countries. Said says that

> the representation of other societies and peoples involved an act of power by which images of them were in a sense created by the Western observer who constructed them as peoples and societies to be ruled and dominated, not as objects to be understood passively, objectively or academically.
>
> (Said 1987, quotation from the original English typescript)

Said (1993) sees the position of the United States as unique in this context. As he puts it, "all cultures tend to make representations of foreign cultures . . . to master or in some way control them. Yet not all cultures make representations of foreign cultures *and* in fact master or control them" (1993, p. 120). Hollywood can be seen as an ideological tool that maintains American domination in world politics.

While Orientalism is important as a framework for understanding the workings of the East/West divide, it carries several shortcomings, which have triggered an intellectual debate outlining this criticism. First, as Porter (1994) and Windschuttle (1999) argue, Said implies the uniformity of Orientalist discourse over time and hence makes "nonsense of history" (Porter 1994, p. 152). Porter argues that, when social and historical differences are transformed into universal differences, when, for example, moral difference is constructed as inferiority, we fail to look at hegemony as "process." Hegemony is not fixed; it manifests itself in fluid forms which maintain its existence. Thus we can see the cinematic Otherness of Arabs surviving through its transformation from being about the womanizer/seducer of the 1920s in films like *The Sheik*, to being about the terrorist of today.

Second, Landow (2002) adds that Said's discourse makes generalizations about the Orient when it is focused on the Middle East. This view is shared by Kerr (1980), who argued that Said's conclusions are limited and therefore cannot be generalized as applying to the whole of what he defines as the "Orient." Third, Said's view on Orientalism implies that the West is ideologically uniform. Porter (1994) argues that the hegemonic unity perceived by Said in Orientalist discourse blinds him to the heterogeneity of such discourse and the possibility that this discourse itself contains ideological contradictions. This can, for example, be applied to the ambivalence experienced in American foreign policy as portrayed in the Hollywood films analyzed in this book. On one hand, the United States has taken what seems like a tough disciplinary stance, illustrated in films like *Navy Seals*, where military action is America's preferred method of maintaining world order. On the other hand, with the New World Order, the United States has had to justify its military action as being about rescue rather than conquering. Films about the Gulf War, *In the Army Now* and *Three Kings*, illustrate this by portraying American military presence in the Gulf as a rescue mission.

Fourth, Porter (1994) moves to saying that Said's discourse eliminates the possibility of the existence of resistance or counterhegemonic practices within Western discourse. While Hollywood, as analyzed in this book, appears to have adopted an Othering stance towards politics in the Middle East, we should not assume, to emphasize a point by Sardar and Davies

(2003), that that is the only stance projected from the United States through cinema in particular and popular culture in general. Examples that spring to mind are Michael Moore's documentaries *Bowling for Columbine* and *Fahrenheit 9/11*, and Bill Hicks's stand-up comedy shows, which have often been televised and sold on video. Those products, in addition to various others, from books to music, challenge dominant American discourse on the Middle East. Therefore, while this book concerns itself with Hollywood, it is important to bear the limitation of this selection in mind.

Fifth, another complication in Said's discussion of Orientalism is the idea that the West writes while the Orient is written about. In the first place, this view implies that Western colonialism is unique, and therefore disregards how colonialism may be exercised by the East as well (like the Ottoman Empire) (Landow 2002). In the second place, not only does focusing solely on the West's depiction of the East enforce the notion of the East as an object, but such a totalizing notion also eliminates any chance of resistance by the non-West. This complicates arguments such as Sardar's, where he states that "Western culture has always been obsessed with representation" (1998, p. 28). Western culture has had a history of placing the East as the object of the gaze, but this does not deny the active role of the non-West in engaging in representation itself. However, while this book shows how the East is also capable of representation (whether of the Self or the Other), it does not infer that the East is "innocent." Halliday (1995) agues that the Middle East is as much responsible for perpetuating myths as the "West" is. Halliday warns about the existence of what he calls "Eastoxification," "the uncritical reproduction of myths about the region in the name of anti-imperialism" (1995, p. 214). The non-West therefore has the capability of looking at the West as an Other as well (as demonstrated by the Egyptian film *Hello America*, for example, which demonizes the United States as a land of crime and immorality). As Porter (1994) argues, this point unsettles subject/object binaries by alternating who is cast on each side of the binary.

Finally, underlying Said's discourse on Orientalism is the assumption of the East's innocence, not only in relation to the West as mentioned above, but, perhaps more importantly, in the context of the Orient itself (Ahmad 1994). Said's discourse on Orientalism discusses in great detail how the West sees the East as an Other, but it does not examine—though it recognizes—the vast differences and conflicts that exist within the East itself. By this I mean that, although Said did mention that the Orient is not *an* Orient (as discussed earlier), he did not take his discussion further. He did not look at how there are power struggles within the Orient itself, and how these power struggles have represented a logic that is not so different from that of Orientalism. The Orient encompasses various socio-economic, gender, and political stratifications that Said's theory does not pay attention to (Landow 2002). These power struggles demonstrate how each side in a struggle views the rest as Others. Within the Arab world, for example, Arab countries have often engaged in struggles among themselves, and tensions and attempts at domination have existed among several countries until today.

Applied to cinema, those shortcomings have meant that, while a significant number of *Orientalism*-based studies have been conducted on representations of the Middle East and the politics behind them, the number of studies done on the way the Middle East represents itself cinematically, namely the way it represents politics, is comparatively infinitesimal. This does not mean that the Middle East has not engaged in such cinematic activities. Part of the problem lies in the culture of victimization that has spread across the Middle East, and that has catalyzed several projects on the stereotyping of Arabs and Muslims, but has turned a blind eye to the other side of the formula. Paradoxically, this has meant that those studies have involuntarily sustained the legacy of Orientalism, by fixing the Middle East as defenseless and objectified. This has also meant that the gap between the "East" and the "West" has been maintained. To sum up, the issue of "us" versus "them" is far more complicated than any theory can summarize. For within the "them" there could be several more "thems." And certainly any attempt at analyzing the East versus West issue that starts with assuming that the East (or the West) is "struggle free" is romanticizing and simplistic. We need to examine how both sides have engaged in representation and in constructing the Other, and how this representation is part of a broader nationalist/resistant agenda.

In what follows, I will therefore be examining how Middle Eastern politics is represented in 70 American and Arab films. The research covers virtually all the Hollywood films from 1980 till 2005 about the subject— 23 films in total—while most of the analysis of Arab cinemas focuses on

Egyptian cinema, as this industry has been the most prolific in producing films about Middle Eastern politics, releasing around 24 films about the subject in the last 25 years. Palestinian cinema, though a young cinema compared to Egypt's, is fast establishing itself as an important contender in the region, producing a significant number of feature films representing the Palestine issue, 12 of which are analyzed in this research (as it has been difficult to obtain copies of or to view some of the others, like Kassem Hawal's *Return to Haifa* [1980], considered to be the first Palestinian feature film ever made, and Rashid Masharawi's *Haifa* [1990]). The rest of the Arab cinemas have produced a few relevant films, which are examined in this research: three films each from Syria and Tunisia (the latter including two short films released as segments in the multi-directed *The Gulf War . . . What Next?*); two films each from Algeria and Lebanon (one of the latter's again being part of the above collection of shorts); and one film from Morocco, also released as part of *The Gulf War . . . What Next?* Therefore, although the word "cinema" is used to refer to the films from different countries, it is important to recognize that the films do not always represent industries as a whole, and do not necessarily reflect the Arab world as a region. Furthermore, a number of Arab cinemas have not engaged or have limited their engagement with the politics of the Middle East because of censorship, the desire to avoid sensitive issues, the concern with attracting wide audiences, or industry limitations (for example, there are no cinema industries to speak of in most of the Arab Gulf). The analysis poses a number of questions: How do the representations of aspects of Middle Eastern politics differ between the different cinemas, and how do they converge? Taking into consideration the global transparency of Hollywood narratives, what challenges do Arab cinemas produce in their representations of the same issues covered by Hollywood? How are the representations of the various political issues covered by the films linked to their countries' national agendas?

Much of the political debate on the Middle East revolves around space. Space in this context is not only part of people's identity, but also a dynamic tool often utilized to define the identity of nations. *Chapter I* analyzes the different ways the films construct and understand space in the context of Middle Eastern politics. Hollywood's relationship with space— a relationship about mastery, mirroring America's "from above" approach to Middle Eastern politics—is contrasted with the Arab films' more intimate portrayal of space, where conflicts are more localized and closer to home. Thus space is explored as both a physical and a mental/imagined/lived entity. Through analysis of issues like the representation of the Arab–Israeli conflict and Islamic fundamentalism in the films and their spatial manifestations, it is demonstrated that political space is not a matter of core versus periphery, where "we" reside within a space and "they" outside it; rather, old boundaries have been erased while new ones have been (re)drawn.

Chapter II discusses gender as a tool of nationalism across the films. The chapter explores gender representations of Arab countries and the United States in their respective cinemas. The Egyptian films construct a mother/whore binary where the Egyptian nation is symbolized by wholesome femininity, while sexually aloof women are used to symbolize the foreign enemy: Israel and the United States. At the same time, Algerian and Egyptian films use gender as a mark of modernity, the latter symbolizing the oppression of Islamic fundamentalism through the representation of silent, veiled women while highlighting fundamentalism's immorality through depicting the hypocrisy of Islamic fundamentalist men in their relations with women in general. In contrast, the films present images of modern, active women who symbolize the modern face of Egypt and Algeria. Palestinian cinema, on the other hand, links the liberation of the country with that of women. Hollywood constructs the American nation as male. There has been a historical/political shift in the way this male has been imagined, moving from the image of the virile, statuesque male in the 1980s that constructs the American nation as the world policeman, to the image of the "new man" in the 1990s and beyond, where the United States is placed as a tough yet caring global force. Essential Arab enemies are also represented as male in the Hollywood films, making the conflict between the United States and Arab countries in the films one between masculinities. The lack of communication between the imaginations of the United States and the Arab countries and their Others in their respective cinemas is demonstrated.

Chapters III and *IV* analyze the three main political themes portrayed in the films: the Arab–Israeli conflict, the Gulf War, and Islamic fundamentalism. Those themes are analyzed not only because most of the films focus on them, but also because they form the core of Middle Eastern politics throughout the historical period covered by the study. *Chapter III* focuses on the representation of the Arab–Israeli conflict and, to a lesser extent, the Gulf War in the films. It explores Hollywood's construction of the Arab–Israeli conflict as an ethnic one, where Israelis and Palestinians are portrayed as clashing ethnic groups fighting over the same homeland, while largely ignoring the oppression of Palestinians by Israeli settlers. The role of the United States is represented in the films as a godfather aiming at restoring peace in the region, and therefore as a superior political actor. This is compared with the Egyptian, Syrian, and Palestinian cinemas' focus on the plight of Palestinians on one hand, and the role of Syria and Egypt as Arab leaders within the conflict on the other hand. The resurrection of pan-Arabism in this context transforms the latter's films into an ironic statement that ignores Egypt's peace treaty with Israel. In this sense, the various sides' representations of the conflict ultimately serve nationalist agendas, emphasizing the role of the United States as a world leader on one hand, and that of Egypt and Syria as crucial Arab players on the other hand. The limited representation of the Gulf War in Arab cinemas is also discussed as an example further destabilizing the ideal of pan-Arab nationalism.

Arab culture has often become a synonym for Islamic fundamentalism in contemporary Western culture, from films to news to social theory. *Chapter IV* focuses on the representation of Islamic fundamentalism in the films. Islamic fundamentalism is examined not as a "reaction" to global-ization and its discontents, but as being global in itself and bearing its own "discontents." Egypt, Algeria, and the United States have both different and convergent points of view on these "discontents," constructing Islamic fundamentalism as an enemy yet configuring this enemy differently. So while Hollywood seems to create/reflect the idea of Islam/Arabism/Middle East as terrorism, Egyptian and Algerian cinemas present a more complex and psychological view of Islamic fundamentalism. Islamic fundamentalism is thus presented as the prime manifestation of the complexity of power relations in the Middle East as highlighted by the films. Its Otherness status makes it not only an enemy to the West, but also a threat to national integrity in Egypt and Algeria. It thus shows that the Orient's Others do not come only from the outside, but that the Orient can also exclude elements of "itself" as an Other as well, therefore taking us beyond a simplistic East/West divide.

The Politicized Landscape

I

The Politicized Landscape

Why space matters

Much of the political debate in the Middle East revolves around space. Space, both physical and imagined, is not only part of the identity of people, but also a dynamic tool often utilized to define the identity of nations. As Lefebvre argues, "space is produced by social relations that it also reproduces, mediates, and transforms" (Natter and Jones 1997, p. 148). Space thus is constantly in flux and carries multiple meanings. It is not a given, a neutral stage upon which history is played out. It is part of history and culture, constantly being defined and redefined. In other words, space is a cultural process through which "pasts erupt into the present" (Gregory 1997, p. 228). There has been a considerable degree of conflict over space and, indeed, (re)defining space is an act of power (this has most obviously been seen in the mapping done by Europe on other parts of the world).

Cinematic representation of space is here analyzed as an example of the exercise of power. The ways different cinemas understand space are different. While Hollywood seems to attempt to use space as the stage upon which political conflicts are fought, i.e. space as background, Arab cinemas pay more attention to the way space is part of political conflicts, i.e. space as foreground. The term "background" here is not used to imply that space in Hollywood has no meaning; rather, the term is used to indicate that space in those films plays a secondary, or a supplementary, role to that of "historical" (or action) events. This view of space as background is an example of the obsession with history as "playwright" (Carter 1995, p. 375) as pointed out by Soja and Foucault. Carter (1995) argues that this reduction of space to a stage is an illustration of what he calls imperial history, a history that ignores the lived experiences of space by the people who inhabit it.

Most of the American films analyzed belong to the action genre, a genre characterized by a masculine, open space. Hollywood's relationship with space here is one about mastery, relying heavily on open, wide, and aerial shots of action occurring outdoors. On the other hand, the Arab films are dramas and melodramas. The Egyptian melodramas are largely confined to feminine, indoor spaces. The rest of the Arab films look at space, whether indoors or outdoors, from the inside. It is a much more intimate portrayal of space. This use of space is parallel to the ways the two sides deal with the various political issues involved. Thus, America's approach to Middle Eastern politics as portrayed in the films is from "above," suggesting mastery over the politics and over the Other regions where the conflicts are played out. It parallels the United States' constantly expanding political frontiers. The Arab countries' approach, on the contrary, is one from "below," where the conflicts are naturally more localized and physically closer to home.

This empirical analysis aims at problematizing the representation of space in the cinemas. Space often passes unnoticed in cinema, becoming naturalized and/or fixed in our imagination as a given. The analysis will "denaturalize" space through contrasting the cinemas' use of space and how that is related to the films' political nature. The cinemas' use of space, while not necessarily oppositional, reflects different approaches to common political issues. The spatial manifestations of representing Middle Eastern politics thus underscore the countries' divergent political agendas.

Space, identity, and culture

Space is a question of power (Foucault 1970). Where once the colonizers' representation of the Other landscape was an example of knowledge as power, through practices like travel writing, mapping, and naming, the films' portrayal of space is a more recent, yet parallel, illustration. Films enable the criticism and the reordering of the geographical imaginations of the world (Lury and Massey 1999). In doing so, films can create space as well as deny it. The films analyzed here represent and classify space in different ways, but the inherent similarity in both the American and the Arab films is the importance of the role that space plays in the construction of national identities and in fighting political battles.

The main idea to remember when analyzing space is that space is not fixed; its dynamic representation in the films is an example of how space is constantly in the process of being produced (Lefebvre 1991). This means that space is "an active component of constructing, maintaining, and challenging social order" (Liggett 1995, p. 245). Moreover, space itself is a cultural construction. The meanings of a space are based on the social power structure of the culture representing those meanings (Rose 1992). Space becomes a question of difference, where differences between cultures/spaces are socially constructed (Soja and Hooper 1993). The concept of space as difference draws attention to the instability of space and how it is differently configured by different people in order to affirm different identities. Space is not just a tool for constructing identities; it is here that spaces become places that have personalities that are part of the people's identities (Nietschmann 1993). Space thus is contested. The same space that is a source of identity for one group (for example Palestinian land for the Israelis) is used as a point of differentiation from Others (Palestinians), while it is also a source of identity for those same Others. The same applies to Islamic fundamentalists in Egypt and Algeria. Cairo and Algiers, for example, are physical and cultural centers for the actions of the countries' moderates, but they are the same spaces that host their Others. In this way, we can no longer speak of perceived or conceived space (Lefebvre 1991) in uniform ways. It is no longer a matter of core versus periphery, where the "us" reside within the space and the "them" outside it. For we are speaking about the same space here. The issue is that this space is constructed subjectively as place. Space thus is not an *object* of discourse that is spoken for (by the films, by the people [re]claiming it) and that does not represent itself (as argued by Beauregard 1995). Space is dynamic and demands attention.

Hence we cannot speak of an "abstract" landscape or space without also paying attention to its "lived" constituents (Lefebvre 1991). This has prompted Sauer to formulate the term "cultural landscape" (in Hirsch 1995, p. 9). This is because a study of space cannot be reduced to "an empirical notion of objects-in-space" (Shields 1997, p. 186). In other words, it is important to examine space not only as material but also as a socially produced system of representation "through which that materiality both embeds and conveys social meaning" (Natter and Jones 1997, p. 151). Moreover, if we are to argue that all places have an identity, we should pay attention to the location of this identity not only in a larger social and historical framework (Soja 1996), but also within a framework of other spaces' identities. Morley (1999) explains that we should not turn to separate, internalized histories in order to discern the identity of places (as, I argue, in the Hollywood films), but rather see a place's uniqueness as "a point of intersection in a wider network of relations" (p. 157). This does not refer to understanding place as antagonistic to other places, but as linked to them. The Other place here is not seen as a threat from which a place should be protected, but as forming part of the identity of the place. This challenges existing dichotomies about inside/outside, center and periphery, because the line between the two is hard to define. This is perhaps best illustrated in bell hooks's (1990) ideas about margins, in her book *Yearning*. She argues that, when the people on the margin actively engage with the center and the margin at the same time (by that I mean recognizing the political complexities of the relation between margin and center and trying to make sense of it), i.e. when the margin becomes a site of resistance, it no longer is an Other space. This is because the notion Other invokes objectification; hooks undoes the inside/outside binary by arguing that the margin can also be empowering.

Hollywood's spatial political stage

In his book *Orientalism*, Edward Said introduces the term "imagined geographies" (1978, p. 55) to denote (to borrow a phrase from Driver and Rose 1992, p. 4) the "maps of meaning" that colonizers created to make sense of Other land(s) like the Middle East. In this sense, countries become subjective creations (Freeman 1999). Yet the colonizers' view was that their imagined geographies were scientific and objective (as in the writings of Mary Kingsley; see Blunt 1994a and 1994b). Hollywood's representation of Other spaces does not diverge greatly from this path. The Middle Eastern Other spaces represented in Hollywood are political and ideological, yet viewed from a distance that invokes a sense of objectivity. This is established through the use of various camera shots that in turn constitute space in this particular way: aerial shots, wide-angle shots, radar views, "targeting" views, penetration views, and panning shots. The different camera shots in turn construct the Other space in various forms: as an object, as a target, as wilderness, as an urban jungle, and as a barrier/border to be crossed. In what follows, I will examine each of those forms with reference to the particular films analyzed.

Imagining the landscape

Objectifying the Other space

Our first experience of San'a in *Rules of Engagement* is a feeling of floating over the city. Masses of solemn houses, yellowish in the twilight, appear suddenly on the screen and jerk us from Wake Island in the Indian Ocean to Yemen. We soon realize that the view we are seeing is that of the American marines arriving in helicopters after a Yemeni terrorist attack on the American embassy in San'a. The helicopters' descent upon the city recalls the opening of Riefenstahl's *Triumph of the Will*, where the first thing we see is an aerial view from Hitler's plane as it flies over and comes down on Germany. Just like Hitler is positioned as God, the American marines' spatial representation bestows upon them an element of glory. At the same time, this representation invokes a sense of mastery over the Other landscape. The Other landscape is thus objectified by the American gaze. This scientific gaze denies a representation of the intricacies of the Other space, and hence its "lived" aspects. Keiller comments:

> the higher we ascend . . . the more we can see, but the less we know
> about events beneath . . . it seems that it is the things that we don't

Figure 1   American helicopters descend on Yemen—*Rules of Engagement*

see that are most important to the depiction of spatial experience in the films.

(1982, p. 48)

The invocation of American mastery is also established through the use of the radar view as seen in *Iron Eagle*. The film presents several images of American fighter plane radar screens depicting computerized images of Other landscapes that are intercut with aerial shots of the Arab deserts below. The opening sequence of *The Siege*, a film depicting Islamic fundamentalist terrorism in the heart of the USA, contains images of radar screens monitoring the movement of an Islamic fundamentalist sheikh's car in the Saudi desert. The radar view shots do not depict the car in its actual form, but rather as a point in motion on the radar screen. As if to validate the radar's view, shots of the sophisticated radar screen are intercut with shots of the Mercedes as it glides through the sand dunes of the expansive Saudi desert. High angle shots of the car moving in the arid land from the right- to the left-hand side of our screen further establish the car and the sheikh, who is meant to represent Osama bin Laden, as objects of American scientific scrutiny. Blunt (1994a) sees this surveillance as an act of authority. *The Siege*'s spatial depiction of this mastery is then twofold. First is the above-mentioned surveillance; second is the enabling of a physical pene- tration of the desert, with American spies having gone through the desert to set up a trap to capture the sheikh. In this sense, the unknown Other space is defined in terms of lack (of power) (Massey 1993), which legitimates control over the landscape (Rose 1992).

Targeting the Other space

Sometimes the Other space is represented as a target. This is particularly seen in situations where American soldiers go into Other countries/ landscapes. *Navy Seals*, a film where American marine troops are summoned to Lebanon to rescue a load of American missiles from the hands of militants, is an illustration. The film emphasizes the superiority of the American Seals over the Lebanese militias in the various fight sequences. The fighting takes place in Beirut, depicted as not much more than a mass of rubble and a shambles. Beirut is meant to function as a generally passive background in the film, where the Americans victoriously encounter the Lebanese militias. Seals penetrate the unknown landscape, hiding behind crumbling walls as they shoot their enemy. In their search for the missiles, they break into warehouses, slamming the doors open, and examining the space from every angle. The camera follows the soldiers as they go in, pans their angered faces, and lingers on the damage caused by their urgent search. When the soldiers shoot, the camera takes their side and portrays their targeting point of view. The Seals' bullets hit their targets, but also penetrate the urban landscape, adding to its existing symptoms of war: bomb and bullet holes penetrating everything, the walls, the buildings, even the roads. The space may be a background in the story, but it does carry with it the horrific aspects of war. The film does not explain how or why the missiles got to Lebanon. The focus remains on the pleasure derived from action sequences and on glorifying America (with the Seals finally succeeding in their mission).

The conflict could have been anywhere, and the narrative is a classic one about the fight between good and evil.

Yet the space need not always be visually present to be targeted. Sometimes targeting is invoked in the unseen. An illustration of this is found in *Courage under Fire*, a film depicting the quest of an American colonel to find out whether a pilot killed during the Gulf War deserves the Medal of Honor for her courage. Iraq during the Gulf War in the film is never given the privilege of a mid shot or closer. Instead, we see hazy images of arid landscape where fighting is taking place between American and faceless Iraqi soldiers. That the landscape is at the heart of the conflict seems to make little difference in the film. Again, the focus is on American heroism, relegating space to a secondary position. The targeting thus is represented indirectly, resembling military computer games where the enemy is reduced to a symbolic representation depicting a "clean war" (Ryan and Kellner 1990).

The ideology of wilderness

One of the most commonly used images of Arabia is that of the desert. The desert is a classic example of the opposition between nature and science (Rose 1992), between wilderness and civilization. Sometimes this distinction is depicted literally, with juxtaposing images of progressive, (sub)urban space and desolate wilderness (Short 1991). *Rules of Engagement* heavily relies on this, with sharp editing that moves between the jungles of Vietnam, leafy American suburbs and the Yemeni desert. The desert is also used as a signpost that serves both the narrative and the American political agenda. It acts as an icon (Nietschmann 1993) that is reduced to a set of transferable "imaginative associations" (Freeman 1999, p. 58). The narrative is served because the desert is an example of a classic binary (barbarism versus civilization); the political agenda is served because the desert is invested with ideology. It is not only—being "foreign"—a "condition of excitement" (ibid.), but also a condition of fear. Fear is transposed to the people who inhabit the desert. They are seen as "native" to the desert, i.e. they are naturalized as part of the landscape (Gupta and Ferguson 1992), or as a reflection of what wilderness represents (Short 1991). In *In the Army Now*, American soldiers Bones and co. find themselves on a mission in the Libyan desert, trying to evict invading Libyans from Chad. The desert is inhabited by soldiers who are as savage as the land they occupy. Speaking roughly, dressed roughly, and treating the Americans roughly, they seem to display the qualities of what is seen as the opposite of civilization, even though they possess such technological advances as weapons and television (which they use to get news from CNN). In *Into the Sun*, the desert is compared to the American Wild West. After American fighter pilot Shotgun's plane is shot down in an "Arabian" desert, he is taken by Bedouins to a military base. The Bedouins transport Shotgun and his mate Tom Slade in a jeep through the desert, playing a country music track on the car radio. The Bedouins sing along "you're looking at me, you're looking at country" as they refer to their hostages as "American cowboys." Here, as Baudrillard explains, the desert can be associated with the figure of the non-human or anti-human who is outside the social order (1983; see also Short 1991). Bones and co. get lost in the desert, and see their situation as being "nowhere" (Schaffer 1994). Arabia as desert is thus denied its privilege as place. It becomes mute (Freeman 1999), only spoken for by the (cognitive) mapping of the United States. But perhaps the most striking example is *Three Kings*, which depicts the experiences of American soldiers at the end of the Gulf War as they embark on an accidental rescue mission of Iraqi civilians. The Iraqi people in the film, fleeing from Saddam and hiding in underground caves, seem to be enslaved by the land they inhabit (Budley and Safran 1983). The Iraqi land itself is not seen as the carrier of the Iraqi people's pain, but rather as inflicting this pain upon them. This parallels the United States' stance towards Iraq after the Gulf War, seeing Saddam Hussein, and not UN sanctions for example, as the sole cause of his people's misery.

In contrast with the depiction of the Other wilderness comes that of the American wilderness. In the American case the attitude is shifted from one about fear to one about pride. Instead of seeing wilderness as something to be defeated, it is viewed as something to be preserved and saved. This concern with environmental conscientiousness is best represented in *Power*, where there is a clear shift from focusing on the Other/Arab landscape to focusing on saving the American landscape from threat by the same Arabs traditionally associated with the menacing wilderness of Arabia. The film revolves around political consultant Pete St John, played by Richard Gere, whose conscience prevents him from supporting the American presidential candidate he is supposed to be working for in favor of another "green" candidate. St John's concern about the environment in the film is a reflection of his spiritual growth as an individual and also of the spiritual growth of the nation he represents. In other words, wilderness here is seen as a sacred space. *Power* is a reflection of the Reagan administration era, where battles were fought (and still are) between environmental and business and government interests, and where material gain was ultimately overshadowed by the environment as the most valued prize. Environmental politicians played on the traditional (and religious) ethic associated with the countryside to cultivate this new sense of morality in society (Short 1991).

The ideology of the urban

Perhaps the most interesting shift that can be seen in the American films is the displacement of the condition of wilderness from actual natural settings to urban ones. In other words, the (Other) city now is portrayed as a negative space, a modern wilderness or a "concrete jungle" (Short 1991, p. 26). In many of the films, like *Rules of Engagement*, *Navy Seals*, *Killing Streets*, *Spy Game*, and *Programmed to Kill*, a film about American scientists implanting a female android amidst Lebanese terrorists in order to eradicate them, there is a stark contrast between the depiction of scarcely inhabited American landscape and crowded Arabian landscape (Budley and Safran 1983). The American landscape is usually green (*Rules of Engagement*) yet urban (*The Siege*). Arabia, on the other hand, is a condensed hustle and bustle of seemingly overlapping houses (*Rules of Engagement*, *Killing Streets*), narrow alleys (*The Insider*, *Programmed to Kill*, *Spy Game*), and graffiti-covered walls (*The Delta Force*, *Navy Seals*). The "difference" of Arab cities is not represented positively; instead of the cities being portrayed as "buzzing," they are depicted as cramped. This suggests a sense of claustrophobia and chaos (Naficy 1996) that can be projected upon the Arab political scene.

The most significant example of the concrete jungle in the films is the depiction of Beirut. Beirut is similar in the films that depict it: in *Killing Streets*, a film about an American man who goes to Beirut to rescue his marine twin from his Lebanese militia kidnappers, Beirut is a city of rubble, shabbily veiled women, sandbags, bombed buildings, checkpoints, and exploded cars (similar representations can be found in *Navy Seals*, *Programmed to Kill*, *Spy Game* and *The Insider*). *Spy Game*, like *The Insider*, uses Beirut as a tool to demonstrate the prowess of American heroes. Telling the story of two such men, CIA officers Muir and Bishop, the film illustrates their superior skills through flashbacks depicting them on a number of missions in places like Vietnam and Beirut. Beirut in the film is a cliché of rows of men praying outdoors and veiled women, a mayhem of slums where rooftops are covered with hanging laundry and bird cages, and where random shooting by militias in jeeps is an everyday activity. The cityscape is no more than a mass of rubble, its streets covered with rubbish and burning cars, and its boundaries framed by coils of barbwire. Beirut is an example of city as crisis (O'Healy 1999). Freeman (1999) speaks of the internal consistency that occurs throughout films and that utilizes the same symbolic locations; in the case of Beirut, these have created and consolidated myths about the city and the people who inhabit it or are linked to it. Beirut is a city that is "fossilized" (O'Healy 1999, p. 241), its overrepresentation fixing it as a site of ruin, terror, and chaos. Beirut thus belongs to a system of fossilized icons often depicted in cinema, like Cairo and the pyramids or the Arabian desert. This recalls Baudrillard's notion of simulacrum, where "codes have superseded signs and . . . the difference between the real and the reproduction is erased" (quoted in Freeman 1999, pp. 61–62). Beirut (like Other Arab places) in the films is a bearer of anti-American sentiment, physically displayed through graffiti. Slogans like "Death to America" are splashed all over the Arab cities (San'a in *Rules of Engagement*, Beirut in *Navy Seals* and *The Delta Force*), their foreign ambiguity (as they are written in Arabic) providing a further sense of threat to a non-Arabic-speaking audience. The walls of the Beiruti space are thus reflectors of the political sentiment in the city as portrayed in the films. Beirut is also essentialized as a place where "normal" life does not seem to exist; the people living in that space are the fighters and the militias. It almost seems empty of civilians (the same can be said about San'a in *Rules of Engagement*, where the apparent civilians, including women and children, turn out to be anti-American "terrorists"). In this sense, the films deny Beirut its "lived" existence.

Beirut is an ambivalent space. It is "different," and this difference provides an element of anticipation that, when fulfilled, may or may not bring pleasure (Urry 1990). Often described as the "Switzerland of the

Orient," Lebanon had been a tourist site before the Civil War. The Lebanese landscape, which combines snowy mountains and sandy beaches, had been a sign of interconnectedness—of seasons and topography and of cultures. This is evoked in *The Delta Force*, a film about American rescue of an American airplane hijacked by Lebanese Islamist militants. A male Israeli Hizbullah captive in the film is taken to an unknown place in the southern suburb of Beirut after the flight he was on is hijacked. As he is being dragged across the city's streets, the man nostalgically (and rather ironically) reminisces about the pleasure with which the pre-war Lebanese landscape had provided him. Lebanon is thus mentally represented as a place that used to welcome Israelis until it was "taken over" by Hizbullah and other Islamist groups (though we do not see that place). The result of this takeover is a radical change of the Lebanese landscape. Now, the country is essentialized as a chaotic mass of rubble. The metaphor "Switzerland of the Orient" thus becomes more than just about landscape. It carries with it an ideological meaning that renders Lebanon a Westernized oasis in the middle of a tumultuous Middle East. The Lebanese landscape thus is politically charged, with the film displacing the "blame" for the changing face of Lebanon on to Islamic fundamentalists. The conflict is internalized, surgically removing the Israeli (foreign) contribution to the effacing of Beirut in particular and Lebanon in general.

The Other space as a barrier/border to be crossed

The Other landscape in the films is subjected to different acts of authority by America. Mapping and surveillance are two examples, but perhaps the most important case is that the Other landscape is often physically penetrated by the Americans. We see the Americans traveling to Lebanon in *The Delta Force*, *Killing Streets*, *Programmed to Kill*, and *Navy Seals*, and to Iraq in *Courage under Fire*, *Three Kings*, and (figuratively) *In the Army Now*. Keiller (1982) argues that the penetration of landscape reduces it from space to object. Being objectified traditionally means that the space can be a site of either desire (for example in the case of tourism) or fear (in the case of anti-terrorist military/intelligence action). Penetration by the masculine American nation can be seen as raping the feminized, weak landscape. But the Other landscape here is also a barrier to political mastery. It has to be crossed, overcome, to ensure American victory; in other words, it has to be (re)territorialized. This implies three things. First, border/barrier crossing involves a physical penetration of land and its impregnation with another culture. Young (1995) explains that this is a seizure of cultural space. Second, this territorialization by Self over Other can be seen as enlighten-ment, as the start of civilization and the end of primitivism. Finally, as Young (1995) puts it, "[c]olonization begins and perpetuates itself through acts of violence, and calls forth an answering violence from the colonized" (p. 173). Those three implications can be clearly seen in *Three Kings*. The mastery of science over nature is also displayed in *Three Kings*. At the conclusion of the Gulf War, American soldiers in the film find themselves rescuing Iraqi civilians even though that means defying American army orders. The American scientific mastery over the Other nature is seen in the film's main character, Archie, and his mates' passing through the mountainous land-scape of the Iraq/Iran border in order to deliver the Iraqi civilians to safety. Mountains are traditionally viewed as the most inaccessible parts of land-scape (Short 1991), and so conquering them infuses the American soldiers with power over the Other landscape and consequently over the people who inhabit it. The film is full of images of American military vehicles and soldiers roaming the desert. When it ends with crossing the Iraqi border and with the Americans reincarnated as saviors of the oppressed Iraqi civilians, America's political frontiers are further expanded. Frederick Jackson Turner argued that the elimination of frontiers is "the significant fact in the American identity" (Turner 1963, quoted in Short 1991, p. 93). The American identity is thus viewed as one projected externally, an all-embracing identity that seeks to better the Other landscapes and their people. This is reflected in American foreign policy (Williams 1972), from Vietnam to the Gulf War to the Arab–Israeli conflict.

The American presence in Iraq is portrayed as bringing with it a new hope that is carried forward the further the soldiers move into and appropriate the Iraqi land. They bring with them physical prowess as well as humanity, and give the Iraqi people a chance of survival away from their primitive caves. Needless to say, the American presence involves a degree of violence, but the violence here is depicted as being directed at the Iraqi oppressors rather than at the oppressed Iraqi civilians. Cultural violence is glossed over through the depiction of a member of the American squad praying with the Iraqis in one of the caves. But the film cannot hide its self-aggrandizement. The camera works with the American soldiers as they cross the Iraqi barrier, with cameras placed on army vehicles traveling through the desert, allowing us to see the landscape unfold in front of our eyes and giving us a taste of the American sense of mastery. The camera also travels on ground level with the soldiers. This is not to give a sense of empathy with the land (by not objectifying it from above, for example), but to give that empathy to the soldiers as they explore unknown landscape.

Penetrating the American landscape

The threat of the Other is not confined to foreign lands. Sometimes the threat happens at home. This is seen in *Executive Decision*, *Hostage*, and *The Delta Force*, where home is transported on to airplanes carrying American passengers, and *The Siege* and *True Lies*, where terrorist activities are carried out in New York and Florida. The depiction of terrorism on board airplanes is obviously inspired by actual hijacking events in the 1980s (like the case of the TWA flight in 1985). But the cinematic portrayal is interesting because it invokes a sense of urgency and claustrophobia that is more clearly represented here than in any other kind of space. This can be seen in *Executive Decision*, *Hostage*, and *The Delta Force*—three films depicting almost identical hijacking situations by Arab terrorists.

On board an airplane, there is no escape. This heightens the drama of hijacking/rescuing situations and, when resolved, also heightens the heroism of the saviors. The camera is more confined on airplanes, and so the variety of shots used is limited. But this also functions to portray the feeling of limitedness experienced by the hijack victims. In all three films mentioned, there is a heavy emphasis on low angle shots when portraying the hijackers, thus making them appear larger and more menacing compared with their confined environment. There are also plenty of close-ups, both on the hijackers' and on the victims' faces. This serves to increase the degree of horror illustrated. Mid shots are also used to give a more collective feel of the terror inflicted, where we see the hijacker(s) in the aisle bordered by seat rows of frightened passengers. The sense of chaos in this situation is also often depicted through hand-held camera work and quick editing that sharply moves from the hijackers to the victims and vice versa, and from one side of the airplane to another or from above to below.

Yoshimoto (1996) points out that the representation of America is not confined to an inert set of images; on the contrary, representing America constitutes a set of conflicting images that are partially responsible for the emergence of the identities of other nations. This is the case for the identity of Beirut in the films, for example. At the same time we cannot analyze America's portrayal of itself as a nation as an isolated matter. As O'Healy puts it, "[i]n order to constitute itself, the subject needs to recognize, expel and disown what it is not. It needs, specifically, to demarcate its boundaries" (1999, p. 250). Boundaries are not confined to borders with other nations; they can exist within the nation as well, as seen in the case of the Arab terrorists living in the United States in *True Lies* and *The Siege*, but more specifically the case of the Arab-Americans in the latter.

Foucault contends that the apparently "natural" spatial oppositions such as inside (familiar)/outside (strange) are invested with ideology (1970; see also Lewis 1991), and hence are "still nurtured by the hidden presence of the sacred" (quoted in Dumm 1996, p. 38). In this way, the sacredness of a space implies the existence of boundaries that deny that space to Others. Hence, the Other's presence in a homeland (physically or culturally) is deemed profane. Morley (1999) explains that members of society produce imaginary geographies that locate them at the core, representing those outside as different and threatening. Sibley terms this the "geography of exclusion" (quoted in Morley 1999, p. 161), inhabited by "imagined communities" (Anderson 1983). Natter and Jones (1997, p. 150) explain that any

> (social) process of centering entails a structuring [that] . . . implies the assignation of a periphery. Assignment to the periphery "provides a home"—one of terror—for the "other", the mere existence of which was both a provocation to, and the raw material for, the center.

In *The Siege*, Arab-Americans living in New York are summoned by the American army in order to capture those behind a series of terrorist attacks. The army herds all Arab-American New Yorkers, old and young, male and female, to massive cages on the streets of the city. Even Frank

Haddad's (an FBI agent of Lebanese origin) son is taken to the camp. Aerial views of thousands of screaming Arabs in the cages are followed by panning shots of the seemingly identical faces and attire of the Arabs. While on one hand the film's use of cages and its criticism of military action are part of an anti-totalitarianism message, cages also act as a vehicle of containment that constructs an internal barrier between Self and disease. The political conflict between the United States and the Arab terrorists in the film acts as a transforming factor on the American landscape. It moves from being a land of inclusion (America as a cultural melting pot) to becoming a land of exclusion (the "authentic" American imagined community rejecting outsiders) (Soja and Hooper 1993). Thus, the Americanness of Arab-Americans in America is "unnatural" and unsettled, subject to being revoked at any time. The usual myths of mastery over the Other apply here, with the idea of the "terrorist within" causing a great deal of distress to an American landscape that is (cinematically) traditionally "non-penetrable."

Figure 2 Arab-Americans forced into camps in *The Siege*

The process of differentiation in the film is an attempt to reclaim this land-scape. Of course, this differentiation is an attempt at denying the power embedded in the periphery, and that can "deconstruct any center of which it is part" (Natter and Jones 1997, p. 151).

Space and power

Whether inside or outside America, the action in all the above-mentioned movies occurs outdoors (with the exception of airplanes). This is related to how the American films mainly belong to the (masculine) action genre. Yet there is a distinction between the American and the Other spaces in the films. While the exterior space of America is masculine, refusing to kneel down and non-penetrable, the exterior space of the Other is feminized through mapping (*The Siege*), invasion (*In the Army Now*), and exploration (*Three Kings*). In other words, it is a passive space. Other landscapes are reduced to imagined spaces. McQuire (1998) argues that Hollywood is notorious for its use of other countries and places as mere background locations for its story lines. Indeed, the common theme of the films seems to be the glorification of America. The director of the film *Collateral Damage* (2001) changed its terrorists from Arabs to Colombians (pre-September 11) because he thought Hollywood was saturated with Arab terrorists. The action in and the main plot of the film remained the same. Only the locations and ethnicities were different. Other spaces thus operate as a stage upon which human struggle occurs and political battles are fought (Budley and Safran 1983). Gottheim (1979) argues that this is a passive relationship to landscape.

Both Soja (1996) and Lefebvre (1991) agree on the concept of "trialectics of spatiality." There is not just a center and a periphery; there is always an-Other (space) (*"il y a toujours l'Autre"*). While First Space is the physical space that can be empirically mapped, that is perceived, Second Space is the imagined space. Lefebvre (1991) argues that Second Space is that of the production of spatial knowledge, where certain orders are imposed on space. Soja (1996) explains that order is constituted through control over knowledge, signs, and codes. This space is the space of power, ideology, surveillance, and control. Third Space, on the other hand, as

Spivak (1988) argues, is the space of critical awareness of the space-blinkering effects of historicism. This is why, in order to understand space, we have to study it hand in hand with the historical and social processes that are inevitably linked to it.

From the above analysis of the Hollywood films, we can see a heavy emphasis on the issues of space, power, and knowledge. Space is sometimes mapped and measured, often imagined. We have to understand here that, even as a victim of Other terrorist attacks, the United States remains the stronger side. It is not marginalized; it marginalizes others. Thus, the imagined geographies of Other spaces are a result of the processes of control exercised by the imagined community of the United States over the Other imagined communities. First Space exists to the extent that the material form of social spatiality exists, as seen in representations of New York for example. However, what envelops this perceived space is the conceived one, the imagined space of Self and Others. The imagined space of Others is homogenized, but most importantly devoid of history, in the sense that it is a fruit of the ideological representation of the American political view. It is not idealized, but essentialized to serve the American political agenda, which is to establish the dominance of the United States in Middle Eastern (world) politics. Hence, space is reduced to a tool, a stage. The Other space does not allow the Other subaltern to speak; indeed the space itself does not speak. It is a passive space, a subaltern itself.

Thus we can see that there are "hegemonic cultural practices" (Natter and Jones 1997, p. 150) operating in the films, in the sense that the social space depicted is essentialized. The films "attempt to fix meaning of space, arranging any number of particularities, disjunctures, and juxtapositions into a seamless unity: the one place, the one identity" (ibid.) (here Arab as terrorist). But Natter and Jones (1997) emphasize that "hegemony, as the process that naturalizes both space and social relations, is like any form of power: never fixed or inevitable but always open to exposure, confrontation, reversal, and refusal through counterhegemonic or disidentifying practices" (p. 150). This counterhegemony will be explored through the spatial representations of the other side, that of Arab cinemas.

The spatial contradictions of Arab cinemas

Space in the Arab films remains a tool of demarcation between the inside and the outside, but is also a space of resistance. In this sense, it can be both an essentializing and a counter-essentialist national space, the first in the case of Egypt's Others (namely Islamic fundamentalists in *The Other* and *The Terrorist*), the second in the face of an invading enemy (namely Israel). This parallels Liggett's (1995) idea that space is about separation. Conceived space erects walls to separate the inside from the outside and its Others. This is similar to the representation of cosmopolitan New York in *The Siege* where—with the (r)ejection of Arab-Americans—the city becomes a kind of fortress society. This calls for the confrontation of the Arab landscape as problem(atic) (Gottheim 1979). It is a site of contradictions and conflicting spatial practices. Our relationship with that place becomes ambivalent; it is at once a fortress and a carnival (Judd 1995). In both cases, the films try to present a unified image of the nation (and hence a coherent space) that is plagued by the difference it harbors. This difference (for example, illustrated by the presence of Islamic fundamentalists) emphasizes the failure of spatial totalization. As Natter and Jones (1997) argue, structure cannot subsume difference.

In this context, the space of Other is contrasted with the moderate national space. The dominant national view of Arab countries feminizes them (Egypt, for example, is the "mother of the world"). Indeed, the Arab spaces depicted in the films can be seen as feminine. This can be linked to the generic aspects of the films, as they are mostly melodramas, traditionally a feminine genre with emphasis on interior spaces, which makes the characters in the films comparatively less mobile than their American counterparts in Hollywood (Naficy 1996). This also applies to the few outdoors spaces depicted in the films. The physical space of Cairo in the films, for example, is largely portrayed as enclosed, womb-like, with narrow, interlocking winding roads that seem to protect the people living within the city. However, this does not deny that "the symbolic agency that controls this space is clearly masculine" (O'Healy 1999, p. 254). Landscape in the Arab films is focused on from the inside out. So while the American films present "a panoramic gaze objectifying the landscape through the imperial power and authority of an external observer" (Blunt 1994b, p. 97), the Arab films' representation is more subjective, with the observer located within the landscape.

The outsiders inside: Islamic fundamentalists in the Egyptian and Algerian landscapes

Naficy argues that "the inside and outside spaces express not only gendered subjectivity but also often national or ethnic imaginings and longings" (1996, p. 128). Islamic fundamentalists in the Egyptian films are ascribed a position outside the Egyptian national imagination, so it is not surprising that they are also outside spatially. By this I do not mean only physically, but also mentally. In Algerian cinema, on the other hand, Islamic fundamentalists are perceived as a threat through their dominance over the national landscape.

Islamic fundamentalists in the Egyptian films *The Terrorist*, *Birds of Darkness*, and *The Other* are shown to live on the "edge of society." Even though they physically exist within the Egyptian landscape, they operate outside the society surrounding them. I say surrounding because they are not seen as part of that society, but as a threat to it. The physical representation of the fundamentalists' existence is always indoors. Closed space can be looked at as a way of symbolizing the Islamic fundamentalists' closed mind. Naficy's (1996) argument about films' invoking of "confining but comforting claustrophobic spaces" (p. 131) can be applied to the way Islamic fundamentalists in the films are shown to regard their confined spaces as shelters from what they perceive as a hostile foreign culture. The fundamentalists live in minimalist, even barren, enclosed spaces. Ali's room in *The Terrorist*, a film about a disillusioned Islamic fundamentalist man, is perhaps the best illustration. A dark room with a grenade chest as a seat, a small bed, a rug, a faint light bulb hanging from the ceiling, and a plaque engraved with the word "Patience" on the wall, the room is a reflection of Ali's dark existence. It serves to isolate him from the outside world. Denied the shelter of the womb of the city (Cairo), Ali turns to his own shelter.

At the same time, Ali's shelter creates a cocoon for him to retreat in from the pleasures of society. This contrast is best portrayed by Ali's

Figure 3   Ali in his barren space—*The Terrorist*

walk down the Cairo street leading to his rigid room. The street buzzes spontaneously (Pidduck 1998) with movement, color, and human inter- action, with street vendors, people in colorful attire, and neighbors chatting all crossing Ali's path (or rather, Ali crossing their path, as he is an intruder). The street also provides sexual pleasure, with a voluptuous woman walking straight in front of Ali and unknowingly offering an experience denied to Ali in his confined space. The walk down the street thus is a metaphor for a passage through (outer) life. Ali quickly hides from life's temptations in his room, a room linked to the outside world only by sounds coming in through the shaded window. The space between the blades of the window blinds becomes Ali's only physical access to the pleasures of the outside world. Ali uses it to peep on his female neighbor who resides in the building across the street, and who is shown as wearing a low-cut bright red dress. Ali fantasizes about the woman—a metaphor for all the pleasures he desires but is denied. Ali's experience is best summarized by Adrian Searle's words:

> Going to the window . . . becomes a figuration of disconnectedness
> from one's surroundings, but it is also the first step, (get up and go to
> the window) of finding, or re-finding one's place in the world.
>
> (2000, p. 3, catalogue essay in Still, Site Gallery:
> Sheffield, quoted in Betterton 2001)

Thus, Ali's window experience becomes an attempt at entering the denied Egyptian space. At the same time, it emphasizes to him his exclusion from it. The window becomes a "transparent filter" (Pidduck 1998, p. 382) between Ali's life and the outside world, and marks his physical and sexual constraint. The camera in the scenes uses a lot of point-of-view shots, panning and tilting around the room, zooming in and out at the length of the street, and looking down on Ali's neighbor. Therefore, the transformations of everyday space for Ali that we see are almost entirely subjective (Keiller 1982). This subjectivity highlights the various juxtapositions of Ali's life and the outside world: his is colorless, the world's is colorful; his is silent, the world's bustling with sound; his is closed, the world's comparatively open and full of possibilities. These juxtapositions are constructed through camera work that pans the walls of Ali's room as they are closing in upon him, allowing us to see what Ali is seeing when he peeps on his neighbor.

A similar yet at the same time different space to Ali's is the room that the liberal-prince-turned-fundamentalist Abdullah is made to sit in by the enlightened friends and family of the progressive-thinking philosopher Averroes in *Destiny*, a historical epic about the battle between Averroes and opposing Islamic fundamentalists in twelfth-century Andalusia. Abdullah, who is lured by fundamentalists into abandoning "blasphemous" song and dance, is tied up by Averroes's friends to a chair in the room and made to listen to the songs performed by the dancing crowd outside. The room's window is also the opening on the outer world and its pleasures, which Abdullah tries to resist. However, the space he is confined to this time serves as a site of liberation. For the people outside, the room is the only way in which they can liberate Abdullah from himself. The room becomes a site of power.

Andalusia in the film is used as a metaphorical representation of Egypt. A land of prosperity with considerable material beauty, its mountains, waterfalls, and gardens reflect not only the material wealth of the place, but also its spiritual wealth (Atef 1997). Andalusia is made to carry the values of the idealized Egypt, bestowing on the country a certain degree of sacredness. At the same time, with its rejection of Islamic fundamentalists, Andalusia bears the politics of the motherland it is standing for. Both landscapes thus are open yet enclosed, drawing boundaries between Self and Other. However, both films offer the fundamentalists a chance to become absorbed in the Egyptian social space. While this is done through coercion in the case of Abdullah, Ali is slowly drawn back into non-extremist society through the compassion of a family that ends up hosting him and showing him an appealing, alternative way of living. In this way, enclosed spaces of the mind are opened up, at the same time emphasizing Egypt's national identity as open, and idealizing Egypt as enlightened. Algerian cinema differs from Egypt's in this context, as Islamic fundamentalists are portrayed as a threat due to their growing control of the national space. In *Rachida*, a film about a school teacher attacked by fundamentalists for refusing to plant a bomb in her school, the main character, Rachida, and her mother are forced to leave Algiers to escape the fundamentalist control of the city, only to find that fundamentalist power has reached the remote village where they have sought refuge. In *Bab el-Oued City*, fundamentalists and their government-affiliated leaders control the Bab el-Oued neighborhood in Algiers. At the beginning of the film, the control of the city is revealed through a wide shot of the crammed houses in the neighborhood. Similar wide shots of the urban space are used regularly in the film, evoking a sense of dominance by the fundamentalists. Dominance is emphasized through a point-of-view shot of two government officials standing alongside the Islamic fundamentalist leader Said on a cliff overlooking the city, and other point-of-view shots of the streets of Bab el-Oued as the government officials ride through the neighborhood in their black car. The fundamentalists also control the ideological space of the city. The film revolves around an incident which the fundamentalists interpret as an attack against them, "an attack on the honor of Muslims, an act of the devil": the removal of a loudspeaker from a rooftop. The speaker is one of 16 in the neighborhood used to transmit religious preachings by the local imam. The camera zooms in on the speaker as a speech on cleanliness is transmitted, and then pans over the houses of the neighborhood, symbolizing the fundamentalists' surveillance and control. Said also exerts control over the space inhabited by his sister Yamina, objecting to her standing at the window, and confining her movements to the house, the public bath, and the mosque. Said and his accomplices are often seen in long shot as they wander about the neighborhood streets, enforcing their way of living. Their power even reaches the beach, where they interrogate a group of young men listening to rai music about the disappearance of the speaker. In this controlled space, Boualem and Yamina, who are in love, can meet only on a rooftop or in the cemetery, and even there they are not safe from the prying eyes of the fundamentalists. One of them, Rachid, reports to Said seeing Yamina with Boualem in the cemetery, and hearing the latter declare his responsibility for removing the speaker when its loud messages prevented him from sleeping after his long shift working at the bakery.

The film satirizes the transformation of space in Algiers as well as former colonial presence through the depiction of an old Frenchwoman who used to live in Bab el-Oued during colonial times, and who has returned to the place to visit. The Frenchwoman is now blind, and is led around the place by her grandson who is shocked by the change but who wants to

Figure 4 Said and his fundamentalist men—*Bab el-Oued City* (photo courtesy of Arab Film Distribution)

preserve his grandmother's nostalgic memory of the landscape. Thus we see them walking through the cemetery, which used to be a garden, with the young man turning on a tap as his grandmother says the sound of water reminds her of the (now non-existent) fountain, and him reassuring her that it hasn't changed. Later they stand on a rooftop overlooking the cramped houses as women can be seen cleaning rugs and hanging laundry on the balconies. The man tells the old woman, "If only you could see it! It hasn't changed. If I were a painter I'd come here for inspiration!" The grandson later likens the derelict local beach as he and his grandmother walk by it to Miami Beach. The film depicts Said as having a low view of the French, blaming them for "teaching us hatred." Thus, the film links Algeria's colonial past with the presence of fundamentalists who still use this issue to fuel their causes. The film is also full of references to immigration: Boualem's brother Kader wants to leave for Canada, his friend Mabrouk dreams of going to Marseille, and Massoud, an Algerian man who has to pretend to be a fundamentalist after finding himself in Algiers without his French passport and with no one else to support him, spends the whole film trying to go back to France. In the end, Boualem decides to leave too after being prosecuted by Said and his accomplices. The grip of Islamist fundamentalists is thus shown to grow and become stronger, fueled by corruption in the government that uses individuals like Said as tools and discards them when they are no longer needed, to the extent that the only way of escape is abandoning the national space and embracing the colonial dream. The fundamentalists then are the ones responsible for this destruction of national space, for the transformation of the garden into a cemetery, for replacing life with death.

Cyberspace, marginality, and globalization

The Other is the only Egyptian film that moves beyond physical space and into cyberspace as a site where political struggles are fought. Cyberspace is also represented as a site for the realization of fantasy, whether personal or political. In particular, the film represents a constant connection between Islamic fundamentalists and the United States, conducted through e-mail and internet chat. Cyberspace thus allows an otherwise undetected convergence between the terrorism of the first and the imperialism of the second, with disastrous results.

The film revolves around a young Egyptian journalist, Hanan, who falls in love with a half-Egyptian, half-American man, Adam. Adam's mother, Margaret, is an American businesswoman who detests Egypt yet is engaged in fraudulent business plans that would allow her economic control over the country. She is also obsessed with her son, whom she turns to to provide her with the love and attention she lacks in her marriage. She opposes his marriage to Hanan, and forms an unholy alliance with Hanan's brother, the Islamic fundamentalist Fat'hallah, who also opposes the relationship and promises Margaret to force the couple to divorce. Fat'hallah also aims at controlling Egypt, through the establishment of an Islamic fundamentalist regime. Fat'hallah and Margaret are revealed to be partners, using the internet to communicate and conduct their personal deals, as well as illegal arms and immigration deals. Cyberspace is thus represented as a site for the realization of fantasy, not only politically but also personally.

For both, cyberspace is a space where they can exercise power. It gives Margaret the chance to control her son's life by keeping a computer

Figure 5 Fat'hallah chatting to Margaret on the internet—*The Other*

file on his life (that includes a database of all his ex-girlfriends). Adam in the film is an Egyptian nationalist; hence cyberspace becomes a tool that allows symbolic control by American imperialism over Egypt. For Fat'hallah, power is exercised through his use of cyberspace as a space of sexual fantasy. In an online conversation with Margaret, Fat'hallah chooses Paris as the virtual location of their "meeting." Images of Montmartre prostitutes as well as the Eiffel Tower are here reproduced as national symbols of France and specifically of Paris. Paris acts as a metaphor for Fat'hallah's repressed sexual fantasies, invoked through the city's mythical association with sexuality and permissiveness (Phillips 1999). It also acts as a metaphor for Fat'hallah's view of the West as promiscuous. As Baltazar argues, cyberspace allows the subject to manipulate space to fit their needs, rather than "fragmenting the identity" (2001, p. 28) to fit the space. Cyberspace is an ideal, imagined space that allows Fat'hallah to transgress the constraints he has imposed on himself as an Islamic fundamentalist and thus guarantees him a virtual victory in his struggle with himself. In this sense, cyberspace can be seen as an example of what Soja (1989) terms mental space or Second Space: a space that is generated by and conceived in the minds of those who consequently "inhabit" it.

The internet is an agent of anonymity, where anyone can be whoever they want to be, an enabling medium that allows the individual to go beyond their social self (Turkle 1996; Hjarvard 2002). It also confuses or blurs the boundaries between the spaces in which those in "dialogue" exist (Freeman 1999). Cyberspace has created communities that are not necessarily physically or nationally bound, but which transcend the sacred boundaries of home and nation (like the subgroup of fundamentalists and Americans), forming their own private spaces (Morley 1999). Yet we have to remember here that, even though cyberspace communities are not national, they are not detached from the nation (Bhabha 1999). Indeed, the political arguments conducted between Margaret and Fat'hallah are inherently about Egypt as a nation (as they both ultimately aim at controlling it, economically for Margaret, and politically for Fat'hallah), and at the same time a reaction to the "nature" of this exclusive nation that denies the fundamentalists political representation (as Islamic fundamentalist groups are denied parliamentary participation in Egypt). Cyberspace thus is a way for both sides to (re)claim the nation. However, closer inspection reveals the artificiality of the "dialogue" between Margaret and Fat'hallah. Although the two sides are communicating, they are both setting traps for and deceiving each other. Margaret informs the police about the physical location of Fat'hallah, while he lies to her about helping divorce his sister from her son. The internet here acts as a theater for the operation of those global actors, allowing them to escape the bounds of the nation-state and form a subculture (Sassen 1999). However, in this particular context, the outcome of this is that the internet is not operating as a site of freedom and resistance. On the contrary, it is a site of oppression where two villains meet.

The internet can also be looked at as allowing individuals in different physical spaces to interact "privately" in exclusive chat rooms. The discussion between Fat'hallah and Margaret is a "private" one, making their politics an exclusive spatial activity denied to any outsiders. The internet in the film is not seen as being open to the non-villains, the Egyptians; it is vilified. So Adam, Hanan, and their friends are depicted as not using the internet, although they have the means to. Technology is thus "theirs," and not "ours," giving it a sinister meaning, with the internet becoming a criminal/imperialist web. Yoshimoto (1996) explains that, with no more physical space to conquer, virtual space is colonized. The film depicts cyberspace as a new frontier that the United States is attempting to colonize.

So even though cyberspace has constructed what Morley labels virtual geographies, where, in the words of Wark, "we no longer have roots, we have aerials" and "we no longer have origins, we have terminals" (quoted in Morley 1999, p. 158), it has not erased the affiliation to the nation. Shohat (1999a) says that cyberspace provides an imaginary home; she does not say whether cyberspace provides an imaginary homeland. This can be applied to the case of the Islamic fundamentalists in *The Other*. Despite limiting their interaction with the outside world to the internet, they do not use cyberspace as a substitute homeland. Yes, it is an imagined home, conceived in the absence of a physical one (as the film portrays the fundamentalists as living outside society), but it is mainly used as a tool to reclaim the homeland that they are exiled from (Egypt). Cyberspace then is not detached from physical space (the Egyptian landscape). This is in line with Shohat's (1999a) argument that cyberspace is another zone in which conflicts are carried out, and that is connected with the corporality of its users. She also stresses that, by being another space and not a substitute space, existing local and global power relations are merely extended to this new space, rather than being displaced from the physical one. Therefore, rather than being an interactive global space that connects people, cyberspace is viewed by the film as a global network of villains, and globalization as a threat and as corruption.

Treading on the Egyptian landscape: the case of Israel

Egyptian landscape is transformable and contradictory in relation to Israel (Hirsch 1995). This is best seen in the representations of contested places like Taba. A part of the Egyptian Sinai, and directly on the Red Sea, Taba had been seized by Israel in 1967 and returned to Egypt in 1989 after the success of Egyptian–Israeli peace talks. Taba since has become a metaphor of Egypt. It is a site bearing the history of the fighting between Egyptians and Israelis, and thus a site of pain. It is also a site of pre-war nostalgia, perceived with a sense of lost authenticity that idealizes its past, thereby implying an "original purity" (O'Healy 1999, p. 243) that is now disfigured. In this sense Taba is a memorial, a representational space that acts as a cultural indicator (Liggett 1995). It is also a site of the uncertainty of Middle Eastern peace treaties; a popular place with Israeli tourists, Taba has caused a degree of confusion among many Egyptians, who within it have had to encounter those they used to consider the enemy now enjoying their country's resources. At the same time, Taba itself, with its spectacular views, is gazed at romantically by the Egyptians. It is a spectacle to be viewed, consumed, and admired (Urry 1990; Phillips 1999) by both sides, with much ambivalence.

Girl from Israel represents this ambivalent relationship with Taba. A family holiday in Taba brings national pride as the Egyptian family admires the beauty of the place. At the same time, being in Taba brings back flashbacks to the mother of her soldier son being killed by the Israelis in that location. Also, Taba offers a rather intimate encounter with Israeli tourists, some posing as Americans, who try to befriend the family. An Israeli girl succeeds in seducing the family's younger son, and convinces him to cross the sea with her to Israel. The sea carries many meanings. It "offers a horizon of freedom and possibility" (Pidduck 1998, p. 395) to the son. The sea can also be seen as a symbol of the tranquility and purity of the Egyptian nation. At the same time, it offers a natural and symbolic frontier between Egypt and Israel (Haffner 1997). Beyond this horizon lies Israel; in this sense, the line of water becomes an "indifferent horizon of disease" (Haffner 1997, p. 35). The film plays strongly on the symbolic evil of what crossing the sea represents vis-à-vis the myth of the ideal Egyptian landscape. It is here that landscape is transformed from being a stage to political conflicts to being a crucial player. Yes, it is imagined, but it is also a "lived" space that carries with it the experiences of the people within it. Combining elements of the physical and the imagined, Taba becomes something that also goes beyond the two; it is a space with a political subtext (O'Healy 1999).

The contested space of Palestine

The most intricate illustration of the complex role that space plays in represented political conflicts is the case of Palestine as imagined in the films. The Palestine problem itself is one largely about space, where the same landscape is fought over by conflicting parties. However, the importance of space here is not just because of the physical space of Palestine; more important are the ideological connections that that space carries. Specifically, Palestine is a bearer of history, religion, and myth (for example Arabism). Yet its most important face is as a homeland. The Arab films closely focus on imagining Palestine as a lost homeland. In doing so they play on nostalgia, but also on resistance. All this is played out against broader issues such as diaspora and exile, and also the myth of Arab unity. In 1990s Egyptian cinema, the Arab world emerges as a solid unit in the face of the Israeli aggressor (as seen in *Nasser, Nasser 56, Naji al-Ali,* and *Road to Eilat*). But this myth is shattered in later Arab films.

The importance of Palestine as a place lies in its position as one of the major carriers of meaning for the Palestinians and Arabs in general. Nietschmann (1993) explains that it is this position that emphasizes the importance of place for invaders. Place is infused with the identity of people and their inherent power. Therefore, "[p]eople, institutions, and resources may be captured, but if place can't be erased, then the occupation will never be victorious" (Nietschmann 1993, p. 8). An example of this is the renaming of Palestine as Israel. Nash (1994) sees naming (like mapping: Blunt 1994a; McEwan 1994) as an act of authority that reflects the fluid, unstable, and open nature of space, rendering it open to the strategic/manipulative use by marginal/dominant groups. It is precisely this idea that we see in the Arab films in their stance towards Israel, and hence their attempts at reclaiming Palestine. The following analysis of the Palestinian landscape is not about Palestine as First Space, but rather about the Arab films' imagining of Palestine as Third Space.

Homeland as nostalgia

At first glance the case of Palestine seems like an excellent representation of the characteristics of place as dynamic and contested, challenging any notion of "national naturalisms" that "present associations of people and place as solid, commonsensical, and agreed-upon" (Gupta and Ferguson 1992, p. 12). However, it is those authentic claims to the Palestinian landscape (and beyond) that lie at the heart of the Arab–Israeli conflict, with Israelis viewing the Palestinian landscape as their promised land. At the same time, the Palestinian people look at Palestine as their only homeland. As Gupta and Ferguson say, "places are always imagined in the context of political-economic determinations" (1992, p. 11). Egyptian films stand out in invoking Palestine from the Palestinian/Arab point of view, thus portraying the Palestinian people and their lost land as the victims and at the same time the resisters. In doing so, the films rely heavily on alluding to history through methods like usage of actual footage (fighting sequences in *Nasser 56*) and historical biographies (*Nasser*). The importance of this attention to history is emphasized by Soja and Hooper (1993), who argue that a proper analysis of space pays attention to the spatial aspects of the historical processes of those "uneven developments" (p. 185) that result in spaces becoming sites of struggle. Processes of differentiation and division operate in which both the hegemonic and the resistant cultures/nations attempt to reclaim space.

Egypt's role here is as a helper, mainly fighting the Israelis in the 1960s under Nasser (*Nasser, Nasser 56, Road to Eilat*). Egypt as a representation does not feature bluntly in *Naji al-Ali*, except through the character of a disillusioned Egyptian drunken man on the streets of Lebanon who is still waiting for the "Arab forces" to come and rescue Palestine and Lebanon from Israeli aggression. However, the film itself—an Egyptian production with a largely Egyptian cast and an Egyptian director about the life of the late Palestinian caricaturist Naji al-Ali—serves to strengthen the position of Egypt as a sympathizer and supporter of the Palestinian cause (despite Egypt's own peace treaty with Israel). In the films, Palestinians are not people who have no place to call home; they are people who are attempting to reclaim a place they call home that is idealized in the Palestinian and Egyptian imagination. Idealized is a strong word here, as Palestine is imagined as an authentic, "good" landscape/motherland. In this way, the nostalgia experienced by the Palestinian diaspora is seen by Naficy (1991) as a fixation whereby home is fetishized, with the exiles focusing on certain (imaginary) aspects of the lost homeland while ignoring others. Here Naficy conflicts with Anderson's notion of homeland; where the latter sees it as imagined, Naficy sees it as imaginary, to emphasize this idealization. Naficy argues that, by trying to exercise power over the recalled past and lost homeland (by representing them ideally), exiles are actually attempting to control their present space and time.

However, it is not only the Palestinians who are represented as experiencing exile. The whole Arab world experienced a sense of exile after the 1967 War, including Egypt. Exile was not only because of the lost land after that war, but also because of the loss of the sense of a collective Arab identity that President Nasser was trying to revive. The Egyptian films thus can be seen as using Palestine as a tool to reawaken this lost identity. The complexity of the situation of Arabs as exiles, especially in their relationship with what is called home, is expressed by Naficy:

> Today, it is possible to be exiled in place, that is, to be at home and to long for other places and other times . . . It is possible to be in internal exile and yet be at home. It is possible to be forced into external exile and be unable to, or wish not to, return home. It is possible to return and to find that one's house is not the home that one had hoped for, that it is not the structure that memory built. It is possible to go into exile voluntarily and then return, yet still not fully arrive.
>
> (1999, p. 3)

This means that home is not a "real" place (Morse 1999). Rather, home is linked to personal and culture-specific imaginary. Home is thus defined as a protected, stable place that "cannot be understood except in relation to its outside(s)" (Morley 1999, p. 153), which draws attention to public and private constructions of "home" (Blunt 1994a). At the same time, the Arab situation highlights that exile can be internal, and not just external (Naficy 1999). In the case of Palestinians, what adds to this exile is the absence of mobility, whereby the exiled are confined to a place that is not "home" (Durham Peters 1999). An example is the refugee camps in Lebanon represented in *Naji al-Ali*, which the film depicts as tents in 1948, then as haphazardly built concrete slums in the 1960s and beyond. Questions of power emerge here, with a distinction being established between who moves and who does not, who can move and who cannot; the tent-to-concrete transformation acts as a metaphor for the Palestinian diaspora's fixity in space (Morley 1999). Naficy (1991) describes the exile's relation with the lost motherland in Freudian terms, as a traumatic experience of separation. What adds to this trauma is the occurrence of war in the motherland, whereby the distance of the exile from home causes a sense of national loss. This may generate a feeling of guilt among some exiles (living in relative safety away from the war). This may be seen as an incentive for the exile's long-distance national struggle and attempts to reclaim the motherland through various activities (Naficy 1991).

But not all activities are "authentic." The struggle over the motherland is not only one between the exile (Palestinians) and the occupier (Israel). It is also an "internal" struggle among Palestinians themselves. *Naji al-Ali* seems to validate the populist nostalgic perspective as opposed to the elitist one. The division between the Palestinian "lay people" and the Palestinian elites is conceptualized as a struggle over authenticity. Spatially, the lay Palestinian people are represented as existing on the margin of society in refugee camps resembling slums (in the suburbs of Beirut, in the south of Lebanon). They remember Palestine through their nostalgic stories and Naji's political satirical cartoons. The elites, in contrast, inhabit high-rise buildings at the core (center of Beirut). While the lay people are represented as sacrificing their lives and actively fighting for Palestine, the elites are depicted as too settled in their new comfortable lifestyle to care. Their affiliation to Palestine has become no more than lip service. Their claim to authenticity is graphically represented as invalid. The elites' affiliation to the "real" Palestine is replaced with one to a fake one. Naji's anticipation of seeing Abu'l'fawares' Palestinian shrine is devastated as Abu'l'fawares unravels what he calls his own Palestine, a roof garden full of fruit trees on top of his Beirut apartment. That the elites have chosen such artificial affiliations is criticized as what has added to the devastation of Palestine itself. It is the ordinary people who bear the cross of resistance, and who suffer the consequences of those spatial/(un)national affiliations. The authenticity of the lay people's claim to the land here is unquestioned. And the film itself is represented as an authentic discourse on Palestine. As for Abu'l'fawares, he is ostracized for severing his ties with his original/authentic homeland (Welsch 1999).

Homeland as resistance

Thus, the relationship between the exile and the homeland is transformed. Nostalgia is often criticized as being unreal for its invocation of authentic, good landscapes; as Keith and Pile ask, "how can the authentic be authenticated—or more properly, who is to authenticate the vernacular?" (1993, p. 9). But the relationship between the exile and Palestine is seen by Seed (1999) as the opposite of nostalgia. Seed describes nostalgia as "resigning oneself to . . . [an] irretrievable loss" (1999, p. 91). She sees the act of keeping the keys to the doors of the houses the exiles left (as seen in *Naji al-Ali*) as a reminder "to remember and to narrate the history of their losses" (p. 91), mainly the loss of not just home, but homeland. In other words, the exile's relationship to the lost motherland here is seen as an active one. By keeping the "history" of Palestine alive, *Naji al-Ali* can be seen as an attempt to reclaim the lost land.

The film uses a mixture of point-of-view and wide angle shots in this context. Point-of-view shots are used to represent the Palestinian people's individual view of their history (the Der Yassin massacre and their existence in refugee camps). The film establishes that the current marginalization of Palestinians in refugee camps in Lebanon is due to their ejection from Palestine in 1948. To emphasize this, the film goes back and forth in time, representing the point of view of the young Naji both in the refugee camp in the south of Lebanon as he tries to make sense of his barren surroundings, and in his flight from Palestine, as he observes the suffering of people around him. This serves to generate audience empathy with Naji and the Palestinian people, and makes their suffering more intimate. Wide angle shots are used in the depiction of Palestinian resistance through the film's fighting sequences. The camera moves back and upwards as we see men shooting at Israeli tanks that are invading the camp, and women throwing hot water from balconies on the Israeli soldiers' heads. Keiller (1982) argues that such high angle, distant shots do not imply a lack of sympathy for the people experiencing what is being depicted (as seen in Eisenstein's *October*). We do not see the characters' point of view here, but this camera use enables us to understand their experiences of space.

Numerous Palestinian films can also be read in the context of home-land as resistance. In *Wedding in Galilee*, this is done through demarcating the masculine, constrictive space of the Israeli army with the nurturing space of the (feminine) Palestinian home. The film tells the story of a Palestinian wedding that can only take place after the Israeli governor of Galilee insists on being invited to the celebrations, along with his officers. When the Israeli female soldier, Tali, faints as she attends the Palestinian wedding, she is removed from the space of the army—where she was seated at a banquet table, in full uniform, surrounded by her male colleagues—and carried by the Palestinian women to one of their homes. The Palestinian home marks Tali's entrance into a protective, nurturing feminine sphere that is alien to her but that is appealing. This sphere is detached from the world of men, and is protected by the women. When an Israeli male soldier follows the women carrying Tali as they are climbing the house's brick stairs, they stop, stare at him, and start ululating, which startles him and pushes him away. A close-up of the face of one of the women, Sumayya, shows her staring at the male soldier and teasing him by saying "We'll eat her [Tali] after the ritual is over." The women lay Tali on a bed and recite Qur'anic verses. The scene when Tali wakes up is dominated by sensual music and quick shots depicting Tali's glances at jewelry, colored fabrics, and perfume bottles in the room around her. The shots are intercut with others of her looking at her surroundings, smiling, her hair let loose after the women remove her military cap. The Palestinian women enter the room, and Tali willingly lets them take off her uniform and dress her in a red *abaya*. Tali ends up looking just like a Palestinian woman, a sign of the triumph of the Palestinian space over the Israeli space.

Khleifi also focuses on Palestinians' attachment to their land in *The Fertile Memory*. The film tells the stories of two Palestinian women: an old woman, Roumia, and Sahar, a divorcee in her thirties. What links Sahar and Roumia is their attachment to Palestine. Roumia refuses to exchange her land, despite 32 years of Israeli pressure on her to do so. She constantly reminds her son that she "worked to death to save this land. It's your ancestors' land!" She defiantly sits in a wheat field, declaring "Land stays where it is," as the camera pulls back into a long shot of the expropriated Palestinian land. Sahar, on the other hand, expresses her attachment to Palestine by choosing to return after working in Libya, and by refusing to leave Nablus.

Michel Khleifi's next film, *Canticle of the Stones*, continued the theme of land as resistance by representing the Palestinian *intifada*. A memorable sequence in the film is one where a Palestinian flag hangs on an electricity cable in a street. Israeli soldiers try to remove the Palestinian flag from the cable with a pole, but the pole collapses before they can remove the flag, which remains hanging on the cable defiantly. Another sequence shows Israeli soldiers forcing Palestinian men to paint over graffiti they have been accused of writing on a wall. The scene is cut to a panning shot of the now distorted graffiti, but with more graffiti painted between the newly blackened lines. Towards the end of the film, a woman collapses on the ground as an Israeli bulldozer destroys her house. As a long shot displays the bulldozer eating up the left side of the white house, another woman declares "Even if every Palestinian dies, the stones will throw themselves by themselves." The scene is cut to the image of the now flattened house, reduced to just a pile of stones on the ground interspersed with leftover objects. But even this does not stop the Palestinian people. Two women and a child address the camera saying they will erect a tent in place of the house and stay in it. Even curfews fail to curb the Palestinians' respect for and attachment to the land. Hand-held camera shots of a market, full of women and children, show them saying they have come out despite the curfew because it is Land's Day. When the Israeli soldiers arrive, a boy throws a stone at them, and other children burn tires in the street shouting

Figure 6 Graffiti in *Canticle of the Stones* (photo courtesy of Arab Film Distribution)

"PLO! Israel no!" The film's adherence message is pertinent, as it is one of the first Palestinian films made after the start of the *intifada* in 1987.

Curfew follows the path of other Palestinian films (*Wedding in Galilee*, *Canticle of the Stones*) where Israeli-imposed curfews are used to refer to Israel's oppression of Palestinians. Scenes of curfew impositions are similar in the films: Israeli jeeps pass freely through the Palestinian streets, with loudspeakers announcing the beginning of the curfews. Shopkeepers hurry as they close their shops, women shut their windows, and children run back home from schools or playgrounds. But *Curfew* differs in that it offers an account of life under the curfew in its minute details. The film is mostly confined to the claustrophobic space of a modest Palestinian home, where brothers argue and sisters express their boredom. The film's depiction of this restricted life is gloomy. We see the mother dividing the food in the house again and again to ensure it is enough to last the whole, unknown length of the curfew, and hanging the laundry indoors. The neighbor's baby daughter dies, as they are unable to call a doctor. And the family's youngest son, Radar, spends his time guessing the nature of the weapons used from the sound they make when shooting breaks out outside: "These are plastic bullets . . . that's a rubber one . . . that's a blank . . . they're live ammunition! This is tear gas!" The space of the home is transformed into an observation place where the family hide in the dark while peeping at life outside. Therefore, although the family's physical movement is restricted, they are still engaged with events occurring around them. Peeping from a window, they witness the destruction of a neighbor's house and the arrest of their son's friend. However, life does not stop because of the curfew. The mother risks her life as she goes outside in the dark to get a midwife to help a pregnant neighbor about to give birth. Radar teams up with the young girl next door to pass groceries from one house to another through the windows. And when one curfew ends and another begins, its loudspeaker announcement interrupting Radar's reading of a letter sent by his brother from Germany, he chooses to continue reading the letter, even louder than before.

Another film by Masharawi, *Ticket to Jerusalem*, continues the theme of resistant space. The film depicts the story of a man who smuggles a film projector from the West Bank to Jerusalem in order to screen a film to Palestinian children in the city. After meeting a school teacher, Rabab, and her demented mother, Um Ibrahim, he decides to hold the screening in their courtyard. Um Ibrahim's house was taken over by Orthodox Jewish settlers, confining her to one room on the ground floor. They try different methods to expel her, from running naked and exercising in her courtyard, to hanging an Israeli flag on her wall, to locking the building's main door without giving her a key. The film ends with the screening held in the courtyard in defiance, with the settlers reduced to observing the event from the top of the stairs helplessly as Palestinian men, women, and children gather to watch the film.

In this sense, the homeland is used by displaced or oppressed people as a unifying, "symbolic anchor" (Gupta and Ferguson 1992, p. 11). In other words, it is empowering (Bisharat 1997). The place of displacement, or the margin (in the case of Palestinians, the refugee camp or the Palestinian landscape), thus becomes a site of resistance. Bhabha (1990) and hooks (1990) agree that, when space becomes a space of resistance, it no longer is merely imagined, but becomes a Third Space. This means that, according to hooks, being at the margin becomes a matter of choice because it is empowering; people are not marginalized; they *choose* the margin as a space of resistance. This space is the lived space of the people, and carries their

Figure 7 Um Ibrahim in her courtyard—*Ticket to Jerusalem*

present and their history. So unlike Palestine as an imagined utopia, the refugee camp is what Foucault terms heterotopia, a space invested with the complexities of power and knowledge, but also with the lived experiences and histories of the people connected with it. Soja explains that in this context spatial knowledge is transformed into (spatial) action in a field of unevenly developed (spatial) power (margin/center). This is how we may look at this space as Third Space. It is not just a medium through which the marginalized attempt to exercise power; it is also the outcome of their actions. (Third) Space is both an instrument and an outcome of resistance. It reflects the struggle over the right to a space, and also the right to be different, to be on the margin. That is why Lefebvre (1991) has stressed the importance of what he calls the "trialectics of spatiality," that spatiality, historicality, and sociality are overlapping and interactive. So when people choose marginality, both margin and center are deconstructed and disordered. Third Space is thus essential for the survival of the oppressed; the concept allows us to comprehend how they look at the center and the margin at the same time and understand both (hooks 1990). The notion of Third Space is thus useful here because it undoes the binaries of inside/outside, center/margin, real/imagined.

The refugee camp as a Third Space is also an illustration of how space in this context is a foreground. In contrast with Selwyn's (1995) argument that the Palestinian landscape is a space where the increasing Arab population is perceived as a threat by Israelis, Palestine in the films is no longer a stage upon which political conflicts are fought; it is itself part of the conflicts, through the lived experiences of its people. This recalls Shohat's (1989b) observation of an image of a Palestinian fighter in a film who seems to be emerging from the land. In this sense, the land and the people merge into one entity where you cannot separate one from the other.

Bridging the gap between Self and Other

In contrast to the spatial binaries constructed by most of the Arab films, the Lebanese film *Kite* and the Palestinian film *The Olive Harvest* attempt to build bridges between Self (Arab) and Other (Israeli). Lebanese cinema has, perhaps surprisingly, largely refrained from creating films about the Arab–Israeli conflict. Most of the political Lebanese films tend to focus on the Lebanese Civil War itself. However, an exception is Randa Chahhal's film *Kite*. *Kite* stands alone among all the Arab films analyzed here, in that it is the only film establishing a positive relationship between Arabs and Israelis. However, this is done through forming this relationship between the Druze in the south of Lebanon and Israeli Arabs. In contrast to films drawing more boundaries between Arabs and Others, the film uses the Druze community to put across a theme of fraternity. Israel in the film is not a monolith; the film pays attention to the fact that Israel contains Arab citizens who are often hidden from public discourse. *Kite* does not demonize those Israeli Arabs, but it also depicts them as victims of politics that go beyond their powers. The film is set on the Lebanese/Israeli border, and begins with establishing an apparent difference between the Israelis and the Lebanese. The pre-credit sequence moves between showing the Israeli Druze border soldiers surveying Lebanon through binoculars, and Lebanese Druze children flying multicolored kites near the border. One of the kites is made from a Lebanese flag, and is flown by a small boy wearing a traditional *sherwal*. An Israeli commander tells the soldiers that, although they are Druze, the people across the border in Lebanon are their enemies, not their brothers or cousins. He scolds a reservist for listening to a popular Lebanese song by Ziad Rahbani, *Aishi wahda balak*, on the radio.

But division between the two communities is only physical. When a white kite gets loose and lands on the barbwire, a Lebanese girl, Lamia, crosses the border to pick it up. The Israeli soldiers join the Lebanese children in warning her against landmines. Later in the film, Lamia's aunt Jamileh narrates the story of how she was not able to marry her promised man, as the village was split in half, with one side remaining Lebanese and the other becoming Israeli, and the groom happened to be in the Israeli side. We find that the groom is actually one of the border soldiers. He periodically expresses his longing for Jamileh, and curses his misfortune that has driven him to sleeping with a Romanian prostitute to ward off his loneliness. One of the most memorable scenes in the film is one where people gather on each side of the border, passing a baby and a coffin though the dividing barbwire, from one side to another. In birth and in death, and despite the imposed divisions, the community is resilient in maintaining its unity. Women from each side communicate with each other using loudspeakers and color-coded scarves, sharing intimate details about their lives. The film's message of unity reaches its peak with a dream sequence at its end. The sequence sees Lamia magically crossing the wire to be with Youssef, the Israeli reservist who had been watching her through binoculars, and with whom she falls in love. Lamia takes off his outer army jacket, removes the star of David from his army cap, and asks him to take off his military boots. With the removal of such overt signs of nationalist/political affiliation, Youssef is once again only human. Lamia's dream thus metaphorically asserts the oneness of the community, and builds bridges between Self and Other.

The Olive Harvest also builds bridges while remaining critical of Israel's expansionist plans in Palestine. The film tells the story of two Palestinian brothers in an unnamed Palestinian village who fall in love with the same girl. Mazen, the elder brother, is released from an Israeli prison to rejoin his brother Taher, who in turn is in love with Raeda, the innocent local village belle. However, Taher is too involved in politics to demonstrate his commitment to Raeda; in steps Mazen, with his poetry and sweet words, mistaking Raeda's friendliness for affection, and eventually falling in love with her. The film's subplot revolves around the threat of the presence of Israeli settlements on Palestinian life and the peace process, demonstrated by the juxtaposition of the innocent Palestinian landscape, with its olive groves, with the cancerous expansion of the Israeli settlements. The film attempts to put forward a message of peace through condemning the two brothers' division after they fall in love with the same girl. Mazen and Taher are meant to allegorically represent Israelis and Palestinians who are fighting over the same land, represented by Raeda. The film criticizes both the expansion of Israeli settlements and the Palestinian governmental incompetence at dealing with this issue. The opening sequence of the film shows healthy, hilly olive groves in the golden sun. The camera lingers on olives on the ground, and then seems to hug an olive tree trunk as it goes up, in close-up, along the trunk and to the leaves, as if caressing them. The shot is abruptly cut to a close-up of barbwire, after which the camera moves back to reveal an Israeli observation tower and an Israeli flag. We discover that the olive groves are under the gaze of Israel, the discovery leaving the audience to feel a chill after the warmth generated by the scene of the peaceful olive groves.

Later in the film, Israeli settlements are shown being built around and closing in on the olive groves. The film then depicts a bulldozer uprooting olive trees in order to build settlements in their place. This building of settlements is juxtaposed with the weakness of the government, which is seen to be occupied with ceremonies rather than dealing with the issue, which in the film is left to Taher and his colleagues working for the NGO Settlement Watch. A memorable scene in the film is when Taher is discussing the building of new settlements with his colleague Abu Youssef, where we see Yasser Arafat in the background, stepping out of a glossy black Mercedes and being saluted by troops, seemingly oblivious to the pressing issues around him. The film highlights the artifice of the settlements by portraying them as empty, ready-made houses being slotted into place by cranes, their identical shapes standing out in an otherwise harmonious Palestinian landscape. This is emphasized when the lifeless settlements are juxtaposed with the hustle and bustle of life in the Palestinian village, with its old brick houses, streets full of proud men riding horses and cheerful kids on bicycles, and its women happily peering out of windows. However, the representation of Palestine in the film is idealized. Palestine as symbolized by the nameless village is a mythical existence. One scene in the film starts with a wide shot of the vast landscape, inhabited by a grazing flock of sheep as we hear a call for prayer. The scene is then cut to that of Mazen emerging into a garden, sniffing the fragrant leaf of a lemon tree, and surrounded by roses, where he later sits and recites poetry. This idealism is particularly seen in the film's olive harvest sequence. The harvest season begins with the playing of traditional musical instruments and women singing as they harvest the olives, while the children run freely in the groves. It is in the groves that Taher and Raeda steal an innocent kiss behind a tree, the branches framing their union. This all-singing-all-dancing romantic life becomes an over-the-top melodramatic representation of innocence, an Orientalist vision of an uncorrupted Palestine.

This uncorrupted Palestine is imagined as rural; in contrast, the city is frowned upon as a place detached from tradition. Raeda's sister Areen falls out with their father because she has chosen to live alone in Ramallah. Raeda and Areen are visual contrasts: while Raeda, with her tumbling curly locks, wears a series of traditional colorfully embroidered *abayas* in the film, Areen has short hair and is always seen wearing modern dark clothes. In a conversation between the sisters, Raeda expresses her wish to join Areen in the city, to which the latter replies "No, you belong to the groves." When their father falls ill and is visited by Raeda, his first comment to her is how she smells of olives. The film thus becomes consumed with representing an "authentic" Palestine, where a typical day is a carnival, where Woman and Earth are one, and where the "genuine" way of life is that of tradition, not modernity.

When Raeda's father, unknowing of her relationship with Taher, orders her to marry Mazen, all she can do is accept. The result is a physical fight between Mazen and Taher, naturally set in the olive groves. Raeda, in her allegorical role as the motherland, tries to stop the fight by shouting to the brothers that she loves them both, and that "brothers never fight." On the day of Raeda and Mazen's wedding, Raeda escapes into the olive groves, calling for Taher. Taher in turn, in a bout of anger, had burned the grove's oldest tree, which we find is called the "family tree" (as Raeda's father had put it earlier, "a 2,000-year-old tree that belongs to everyone; no one owns it"). As the blue-black smoke from the tree fills the sky, rain pours down, as if nature itself is protesting against the brothers' feud. This causes Raeda to stumble in her white wedding gown. She falls on the muddy ground, her dress becoming stained brown, consequently giving her the same color as the land. Mazen follows, calling after Raeda from her right, while Taher calls after her from the left. Unable to choose between the brothers as they engage in another fight over her, she calls after them both, finally merging their names together: "Maher." The film ends with Raeda's crying as we hear a repetition of her father's speech to her from earlier in the film: "Look at all those trees. This tree is your aunt. This one is your grandmother. They communicate. This is the family tree, the tree of peace." The film's message about Palestinian and Israeli brotherhood is thus repeated at regular intervals throughout the film. For instance, in the final third of the film, Mazen and Taher are revealed to be the children of a man called Abraham, this religious reference further stressing the same point. The message is also communicated outside of the film itself, with its website declaring how the film was made with an Israeli crew and a Palestinian cast, and announcing that the film is "one element of a comprehensive effort to foster peace by building personal bridges between Palestinians and Israelis" (www. theoliveharvest.com).

The Tunisian film *A Summer in la Goulette* differs from the above two films in that it also builds bridges, but this time between Arabs and Jews in an Arab space. North African cinema has not generally been concerned with conflict in the Middle East; it seems that the further one moves away from the Middle East geographically, the less the cinematic representation. Nevertheless, *A Summer in la Goulette* laments the loss of fraternity between Muslims, Christians, and Jews as a result of conflicts in the Middle East. The film opens with a song about how Arabs, Jews, and Christians all lived together in the village of la Goulette in Tunisia. The film hints at existing tensions between the three religious groups prior to the breakout of the Six Day War in 1967, but the film establishes how the three sides were at heart united. A scene in a café portrays an argument between men over the position of Jews in Tunisian society, as one man wonders why Jews have remained in Tunisia when they "have Israel now." The film depicts the main Muslim character, Youssef, defending the Jewish community in Tunisia, saying "What about the Arabs? They're all freedom fighters? There were plenty of traitors. The Jews went to prison fighting for us. Politics is about patriotism, not religion." Shortly afterwards we see the main three male characters—a Muslim, a Christian, and a Jew—on a boat, drinking and

Figure 8   The three men on their boat trip—*A Summer in la Goulette* (photo courtesy of Arab Film Distribution)

laughing together, and later collectively carrying a statue of the Madonna in celebration of the day of the Assumption of Mary. The men seem oblivious to the political cracks forming around them, ignoring news that war was about to break out in the Middle East. When a man carrying a radio runs past the men on the beach, announcing the news, the men declare that "it's the same old song" and pay no attention to him, instead hurrying out of the café to greet the Italian actress Claudia Cardinale when her arrival is announced by another villager. The film ends with the men's last fishing trip on June 4, 1967, as a caption announces that "After the Christians, the last Tunisian Jews left the country of their birth. They'll never forget la Goulette."

Conclusion

Through an analysis of the various roles space plays in the films, one can draw some important distinctions between the American and the Arab films' relationship with space. One of the most distinctive comparisons is the gender/generic aspect. While Hollywood's films take place in a masculine, open space, the Arab ones construct space as feminine. Egyptian films limit themselves to feminine, closed spaces. This is because the American films are generally action films, while the Egyptian ones are melodramas. But Palestinian films use open space as a construction of the motherland. In Hollywood, action usually occurs within the space of the Other, namely Arab countries. Those countries are characterized by their wilderness, whether natural or urban. This establishes two things. First, the Other space is objectified/feminized through penetration by the Americans. The role of American soldiers and intelligence officers in the films is depicted as to discover and conquer the Other landscape. Second, the Other space is feminized as nature versus the American culture or science. The Other space is objectified by the American gaze through practices like mapping and surveillance. This is established through heavy usage of wide and aerial shots that imply mastery over the landscape. The Arab films in contrast use a lot of mid shots, close-ups, and point-of-view shots of landscape, which is a more individual, intimate view of space. Using Keiller's (1982) argument, the contrast between external views of space (wide shots) and individual perspectives of space (characters' points of view) means that, while the Hollywood films depict space, the Arab films depict the experience of space. This can be transplaced on to people, denied their individuality in the Hollywood case, and depicted as people with individual experiences in the Arab one. This is also seen through the focus on history, personal and national, in the Arab films, depicting spatiality as a producer, not just a product, of history, in contrast with the absence of history in the Hollywood ones. And it is the Arab films that dare to construct bridges between the spaces of the Self and the Other, going beyond the essentialism of Hollywood cinema.

As we have seen, cinema is a "national institution which is merely symptomatic of broader political and economic relations" (McQuire 1998, p. 203). In exploring questions of the relationship between space and the imagination (Dumm 1996), cinema utilizes space as "the sphere of the possibility of the existence of multiplicity/difference" (Lury and Massey 1999, p. 231). In other words, space as difference is an enforced concept, a part of a global system of domination that plays on problems of contact and isolation between cultures.

With boundaries still existing between cultures, we can see that territorialization has not disappeared; it has been redefined; space has been reterritorialized (Gupta and Ferguson 1992). This means that identities are also re-(rather than de-)territorialized (for example Naficy 1991). The existence of displaced people (the Palestinian diaspora, for instance) is a case here. Diaspora in general has challenged the idea of fixed homeland. Questions of belonging have been complicated, the line between colonizer and colonized has been blurred, and concepts of local politics are seemingly no longer valid. This creates a sense of anomie, portrayed in the films through the Islamic fundamentalists who are "here" but also "there," the Arab-Americans who are ascribed a marginal loyalty to the American whole, and the Palestinian refugees in Lebanon who are not accepted as part of the Lebanese nation despite the many years they have spent there (Gupta and Ferguson 1992). Diaspora thus "is an invocation of communal space which is simultaneously both inside and outside the West" (Keith and Pile 1993, p. 18) (I add the national space). Hence, boundaries are not disappearing with diaspora. Freeman (1999) argues that such group formations strive to homogenize and maintain social order within their own socially constructed and practiced boundaries.

Thus, the state of displacement does not apply just to those who are physically or culturally displaced (Gupta and Ferguson 1992). Displacement also applies to those who remain in the same physical or cultural place, who find that their illusion of home has been shattered, thus breaking their perception of a natural link between place and culture (the nationalist imagining of the United States and the Arab countries).

Anderson's concept of imagined communities can be applied here, whereby

> imagined communities . . . come to be attached to imagined places, as displaced peoples cluster around remembered or imagined homelands, places, or communities in a world that seems increasingly to deny such firm territorialized anchors in their actuality.
>
> (Gupta and Ferguson 1992, pp. 10–11)

II

Gendered Tools of Nationalism

Gender has been an essential part of the Orientalist discourse. Orientalist notions of the Arab world are invested with ideas of sensual and submissive females (the harem) and violent, yet succumbing, males (the colonized). These notions have sedimented themselves on to the Western imaginary sense of the Middle East. At the same time, gender interlaces political agendas of the East itself. Gender in the films is a national symbol or myth; it is part of narratives through which the United States, Egypt, Palestine, and to a lesser extent Algeria imagine their collectivist identities. While females have been traditionally seen as a *symbol* of the nation (like Marianne in France and Boadicea in England) and as "signifiers of national difference" (Kandiyoti 1994, p. 377), the male has been looked at as an active embodiment of it. However, a closer look reveals a more complex view. There is a major axis dividing how the American and the Egyptian, Palestinian, and Algerian nations are represented and gendered in their respective cinemas. The traditional Egyptian nation is represented as a virtuous, virginal female who does not pose a threat to patriarchy. On the other hand, the Other nations in the Egyptian films, Israel and the United States, are symbolized by sexually permissive females, thereby constructing a virgin/whore dichotomy (Enloe 1990). However, this dichotomy is paralleled by that of the contrast between the representation of repressed Islamic fundamentalist women and that of modern, (politically) active women signifying the modern faces of Egypt and Algeria. Women are also used as symbols of the nation in Palestinian cinema, whereby the liberation of the land is signified as that of women.

This tension in Egyptian and Palestinian cinemas is an illustration of the ambivalence of cinema as a cultural artifact caught between modernity (seen as manifested in a progressive present) and tradition (seen as looking at the past for guidance). The Egyptian films form part of a nationalist movement that is opposed to the West yet at the same time admires it and accepts its supremacy (Elsaddah 2002). As Barthes (1993) argues, myths are discourses that serve to "suppress" history in order to build national identity. This suppression and transformation of history in order to affirm the nation is also seen in Hollywood. Here the imagination of the American nation has moved from the representation of the virile, conquering male that constructs the American nation as the world policeman, to that of the "new man" who symbolizes America's position as a world savior. The Other in this context is also represented as male, making the conflict between the United States and Arab countries in the films one between masculinities. The analysis that follows thus destabilizes the binaries between and within the men and the women represented in the films, showing how gender is a myth transforming "history" into "nation" (Barthes 1993).

The changing face of the American male/nation

It is no coincidence that nearly all American films depicting Middle Eastern politics are action dramas. Action dramas, as a genre, are prototypically male fantasies of mastery, often with military-political undertones. The classic action films, such as *Rocky IV* and *Die Hard*, portray the odysseys of a rugged American male hero against some primordial national enemy, such as the Soviets, the Japanese, and the Arabs. The films establish a mythical association between the strength of the rugged American hero and the nation's strength. The American nation as represented in action films is then clearly a masculine nation. Jeffords (1993) points out that the golden era for such a representation of infallible action heroes was the Reagan era. She argues that that era was characterized by cinematic representations of two oppositional masculinities: the "soft" bodies, signifying immorality and disease, and the "hard" bodies, signifying strength, loyalty, and courage. While the soft bodies belonged to Others, including Arabs, the hard bodies constructed "white masculinity as a kind of default position, ostensibly lacking specificity but defining the universal in the form of the white male" (Davies and Smith 1997, p. 17). Moreover, the characteristics of the hard bodies mirrored America's "hard" foreign policy and stance in the Cold War era.

With the Gulf War came another kind of foreign policy, maintaining the status of the United States as a world policeman but adding another dimension. The United States also constructed itself as a rescuer and liberator of oppressed peoples. Such an allegory was reflected in cinema in the representation of "new men." Jeffords argues that this is a "new" way for masculinity:

> not, as in the 1980s outward into increasingly extravagant spectacles of violence and power . . . but inward, into increasingly emotive displays of masculine sensitivities, traumas, and burdens. Rather than be impressed at the size of these men's muscles and the ingenuity of the violences, audiences are to admire their emotional commitments and the ingenuity of their sacrifices.
>
> (Jeffords 1993, p. 259)

The new men then offered a mélange of masculinity that combined being sensitive with maintaining "manhood," which in essential terms refers to "society's dominant conception of masculinity—man as warrior and conqueror" (Kimmel and Kaufman 1994, p. 270). While the face of the American nation may have changed, its representation remains one about mastery over the Other. Whether an action hard body or a new man, the American male remains a universal savior/hero, while the Arab male is essentialized as a threat to the peace and integrity of the United States and the world at large. The weakness of the Arab male is ultimately established with the physical victory of the American male, and the emphasis on the sexual vulnerability of the Arab.

Tough American men / nation

The representation of the prowess of the United States as exemplified by action heroes is based on portraying the male protagonist as a "spectacular body." The hero's body is the focus of the camera's vision, and is often exaggerated by close-ups, larger-than-life framing, and lingering camera shots (Holmlund 1993). The body's strength can mean that it is "offered as a form of protection . . . within this discourse, the body itself functions as a sort of armour against the world" (Tasker 1993, p. 123). The hero here is a savior who rescues the innocent from terrorism (*True Lies, Hostage, Programmed to Kill, Executive Decision, The Delta Force*), or conquers threatening foreign land (*Navy Seals, Iron Eagle, Rules of Engagement, Killing Streets, Into the Sun, Spy Game*). This can be seen in *Spy Game*, in a sequence where Tom Bishop finds himself at the scene of a suicide bombing in Beirut. As the camera zooms out, showing us the explosion, black smoke dominates the screen. In slow motion, the camera pans on a crowd of civilians screaming in the streets. Then out of the smoke appears Tom, closer to the camera than those around him, and appearing larger than life. A lone hero, Tom calmly leaves the madness of the scene behind him and moves on to his next "spy game."

Figure 9 Spy Game's larger-than-life American hero in Beirut

Perhaps the best example of the representation of the physically powerful American male is Harry in *True Lies*. Harry, the heroic American male (played by Arnold Schwarzenegger), is an FBI agent directly attacked by causeless Arab terrorists, and has to fight back in order to protect his family and his country. The battle between masculinities in *True Lies* is one of the most explicit between "hard" and "soft" bodies, where on one hand we have a symbol of the idealized America, and on the other hand we have the contrasting image of the Other. Harry represents an exaggerated, larger-than-life masculinity that stands out from almost everyone around him (Sobchack 1988). In the sequences where Harry engages in an air battle with the main villain, Harry's body is displayed through his wearing a sleeveless, unbuttoned vest that emphasizes his statuesque, muscular physique.

Camera work also plays a role in this emphasis. One of the longest action sequences in the film starts with a shoot-out between Harry and two Arab terrorists in a male toilet at a department store. Harry manages to kill one of the terrorists, but the other one escapes, crashing out unto the street through a glass display window. The camera lingers as Harry follows, dashing through the glass frame caused by the terrorist's crash. As Harry chases the villain across the street, the latter snatches a motorbike. Harry follows, running and leaping over colliding cars, until he eventually manages to "borrow" a policeman's horse which he rides, chasing the villain along a street leading into the Marriott Hotel lobby. The use of the horse exaggerates Harry's presence even further, and the camera juxtaposes his image with that of the slight Arab figure on a considerably smaller motorbike. The chase continues on horse and motorbike inside the hotel, and larger-than-life Harry has to lower his head several times in order not to hit the ceiling as he pursues the villain. Harry guides his horse in a spectacular jump over a reception desk, his long coat flapping behind him, mirroring classic images of Zorro in his quest for justice. Harry finds himself in the street again, this time having to go through a large fountain in order to get to the terrorist on the other side. The camera portrays Harry's heroic, Western movie-like splash through the water on his horse repeatedly, in slow motion, and from four different angles. Harry ends up guiding the horse through the hotel's glass elevator, and as the two enter the compartment they dwarf an elderly couple on their way to their upstairs room. Not only is Harry (and his horse) made to appear even larger in such a confined space, but the camera also utilizes high angle and low angle shots showing Harry looking down at the couple, and them looking up to him, respectively. Harry ends up on the hotel's roof, still on horseback. After the villain, who had also reached the roof, still on his motorbike, falls down into the hotel's outdoors swimming pool on ground level, the scene ends with Harry standing on top of the high-rise hotel, seemingly even bigger than the city surrounding him. This heavy physical presence lends its weight to the subsequent heavy presence of the American nation.

But the hero's strength does not only lie in his physical prowess; it is also situated in his high mental capability and expertise. In addition to Harry's extreme physique, his "voice" adds another dimension to his muscular masculine performance (Tasker 1993). Harry is not only muscular, but also witty, throwing one-liners at everyone from the horse he snatches to chase the terrorist to the terrorist himself. And he is also a charming talker when in the company of women. Dressed in a tuxedo, Harry goes under-cover to a cocktail party where he meets an attractive female gang leader. As the camera traces Harry's entrance, we see her admiring looks. It only takes Harry a few moments to get her to give him her business card, dance with him, and give him the information he needs about her terrorist network without her noticing. This consequently leads Harry to unravel her and her gang's hiding place and uncover their terrorist plans, and the film ends with the triumph of Americans over threatening Others.

This model of extreme masculinity has acquired a different interpreta-tion in the 1990s and beyond, where the focus has shifted from physical to mental prowess. An illustration is Samuel L. Jackson's character Childers in *Rules of Engagement*. The film's controversial portrayal of Arabs led to its ban in most Arab countries, as the film justifies the mass killing of the Arabs by showing armed Arab women and children who attack the American embassy in Yemen. The American soldier Childers responds by shooting at the Arab crowd, and is consequently charged with breaking the rules of engagement, to which he responds by persistently fighting his case in court until proven right. In this way, Childers's position as protector of the nation is redeemed. A striking scene in the film is one where Childers steps out of court after one of his hearings to see a troop of American soldiers saluting the American flag in the leafy forest nearby. Childers's image joining the salute zooms on that of the raised American flag; the shot is then cut to that of Childers saving the American flag while it is being shot at by terrorists in Yemen, risking his life in the process. Childers's rescue of the American flag is later used in the trial as proof of his patriotism. The film ends with the redemption of America's glory and the justification of its "mistakes," while celebrating the masculinity of the black man who risks his life to rescue the American ambassador, the American flag, and American soldiers.

Thus, the symbolic battle between nations as presented by the films remains one about strengthening the American national identity as invincible. The films eliminate any doubt about the validity of the United States' political/military actions, maintaining its position as a righteous world policeman.

New men, same nation?

Besides the United States' role as a world policeman, the films also construct the United States as a world carer. While "new masculinity" was still overshadowed by the traditional representation of tough men in the 1980s with films like *Rambo*, *The Terminator*, and *Black Rain*, it presented an important turning point that has continued until today. The representation of heroes' internal feelings has replaced the display of "highlighted masculinity . . . as a violent spectacle that insist[s] on the external sufficiency of the male body/territory" (Jeffords 1993, p. 346). The films examined in this section (*Power*, *Courage under Fire*, *Three Kings*) relate to the changing nature of the Arab Gulf from the 1980s till the 1990s, and represent the political conflict in the area through the contrast between the new American man/nation and the backward Oriental man.

Power is a film in which the threatening Arab male makes a short but meaningful appearance, attempting to use his oil power to tilt American congress elections to his advantage. The film was released 13 years after the 1973 October (Yom Kippur) War, in which Arabs fought Israelis in an attempt to recover land taken over by Israel following the 1967 Six Day War. The Six Day War had ended with Sinai, the West Bank, and Gaza seized by Israel from the Arabs. The Egyptian president, Nasser, had failed to recover the land, and his successor, Sadat, was determined to win it back, partly to validate his own position as the new Egyptian president. After two weeks of near loss on the side of the Israelis, the United States offered Israel military support. OPEC Arab countries consequently used their perhaps most important resource, petrol, to exert some pressure. By cutting off Europe's and the United States' supply of oil, oil-rich Arab countries were able to pressurize Israel into giving up some of the land. The war, a defeat for the Arabs militarily, but a win economically and politically, put Gulf Arab countries back on the agenda as powers not to be ignored.

Power can be seen to parody the Arabs' victory, as if saying that, despite being able to use their oil as a political tool once, the Arabs could not succeed in doing that again. While the main spin doctor in the film, Pete St. John, is working for his mainstream presidential candidate, the film presents a rival candidate who is an environmentalist. St. John is shown to be dutiful to his candidate but to prefer the environmentalist one to win because of his conscientiousness. Thus, despite his job, which he performs professionally, he still chooses the benefit of not just his country, but also the environment. He thus mirrors a nation that sees itself as a world savior and (ironically) a supporter of green ethics.

The film is one of the few non-action dramas depicting Middle Eastern politics. A political drama, it does not contain any action sequences; yet revolving around the realm of politics means that the film is largely confined to a traditionally male arena. St. John is the savvy American who knows his way both within and outside of his job. Professional to the smallest detail, such as his tailored suits, he is a symbol of the United States at the beginning of the 1980s. He is calm, preferring to let off steam by playing percussions instead of fighting, and is concerned with image management. This masculinity is different from the one we are presented with in action dramas, whereby a high proportion of attention is given to the hero's physical attributes and prowess. St. John is concerned with physical attributes, but they are not ones about muscles; they are about being fit, an obsession that had taken 1980s America by storm. The film can be seen as representing 1980s driven America as the ethical businessman.

The Gulf in the 1990s became a site of conflict again after Iraq's invasion of Kuwait and subsequent American intervention. *Courage under Fire* is a thriller depicting the perseverance of Gulf War veteran Lieutenant Colonel Sirling (Denzel Washington). Sirling assigns himself the mission of finding out whether a female colonel who died during the Gulf War deserved the Medal of Honor or not. No one else shows interest in his investigation, and he is left to pursue the truth on his own, outside the system. His sense of duty drives him to confront a soldier who tried to prevent the award of the Medal of Honor. Sirling questions the man persistently as they drive down a long country road. The soldier becomes enraged and instantly commits suicide, but Sirling remains calm throughout, keeping control of the car. But he encounters difficulty in keeping control of his life, as his mission puts strain on his relationship with his family. But Sirling does not forget his children. Despite his absence from them, he waits in his car outside his house to watch them from a distance. He eventually proves that the female colonel deserved the medal, and goes back to his normal family life, after his wife finally comes to terms with the importance of duty. Sirling is therefore redeemed as a new man who is a good husband and a good father who is driven by his morals, and thus can be seen as representing the American nation's conscience (Jeffords 1993).

Three Kings, set at the end of the Gulf War, reflects America's changing stance in the region. The film concentrates on a multi-ethnic American army unit containing a range of character types that is established as a "democratic microcosm" of the United States (Sobchack 1988, p. 15). The combination of the individualist leader (Archie), the reasonable black man (Chief Elgin), the family man (Troy), and the naive yet aspiring young man (Conrad) identifies the characters with the "average man" and thus highlights their role as representatives of national identity. The men cruise the desert in army vehicles displaying American flags, and are guided by a nationalism that induces them to pray to God "to protect us as we protect our country."

Archie, played by George Clooney, is the heroic figure in this army squad, emerging "as one who is typically outside, if not actually opposed to, the mainstream" (Tasker 1993, p. 104). This is portrayed in his sexual behavior as well as his military behavior. Our introduction to the "cool" Archie in the film sees him having sex with a female journalist covering the end of the Gulf War. Archie's imperfection is soon highlighted in his temptation by the chance to steal a large amount of gold held by Iraqis. However, he is later presented as an independent thinker and leader who defies the system—eventually becoming a local hero—by saving the lives of innocent Iraqi civilians. He and his mates Troy, Chief Elgin, and Conrad risk their lives, their status, and their future to smuggle the Iraqis into Iran where they can escape Saddam Hussein's dictatorship.

Throughout the trip to the Iranian border Troy suffers from a serious injury, highlighted with anatomical shots of what is happening inside his wound juxtaposed with shots of the Iraqi people. The people's wounds thus become linked with Troy's own, with the message connecting the men's sympathy towards Troy with that of the United States towards Iraqis. At the same time, Troy constantly thinks of his wife and daughter and how he plans to devote himself to them after he leaves the army. Troy's wife and daughter are presented as the catalyst that keeps him going and enables him to tolerate and eventually overcome his wounds. As Jeffords puts it, he becomes an "emotionally and physically whole man," whose family provides "both the motivation for and the resolution of changing masculine heroisms" (1994, p. 143). Troy's injury also serves to show that "the national body can be . . . capable of recovering from a past wound" (Jeffords 1994, p. 51). The American men's masculinity in the film is thus revisionist, portraying them as a helping hand instead of terminators. However, the film does not present the men as totally refraining from violence. The men engage in battle when needed, shooting at and killing a significant number of Iraqi soldiers. This combination means that these "wild yet sensitive (deeply caring yet killing) guys" (Pfeil 1995, p. 5) are "simultaneously feminized and re-empowered" (Pfeil 1995, p. 54). The men thus serve to legitimize the American violent intervention in the Gulf War, symbolizing the United States as a much needed rescuer. As Bingham argues, this representation of new men serves as "an apparent strategy for holding on to power during shifting times" (1994, p. 4); "with the codes of masculinity reduced to a series of roles, sensitivity is just another in the repertoire" (1994, p. 5).

Though masculinities may differ, the underlying attributes are the same. The American nation is manifested in the superior/victorious male who is set against Other nations. The masculinities seem to differ according to historical sensitivities, changing with the highlights of the times. Thus, 1980s environmentalism is highlighted along with the Reagan era's tough approach, 1990s feminism follows with new men and the focus on male sensitivity as opposed to physical strength, and multiculturalism continues at the turn of the millennium, with black actors taking on more major roles as representatives of the changing face of the same nation.

Essential Arabs

In contrast with the greatness of the American male comes the mediocrity of his Arab counterpart. Whether the Arab's political agenda is known or not, the films seem to use Arabs as token enemies, essential for the strengthening of the central hero, and consequently the American nation. In fact, one could easily replace the Arab "bad guys" in those films with anyone from any other background, as their threat and operations are not culture specific. What is fixed about these Arab men though is their essential Orientalist representation as backward, savage, and materialist Others. This masculinity manifests itself in the representation of the Arab terrorist who is on a mission to attack the United States. This terrorist can be a plane hijacker terrorizing the elderly and religious figures (*The Delta Force*), women (*Executive Decision*), or children (*Hostage*); a maniac kidnapping an American family (*True Lies*); or a street militant set on attacking American troops (*Navy Seals, Killing Streets*) or his own people (*Spy Game*).

The terrorists in the films are characterized by extremism, ignorance, and lack of sympathy. An illustrative case here is that of Abdo Rifa'i in *The Delta Force*. A rugged, dark figure with a heavy accent, Abdo launches an attack on the passengers and crew of a "TAW" flight (paying homage to the 1985 TWA hijacking). Abdo's reasons for the hijacking are stated by him as being to fight Zionism and American imperialism. However, Abdo's ignorance is highlighted when he forces the German hostess to read out the names of those he believes are Jewish passengers, assuming that all Jews are Israelis. With mad hair and gun in hand, Abdo orders his captives to gather near the cockpit, and mistakenly forces a Christian man of Russian origin to comply as well because he thought the man's name was Jewish. When an elderly priest tries to calm Abdo down, the priest also ends up joining the on-board "concentration camp." Abdo's political case is therefore stripped of any credibility, and instead we are faced with a representation of a ruthless man who poses a threat to the unity and integrity of an all-encompassing American nation, where people from different backgrounds live in solidarity. This is exemplified in the Russian man's statement that the United States has treated him well.

The representation of the Arab men in general serves to justify the position of the United States in world/Middle Eastern politics. However, this justification does not always follow actual political events. An illustration of this can be seen in *Navy Seals* and *Spy Game*. *Navy Seals* deals with the intricacies of the Lebanese Civil War, pointing out the large number of participants in this war: the "Shuhada" (a fictional Shiite terrorist group mentioned in the film), Hizbullah, Amal (a Shiite group), the Druze (a religious sect), Israel. Similarly, *Spy Game* sees Nathan Muir announcing that in Lebanon there are "17 sects all claiming their birthright," and that the "sheikh [a local militant] is planning a major attack on the civilian sections of West Beirut." The film later tells us that the "Druze and Party of God started a street war in Beirut," a statement supported by a few seconds of gritty, black-and-white documentary-like images of a mob in Beirut. The film, however, does not dwell on historical detail, instead presenting Nathan simply referring to "Lebanese militias," whom Tom calls "cowboys." Thus, the films pay homage to the idea of Lebanonization—how Lebanon has been essentialized as an icon of tribalism rather than nationalism. *Navy Seals* portrays one Shiite militia leader saying they "kill in response to American hostilities." However, the film gives no explanation for the complexity of the situation, nor does it provide much historical grounding, leaving the conflict in Lebanon as a given: something emanating from the intrinsic nature of Lebanon. The argument then is a classic Orientalist one about the issue of nature versus culture (West 1995).

The American intervention in the film is carried out by Navy Seals, anti-terrorism marine troops appointed by President Kennedy in 1962, which the film shows are sent to Lebanon in the 1980s to claim American missiles. The film fails to tell how the American missiles got into the hands of Shiite terrorists in Lebanon, and does not portray American intervention from any other angle. The American presence in Lebanon in the eyes of *Navy Seals*, then, is one linked with a single military activity, and does not necessarily replicate the American participation in Middle Eastern conflicts in general. Yet the film's portrayal of Lebanese militias is not central. None of them is a main character. They just symbolize another threat to the United States, although what they might be capable of is unexplained in the film. This way, the Other masculinity is ambiguous. It operates as an abstract threat to the American nation.

The same applies to *In the Army Now* and *Three Kings* where we are presented with irrational and barbaric Arab soldiers. But in addition to the barbarity of the Arab men in the two films, *Three Kings* presents another dimension to this Other masculinity. The Arab men in the film belong to one of two groups. They are either outsiders who explicitly long for American aid, and thus represent a passive, surrendered masculinity, or are soldiers who blindly follow Saddam's orders and are therefore set to destroy and jeopardize the status of the United States. Yet the Iraqi soldiers are brutal not only to the Americans, but also to their own people, killing them and preventing them from accessing food. An unforgettable scene in the film is one where a container truck filled with milk that is meant to be for the starving Iraqi civilians is shot by Saddam's soldiers, bursting it open. As the milk spills all over the ground and is slowly soaked into the dry earth, women and children gather around the white pool, drinking the mixture of milk and mud in desperation while the Iraqi soldiers watch like stone figures. The film thus is an illustration of Orientalist discourse, whereby the Orient is presented as needing the Occident to rescue it from itself.

The Iraqi soldiers in *Three Kings* are also obsessed with material gain, and harbor vast quantities of stolen, mainly electrical equipment and gold, stored in basements resembling showrooms. The most striking scene here

Figure 10 Iraqi women walk on milk-soaked ground—*Three Kings*

has to be the one where Archie and co. "strike gold." They open, one by one, a long row of suitcases, only to find them filled with stacks of pure gold plates. Materialism is also found in the Gulf Arab man in *Power*, and in the nameless Bedouin characters in *Into the Sun*. Riding in the back of a Mercedes, in full headdress and *gallabiyya*, the Gulf Arab in the first film complains about the environmentalist candidate who is advocating alternative energy sources to petrol. The Arab man's concern is that, if the USA manages to conserve energy, then there would be little or no need for Gulf oil. The Arab Gulf man is not interested in the United States. The film symbolizes this through showing him struggle to pronounce the word "Ohio." All he clearly expresses interest about is his profit and the need for his oil. The film ends with the victory of the environmentalist candidate, with the Arab's defeat symbolized by his absence. In *Into the Sun*, after an American fighter plane crashes into the desert in an unnamed Arab country, American pilot Shotgun and his sidekick Tom Slade are kidnapped by Bedouins who first sell them to the country's barbaric army (whose leader resembles Yasser Arafat with his military uniform, *kaffiyya*, and beard), and then try to sell them again after realizing that Tom Slade is a famous Hollywood actor. The Arab male, therefore, is a symbol of the vulgar, degenerate, materialist, cruel Arabia that is threatening to swallow up the United States. The Arab's defeat in the end revalidates the American national identity as victorious, and Others the Arab further. The absence of the Arab character here is symbolic of the total elimination of "disease" from American society. This is further stressed through the victory of the environmentalist candidate. The message, then, is the battle for a "clean" America, both literally and symbolically.

A slightly more unusual representation of Arab masculinity is found in *South Park: Bigger, Longer and Uncut*. The film is a cinematic version of the television cartoon, and revolves around the portrayal of Saddam Hussein and Satan in a battle over controlling Earth, which they descend to from hell after a dispute between the United States and Canada. Representing an "Operation Human Shield," whereby black soldiers are summoned to fight at the front lines to spare the lives of white soldiers, the film is heavily critical of the alleged allocation of black soldiers to battlefronts during the Gulf War. The film is also self-reflexive in its portrayal of Saddam Hussein, represented as a cartoon with a newspaper cutout for a head, and who thus is as much a creation of the media as an actual threat to American integrity. The film's casting of Saddam as a homosexual having an affair with (and then "dumping") Satan gives a new dimension to the representation of Other/Arab masculinity in American films. This non-mainstream masculinity is satirical, yet it serves to symbolically demonize Saddam further. At the same time, it undermines him as a threat because, in the film, he is too much of a pathetic "loser" who wants to dominate the world but fails.

Yet perhaps the most extreme representation of essential Arab Others is their absence. Despite dealing with the Gulf War, *Courage under Fire* does not portray any Arab characters, male or female. All the Arabs we see are vague black silhouettes of Iraqi soldiers in the background getting shot by the Americans. As Lieutenant Colonel Sirling sits in a circle of ex-Gulf War soldiers to query them about the details surrounding the death of a female pilot, one soldier gets so carried away in his descriptions that he uses the word "fuckers" to refer to the Iraqi soldiers. Staring at Sirling, the soldier apologizes for his language. Here Sirling smiles warmly at him, approving of the soldier's description, and affirming the United States' superiority by saying that compared with the Iraqis "we're a hell of a lot smarter." American policy in the Gulf War is not criticized, and the symbolic absence of the Arabs denotes their relative unimportance in a war tale taken for granted as "right." It also serves to dehumanize them.

Sexuality and the Arab male/nation

The Arab–Israeli conflict is one of the longest on-going struggles in the Middle East, and has extended beyond the Arab world with increasing American intervention. The position of the United States has shifted from relative direct support for Israel (such as American aid in the 1967 and 1973 wars), to acting as a go-between, attempting to arrive at an agreement between the Israelis and the Palestinians which would (in theory) satisfy the interests of all three parties. This role most prominently started in the late 1970s and early 1980s, and thus can be seen as triggering the production of two films, *The Ambassador* and *The Little Drummer Girl* in 1984, that deal with this issue. *The Siege* was released in 1998, and provides a more contemporary look at the manifestation of the Arab–Israeli conflict at the end of the 1990s.

The United States in the films is represented as the rational negotiator which is set to combat terrorism and arrive at peace. This can be seen through the representation of the American ambassador in *The Ambassador*, and the FBI agents in the other two films. Against this moderate masculinity is that of the mad Arab male terrorists, who train in military camps in *The Little Drummer Girl*, terrorize moderates in *The Ambassador*, and blow up the Americans in *The Siege*. Indeed, not all Palestinians want peace with Israel, and various Palestinian extremist groups such as Hamas have engaged in military and suicidal activities against Israel and the United States. The films sometimes make a distinction between those people and the majority of Palestinians and Arabs. However, there is still a major divide between the Arab men in the films and their American counterparts. This division is a derivative of a long Orientalist perspective objectifying and vilifying the Orient as essentially "uncivilized" and uncontrollable.

Perhaps the most interesting point about this contrast of masculinities is about the Arab men's sexuality. In the three films dealt with here, we are presented with the stereotype of the "Arab stallion." The origin of this stereotype as seen in American films dates back to the days when Rudolph Valentino in *The Sheik* lured Western women into his bed. This stereotype evokes images of harems and Arab men who are maybe good at attracting women but who bear a lack in everything else and end up defeated by the Western men. This stereotype can be compared with that of black male sexuality, which in classical Hollywood films was often represented as virile yet savage. In both cases, the sexuality of the Other is primitive, whether overtly (black) or covertly (Arab). This savagery is an explicit symbol of the "essence" of the Other nation/nature, sharply contrasted with that of the West, symbolized not through sexuality but through the use of the Western male's mind.

Both *The Siege* and *The Ambassador* represent American women (CIA agent Alice and the American ambassador's wife, respectively) sleeping with Palestinian men. Alice is asked by an FBI agent "Do you know what they do to women there [in the Middle East]?" to which she answers with a satisfied "Oh yes." Computer-detected scenes of her having sex with the Palestinian Samir are then beamed to the FBI agents who express their admiration at the "stallion's" skills. In *The Ambassador*—a film about the attempts of the American ambassador to Israel, Hacker, to achieve peace between Israelis and Palestinians—Hacker's wife submits totally to her lover, for whom she dresses in revealing Oriental clothing and belly dances. The camera traces her face while they are making love and shows her reveling in ecstasy. The film goes further in adopting the "Arab stallion" stereotype by using that same phrase to describe the man. When the unfaithful wife is asked by her husband whether she "got a good horse" at her supposed riding session (her alibi for seeing her lover), she replies "Yeah, an Arab. Just the kind I like."

A point linked to the above is the film's display of these Arab men's bodies. In all the films where these bodies are shown, naked or half-naked, the American men remain fully clothed. The display of the men's bodies in *The Siege* and *The Ambassador* is purely sexual, whereas in *The Little Drummer Girl*—a film about an American actress, Charlie, who gets recruited by the Mossad to help eradicate Palestinian "terrorism"—it is partly sexual (scenes of Charlie and her "Palestinian" lover Michel, who is later revealed to be Israeli agent Joseph) and partly humiliating (the torture of the always naked body of the revolutionary Samir). Samir's naked body—despite his failed attempts to hide his modesty—is displayed to the gaze of the audience, Charlie, and his captors. The power of the gaze here "traps subject and object in . . . [a] claustrophobic space of ritual and obsession" (Riggs 1993, p. 54).

Samir's Israeli captives, especially, are the ones obsessed by his nudity, which they gradually construct. In a series of intercut shots, Samir in the beginning is clothed, then is wearing a rag, then is lying down in a fetal position which hides his front, then is made to stand up while covering his genitals with his hands, and finally is forced to appear totally naked. The focus of these shots is on Samir's penis, whether it will be displayed or not. In this sense, the penis is "marked as being of extraordinary significance. The discourse of the melodramatic penis still seeks to block a penis from merely being a penis" (Lehman 2001, p. 39). Whether in a sexual context or a humiliation context, the Other body is objectified as a spectacle to be consumed or dominated. As Parpart argues, "individual moments of male nudity [of the colonized male body] may register . . . as . . . affirmative of difference and marginality" (2001, p. 179). But Samir's case is, moreover, one about the progressive conquering and subsequent total submission of the Other. Samir's subsequent murder by the Israelis does not add to their conquering; his naked surrender is a sufficient indicator.

The female nations of Arab cinemas

The woman-as-nation metaphor has meant that in Arab cinemas "women . . . become the battleground of [national] group struggles" (Spike Peterson 1999, p. 48). Anthias and Yuval-Davis (1989) argue that citizenship constructs men and women differently. They state five ways in which women participate in national processes, and which form the framework behind the analysis of the representation of the female Arab nations. First, women are constructed as biological reproducers of members of an ethnic group. Second, they are constructed as reproducers of boundaries of ethnic or national groups. This has necessitated the establishment of codes determining women's acceptable sexual behavior, limiting this behavior within the group. Third, they are ideological reproducers of collectivity and transmitters of culture. Fourth, they signify national difference, and therefore act as symbols in ideological discourses used in the construction, reproduction, and transformation of the nation. And finally, women are constructed as participants in national, economic, political, and military struggles.

Anthias and Yuval-Davis further argue that "[d]ifferent historical contexts will construct these roles not only in different ways but also the centrality of these roles will differ" (1989, p. 7). The analysis of the Arab films shows that notions of gender and patriarchy cannot be applied universally, and therefore highlights the importance of examining the representation of the different roles of women in the films in a historical context. In doing so the analysis challenges the notion of "'Third World Woman' as a singular monolithic subject" (Mohanty 1994, p. 196), where women form "a unified 'powerless' group prior to the historical and political analysis in question" (Mohanty 1994, p. 202).

In what follows, five major points will be discussed. First is the representation of woman-as-idealized-nation. The Middle East has generally invested the female with the task of being the moral gauge in society. The female's role thus goes beyond symbolizing the morals of the family and into being the bearer of the nation's values. In films about late President Nasser, the Egyptian nation is represented as a virtuous female who does not pose a threat to patriarchy. With Egypt imagining itself in terms of honorable, subdued femininity, it is no coincidence that Egyptians call their nation the "mother of the world." Second, Kandiyoti (1994) argues that women's appropriate sexual conduct "often constitutes the crucial distinction between the nation and its 'others'" (p. 377). Thus, in contrast to this image of idealized femininity, Egyptian films representing Israel and the United States as Other nations communicate the representation of Other-woman-as-whore. Other nations are symbolized by sexually permissive females who are presented as summarizing the moral depravity of the enemy. Third is the symbolic use of women as an oppositional tool vis-à-vis Islamic fundamentalism. Here we have two representations. The first is the use of woman as a tool highlighting the moral depravity of Islamic fundamentalist men. The second is the representation of the silent, veiled woman who symbolizes the oppression of Islamic fundamentalism. This is contrasted with the fourth point, the representation of the modern woman/nation, seen in women who are politically active. However, the fifth point argues that this representation of "active" women does not imply that they are central protagonists. The films in the end construct the Arab nations as being patriarchal. The shift from the representation of idealized women to that of modern women indicates a historical move from private patriarchy, where women are subordinated through their relegation to the home, to public patriarchy, where "women are no longer excluded from the public arena, but subordinated within it" (Kandiyoti 1994, p. 377).

Idealized femininity

"Women bear the burden of being 'mothers of the nation'" (Kandiyoti 1994, p. 376). The Egyptian films analyzed are mainly melodramas focusing on the feminine, private sphere, where family honor and national honor are signified by idealized, wholesome women. Thus the females symbolizing the nation tend to be devoted mothers who sacrifice for their husbands and their families. One way of analyzing this devotion is stated by Kaplan, who argues that the mother's passion for her children can be a "'safe' location of female desire" (1992, p. 79). Kaplan also maintains that the mother who sacrifices for her husband can be "blameless and heroic . . . she has ceased to be a threat in the male unconscious" (1992, p. 124). Yet, such a paradigm "uncritically embodies the patriarchal unconscious and represents woman's positioning as lack, absence, signifier of passivity" (ibid.).

Such characteristics are seen in the character Tahiyya, Nasser's wife, in the film *Nasser*. The film is a biographical account of the life of the late Egyptian president, and presents Tahiyya as a selfless mother/devoted wife who not only takes care of her children and husband, but also sacrifices her own personal life with Nasser for the sake of the nation. The film ends with Nasser's death, depicting a mourning Tahiyya alone by his deathbed, saying "It is only now that I have you for myself." Tahiyya's sacrifice means that she is ascribed a heroic status. This status is maintained in her portrayal as being an obedient wife, yielding to Nasser's wish to work long hours despite her concern over his deteriorating health. At the same time, she excels at her role as housewife and hostess. A scene depicting a meeting between Nasser and Deputy Supreme Commander of the Armed Forces Abdel Hakim Amer starts with a panning shot revealing a long dinner table laid with food prepared by Tahiyya. As the three eat their dinner, the men praise Tahiyya's culinary skills, after which she leads them to the living room where she serves them tea. Yet as soon as Amer and Nasser start discussing politics, Tahiyya makes a swift exit, excusing herself as having to look after the children, and taking the sugar bowl from the tea tray with her while joking that she cannot trust her husband with the sugar.

The film's depiction is closely based on the doctrines of the real Nasser. According to Hatem, Nasser was passively ambivalent "regarding the impact of the roles assigned to women in modern society" (1993, p. 39). Officially, Nasser was committed to "the integration of women in the public sphere" (ibid.): despite the shortcomings of the unchanged personal status laws, among others, Nasser's government gave women the right to vote and distributed education and health benefits equally, which women gained from. Yet, Nasser quelled the public Egyptian feminist movement during most of his ruling period, accusing it of being too leftist. This was in line with his suppression of all other independent political groups (Badran 1993).

Nasser's revolutionary struggle relied upon "using Islam to rally the masses for the liberation of their occupied land" (Majid 1998, p. 327). Majid explains that such a "form of Islam was obviously infused with a patriarchal spirit" (ibid.). As Khan puts it, "these politicized, frequently anticolonial, anti-West movements exert increasing social and sexual control on the symbolic and chaste women centered at the core of an identity politics" (1998, p. 468). Moghadam calls such a type of revolution a "Woman-in-the-Family" model (quoted in Wilford 1998, p. 6). The women's role in this context is more complex than that of men, in that, while men and women may sacrifice themselves for the nation, it is the woman who is a symbol of the nation itself (and the nation's honor) (Anthias and Yuval-Davis 1989; Wilford 1998; Joseph 1999). As a woman's morality extends to the nation, Tahiyya becomes a symbol of the pure, nurturing, virtuous Egypt. Her political uninvolvement validates Delaney's point, *"women may symbolize the nation, but men represent it"* (1995, p. 190, italics in original).

Permissive femininity

The Arab–Israeli conflict in the Egyptian context has taken many shapes. The situation has shifted from blatant opposition to Israel pre-1978 to acceptance after Sadat's signing of the Camp David Accords in 1978. Sadat started a long process of peace talks with Israel, ending in 1989 with Israel returning Sinai and other Egyptian territory it had occupied 15 years earlier. Yet, while the Egyptian state's stance towards Israel since then may have been accepting, the general mood in Egypt has not always been. Even with peace with Israel being established, this popular anti-Israeli sentiment is expressed in cinema. All the films portraying various aspects of the Arab–Israeli conflict analyzed here represent Israel as an essential enemy. This representation can also be traced to Egyptian cinema's being the biggest film industry in the Middle East, and hence the need to cater to a wider anti-Israeli sentiment, "using Arab–Israeli politics as a commercial drawing card" (Armbrust 2002, p. 927). Gender is at the heart of this representation. The films representing the Arab–Israeli conflict are guided by essentialist assumptions about Others and about the Egyptian/Arab Self (Sharoni 1995). The films present a sharp opposition between Israeli women and Egyptian women, acting as Israeli spies on the one hand, and nationalist Egyptian women on the other hand. The films can be divided into two sets.

The first set portrays Egyptian women betraying the nation by working as Israeli spies, while the second portrays Israeli women on Egyptian soil.

The first set includes *Execution of a Dead Man* and *Trap of Spies*, films that are similar in their treatment of the subject of Egyptian spies working for Israel in the 1970s. They both introduce young Egyptians allured by the money and status that being a spy gives. The Egyptians in both films hide what they are doing from their families, who in turn condemn the spies when they discover what they do. The spies in the films are also similar in their "immorality." Both films rely on females to represent this immorality. In *Trap of Spies*, the female Egyptian spy who betrays her country even after being caught by the Egyptian secret service is a blatant representative of Israel's reliance on duplicity to achieve its aims. She is a symbol of the immoral Israeli state that is attacking "us" from within and that "we" should guard ourselves against. In *Execution of a Dead Man*, the spy Sahar also gets caught by the Egyptians yet continues working for the enemy. However, her immorality is amplified in that she gets pregnant after having an affair with another Egyptian spy. Here we see the classic use of premarital sex as a sign of moral degeneration.

The second set includes *Love in Taba* and *Girl from Israel*, films that show how Israel's decadence has infested the Egyptians' everyday lives. Both films tackle the issue of normalization between Egypt and Israel after peace was established. Set in the newly freed land of Taba in Sinai (previously Israeli-occupied), the films construct gendered Self/Other dichotomies (Ranchod-Nilsson and Tetreault 2000) that establish women as a battleground in the Arab–Israeli conflict (Anthias and Yuval-Davis 1989). Women are used to establish "the boundaries of the group [Egyptian] identity, marking its difference from alien 'others'" (Spike Peterson 1999, p. 49). Jan Jindy Pettman argues,

> Women's use in symbolically marking the boundary of the group makes them particularly susceptible to control in strategies to maintain and defend the boundaries. Here women's movements and bodies are policed, in terms of their sexuality, fertility, and relations with "others", especially with other men. This suggests why (some) men attach such political significance to women's "outward attire and sexual purity", seeing women as their possessions, as those responsible for the

transmission of culture and through it political identity; and also as those most vulnerable to abuse, violation or seduction by "other" men.

(1992, pp. 5–6)

The films illustrate the above through constructing various binaries. First is the contrast in attire and lifestyle. The Israeli women are represented as heavily made up and bikini-clad, drinking alcohol and taking drugs as they party through the night. The Egyptian women, in contrast, dress modestly and refrain from any such activities, spending their time in Taba playing volleyball and painting.

Second is the sincerity/deception binary. While the Egyptian women are presented as not having anything to hide, the Israeli women are presented as being deceitful. In *Love in Taba*, Israeli women hide their HIV status from the Egyptian men they sleep with. The message is that Israel as symbolized by those women may be attractive yet is diseased, luring "our" men and then destroying them. In *Girl from Israel*, an Israeli woman pretends to be an American in order to get through to a young Egyptian man she eventually seduces, promising him money and status if he leaves his family behind and goes to Israel. In this way, there is a focus on the contrast between the artifice of Other women and the naturalness of the moral Egyptian women. It can be said that the Other women's artifice is a symbol of the artificiality of the State of Israel itself as portrayed by the films. Established in 1948, the State of Israel is seen by the majority of Arab countries (though not Egypt) as an artificial state that they do not recognize—an impostor attempting to replace the "real" Palestine.

Third is the emphasis on women's sexuality. The nation's honor is seen as an extension of the family's honor, which women are also used to signify. The greatest weight in this context lies in premarital virginity, which seems to dominate any other form of expression of morality (Tucker 1993; Tseelon 1995). The Egyptian women in *Girl from Israel* do not have sex before marriage; the Israeli women, on the other hand, attract the Egyptian men through presenting the opportunity of premarital sex. Towards the end of the film, *Girl from Israel* depicts a rape of one of the Egyptian virgins (dressed in a floating white dress) by an Israeli man (dressed in black). As Spike Peterson argues, "the rape of the body/nation not only violates frontiers but . . . [also] becomes a metaphor of national or state humiliation" (1999, p. 48).

This Self/Other essentialism has also been extended to the representation of the United States as an imperialist force threatening the sovereignty of the Egyptian nation. *The Other* represents the imperialist United States as a devouring mother. A wealthy American businesswoman indulging in a world of fraud, Margaret serves as a classical villain: her unholy alliance with Islamic fundamentalist terrorists, and her selfishness, immorality, and total immersion in a constructed cyber-world detach us from any identification with her character, and highlight her contrast with Egyptian purity and simplicity as seen in the character Hanan, Margaret's Egyptian daughter-in-law. Margaret sees the Egyptian people as an Other: she is outraged when Adam, her son, donates blood to Egyptian victims of an explosion: "Why give blood to 'them'?"

Margaret follows the idiosyncratic character of the devouring mother who swallows her children while the father is factually or symbolically absent (for example, as seen in *Psycho*). In *The Other*, Margaret is obsessed with her son and tries her best to be number one in his life, casting on him the "duty" of compensating her for the romance she never had with her husband. Unlike Hanan's devoted mother, Margaret does not only sublimate her desire through her son; she projects her unfulfilled desire on him (Kaplan 1992; Mulvey 1999). That preludes Margaret's latent rejection of Adam's marriage to Hanan, and her consequent endeavors to undo the multi-ethnic coupling (Adam being a Christian Egyptian-American and Hanan being an Egyptian Muslim). The inevitable and classical outcome of this drama is that Margaret ends up destroying her child. Throughout the film, Adam and Hanan's anti-essentialism is caught up between the poles of imperialism and fundamentalism. This entrapment is epitomized in the film's tragic ending. In front of Margaret's eyes and amidst a shoot-out between the fundamentalists and government military troops, the loving couple die holding hands.

In the final third of the film, we find out that Margaret is an alcoholic. She is also portrayed as having a derogatory view of other women, whose purpose, in her eyes, is merely for (sexual) pleasure. Margaret's role is ultimately as a symbol of the United States in all its degeneracy. This symbolism is stressed towards the end of the film in a conversation between Margaret and her Egyptian husband. We hear Margaret reminding him that he would be nothing without her, and at the same time she declares, "He who leans on me, I bust him," while throwing her whisky bottle at a TV set. Using the only distinguished avant-garde technique in the film, the scene is then cut to that of missiles being launched—obviously a sign of destruction.

Oppressed femininity (and masculinity)

As if appearing out of nowhere, a sultry woman in a revealing red dress, with big hair, lots of jewelry, and lots of make-up, appears on the screen. She taps her feet gleefully in a short dance routine, and then, to the background of non-diegetic cabaret music, sashays slowly down a flight of stairs, smiling at the people in front of her and swaying the frills of her dress, like a diva who knows she is making a big entrance. Jaws drop at the sight of her, her colorful aura contrasting with the grayish-yellow background of the place and the dull outfits of the crowd. She explains that she was being interrogated by the police for a prostitution accusation. This scene featuring the Egyptian actress Yousra in *Terrorism and Barbecue* is one of many in which her nameless call girl character is used to juxtapose that of the Islamic fundamentalist man Rashad (whose jaw drops in the above scene as well). That call girl is a classic example of cinema's seductive, "immoral" whore who epitomizes men's suppressed desires, and is an object of the men's gaze, both in the film and in the audience. She literally walks into an armed protest against the government led by the ordinary man Ahmad inside the 13-storey ministries complex. She joins the protesters and, when Ahmad asks her why she did that, she answers that she is too shy to say, to which he reacts, "Do you feel shy like we do?"

Ahmad's spontaneous response epitomizes the call girl's "essential otherness" (Mulvey and MacCabe 1989, p. 57) and the expectation that she—being an "immoral" call girl—is inherently evil and emotionless. The film thus demarcates the simple, innocent, moral Egyptian people who, in a comedy of errors, find themselves being labeled as terrorists, and the call girl who is presented as different, both in the way she looks and in her immorality. The call girl plays a key role in the film, in that she is used to point out the Islamic fundamentalist Rashad's moral dissolution. Gazing hard, eyes almost popping out, at the call girl's breasts, Rashad—a civil servant caught up in the protest—"advises" her to "go back to the right path," saying "All you need is a long dress and a veil and you will be virtuous." The veil thus becomes the passport that will legitimate the fundamentalist's action on his desire. This desire remains forbidden otherwise, and all the man can do is stare, causing the call girl to wonder, "Is this look on your face that of an adviser? And how come you are not advising the rest of the people?"

The scenes containing the call girl in *Terrorism and Barbecue* provide what Mulvey refers to as "scopophilia," defined as "pleasure in looking" (1999, p. 60). The way the camera traces her footsteps as she walks down the stairs, the way it caresses her face while she looks empathetically at a desperate suicidal man who falls for her, the soft non-diegetic music that we hear every time she moves, her husky voice, the slow pace of her speech, her bright red dress, and the way she uses her bosom to store her make-up and accessories all work to emphasize her sex appeal and therefore intensify the gaze of both the male audience and the male characters in the film, especially Rashad (Tseelon 1995; Mulvey 1999). Ahmad, though, is presented as being uncomfortable with her overt sexuality, stammering and diverting his gaze away from the girl. The call girl is therefore used to strengthen Egypt's morality in opposition to the corruption of Islamic fundamentalism.

A similar example is the lawyer Fat'hi's sexy neighbor in *Birds of Darkness*, a film depicting Islamic fundamentalism spin doctoring during Egyptian parliamentary elections. All we know about her is the way, squeezed into a tight dress that emphasizes her ample breasts, she enters his house submitting her chest to Fat'hi to pat in front of his Islamic fundamentalist friend Ali as a form of greeting, goes straight to Fat'hi's bedroom, and starts undressing on his bed, all the way laughing and calling Fat'hi to join her, disregarding the presence of a stranger. Thus the anonymous woman is shown to know her place, which she accepts and submits to robotically and without protest. After Ali asks Fat'hi about her, we find that Fat'hi used to be her lawyer and saved her from prosecution for murdering her husband. The woman has apparently made a deal with Fat'hi: he proves her innocence and, in return, she gives him sexual favors. This immoral woman is later used in the film to juxtapose Ali's suppressed desires with Fat'hi's gratified ones. Ali enters Fat'hi's bedroom only to find the woman's red bra left on the bed.

A comparable ambivalence is found in *The Other*, where a cyber-meeting virtually set in Paris finds the fundamentalist Fat'hallah, who chose the location, in the presence of Parisian prostitutes in the Eiffel Tower. As the meeting is virtual, we know that the presence of the prostitutes is the product of Fat'hallah's fantasy. However, his overt reaction is saying how he wishes to eliminate the presence of these women, whom, in such a realistic fantasy, he can only gaze at. This representation of women as objects to be desired and controlled (Tseelon 1995) ascribes Islamic fundamentalism an Orientalist status where women are constructed as Other (Kofman 1996).

But this fundamentalist desire oscillates between being forbidden and being permissible. The fundamentalist Ali in *The Terrorist* is a man with sexual desires like everybody else. Ali is convinced by his leader that the "possession" of the women of "infidels" is permissible. After he gets run over by a woman whose non-fundamentalist Muslim family welcomes him into their home while he recovers, Ali does not hesitate to follow his leader's suggestion and makes a sexual move on the woman's sister, which she blatantly rejects. Ali is also torn between his religious commitment and his voyeurism. In one scene Ali walks down the street behind a woman wearing a tight dress. The camera displays Ali's gazing at her bottom, which the camera then zooms on giving us Ali's perspective. At home, Ali peeps from his window at the woman, now wearing a low-cut red dress, who is on a lower floor in the building opposite him. Ali fantasizes about having sex with the woman—something that disturbs him and drives him to seek refuge in vigorous exercise and prayer.

Tseelon analyzes such gendered acts of looking/being looked at by saying that in such a distinction "there is an assumption that one position, that of the onlooker, is inherently more powerful than the other" (1995, p. 68). In the case of the woman he harasses, the woman as the object of Ali's gaze is visible. Tseelon argues that being visible does not mean possessing power: "visible as objectified is powerless, but visible as prominent and dominant [here, Ali] is powerful" (1995, pp. 68–69). In the case of Ali's neighbor, both the woman and Ali are invisible to each other. In the same way, Tseelon argues, "[i]nvisible as ignored and trivialised is powerless, but invisible as the source of gaze . . . is powerful" (1995, p. 68). Hence, invisible or not, the fundamentalist man constructs the woman as an object of his gaze and she is therefore always powerless.

In this way, the films show that, according to fundamentalism, the woman is commodified. In *The Terrorist*, fundamentalist leader Ahmad promises Ali a wife if he performs a terrorist activity. In *The Other*, the fundamentalist Fat'hallah promises to let his friend marry Fat'hallah's sister (Hanan) if the friend helps him get her divorced from her husband. Thus, we see that the woman has no say, and that she is used merely as a product in exchange for services. To summarize, women are used in the films as indicators of the corruption of Islamic fundamentalist men. This serves to de-validate their political agenda while at the same time strengthening the Egyptian nationalist agenda that sees Islamic fundamentalism as an Other. This discourse of difference is an illustration of how the nation "utters different narratives for its different inhabitants" (Eisenstein 2000, p. 38).

Moreover, the films portray the oppression of Islamic fundamentalism through the image of the silent, veiled woman (Afshar 1996). It is important to note that the notion of veiling *à la* fundamentalism in these films tends to always be that of the long, loose black chador, perhaps because of its dramatic look (as opposed to a mere colorful headscarf, for example, typically associated with traditional *baladi* women in Egyptian cinema). This image of the chador-wearing woman brings to mind the images of colonized women reproduced in Malek Alloula's (1986) book *The Colonial Harem*. As Khan puts it, "both poles [Islamism and Orientalism] essentialize the ideal Muslim Woman and reduce her to the same symbols and icons" (1998, p. 469). Almost always, with the exception of religious historical films, any such veiled woman in Egyptian cinema is connected with Islamic fundamentalism. The epitome of fundamentalist oppression can be seen in *The Terrorist*, where such women are shown to be blindly obedient to men. There is a scene in which Ali, the fundamentalist terrorist, knocks on the door of his fundamentalist leader, Ahmad. The first shot is that of Ahmad eating with his four chador-wearing wives. We hear knocking on the door, and Ahmad quickly dismisses his wives with a wave of his hand. Words are not necessary for the women to understand where their place in the hierarchy is. In *Birds of Darkness*, however, the oppressed, veiled woman steps out of the house. But that does not take her beyond any "expected" female roles: she is either the fundamentalist lawyer Ali's secretary, or a messenger who gives Ali a letter from his opponents. These women are contrasted with other women in the film, who are seen as successful businesswomen—even if they had either literally or metaphorically "inherited" their businesses from their fathers/(male) partners (like the character Raga'). The film tries to put across the message that, despite their "involvement," fundamentalist women are still oppressed.

There are multiple assessments of the meanings behind the "uses" of the veil, especially the one about the veil being a sign of resistance (El Guindi 1999). However, the Egyptian films seem to concentrate on only one: the veil as a sign of backwardness and oppression. In all these films, if we hear the veiled women speak, their relative passivity sends the message that, in essence, they are silent. In contrast, the films' depiction of the business-women shows that it is unveiling and "liberation" that gives the woman a say in society—hence, being "advanced." This view is resonated in Nawal El Saadawi's argument that "Islamic fundamentalist groups are trying to push women *back* to the veil, *back* home, *back* under the domination of their husbands" (1997, p. 95, my emphasis). The veil becomes a sign of the sexual and psychological repression of the fundamentalist identity—an identity deemed foreign to the Egyptian national one. The veil then is a nationalist tool "through which social difference is both invented and performed" (McClintock 1997, p. 89). The demarcation between Islamic fundamentalism and the construction of the Egyptian national identity as modern and oppositional emphasizes how

> definitions of the "modern" take place in a political field where certain
> identities are privileged and become dominant, while others are
> submerged or subordinated . . . secular notions of modern nationhood
> subordinate and sometimes seek to destroy alternative bases for
> solidarity and identity.
>
> (Kandiyoti 1994, p. 382)

Resistant femininity

Women participating in national struggles form another category that constructs the modern Arab national identity. When the woman, expected to be weak and powerless, becomes a fighter, she becomes a symbol of the ability of the powerless to fight (Waylen 1996). In Palestinian cinema, the liberation of women is firmly connected with the liberation of the land, in a twist on the usual motherland symbol. One such woman is Nahila in *The Door to the Sun*, a film that locates female resistance within the start of Palestinian dispossession in 1948. The film depicts Nahila as a young woman, working in a field with other women, with barbwire separating them from a school where Israeli girls are jumping rope. The illiterate Nahila pulls up her robe in an attempt to transform it to a version of the shorts worn by the Israeli girls. Nahila's symbolic act of resistance is put in practice shortly afterwards, when the Palestinian villagers are driven away from Ain az-Zaitouna. The villagers decide to defy the Israelis and return to their village, and Nahila is the one who leads the crowd back. When Nahila falls pregnant after she meets her husband in secret, she is confronted by Israeli soldiers who inquire about her pregnancy. Nahila succeeds in protecting her husband by defiantly telling the shocked soldiers that she is a prostitute. Nahila's limited acts of defiance in 1948 can be seen as the seed of the more active roles played by women in Palestinian political struggle in the years to come.

The Fertile Memory depicts the lives of two different women who have survived the ordeals of 1948 (in the case of Roumia) and 1967 (in the case of Sahar). The film contrasts the life and thoughts of Sahar, who has broken the chain of patriarchy by choosing to work and raise her daughter on her own after her divorce, and those of Roumia, the old widow who refused to remarry or "have a life" (as her neighbors say to her) for the sake of her children. Lengthy screen time is given to shots of Roumia doing domestic work, from cooking to preparing large, heavy strands of wool for spinning. In contrast, Sahar—who smokes and has short hair—is a novelist and theater director whose novels deal with the occupation of Palestine. Sahar sees her resistance as ordinary, saying that her struggle is not by demonstrating, but through surviving every day. The film links Sahar's struggle for Palestine with her struggle against patriarchy. Thus we find that Sahar studied literature only after her divorce. Marriage to her was a cage: "When a woman is cooped at home, her mind becomes confined to the house, the kitchen, and the children. Not a pleasant experience." She reads an extract from one of her novels, where she writes about refusing to be a woman who marries, gets pregnant, cooks complex meals, and proves her household skills to her husband. The shot of Sahar reading is cut to that of Roumia

Figure 11 Sahar: the liberated nation as liberated woman—*The Fertile Memory*

whipping wool with a stick. The film thus advocates the liberation of women as a prerequisite for the liberation of Palestine. In a prophetic scene, Sahar looks out the window overlooking Nablus. We hear Sahar's voice saying "Nablus is beautiful but painful. Here, when I was a child, I was treated as a woman. It's hard for a divorced woman to live here. Any word or joke can be misinterpreted. But you are never alone in Nablus, in misery and joy. It is therefore not easy to think freely. That's why the religious fanatics are going to cause problems. How can you improve society when you cover half of it top to toe?"

Female symbolic resistance continues in the twenty-first century in *Rana's Wedding*, a film about a young Palestinian woman trying to get married under Israeli occupation in Jerusalem. Rana represents the symptoms of Israel's interference with the Palestinians' private lives, but also Palestinian defiance. She is also used to criticize the clashes between

Israelis and Palestinians. Towards the beginning of the film, a long shot reveals a row of vans stuck in a road block as Israeli soldiers check people's papers. Palestinian children standing on the right of the screen throw stones at the soldiers on the left. The soldiers in turn shoot at them. Rana stands in the middle, her head moving from side to side as if watching a tennis match. She picks up a stone, throws it at the soldiers, and runs. Rana's character summarizes the frustration of Palestinians. As Rana, her fiancé Khalil, and another friend drive endlessly around Jerusalem to try to get to the marriage registry office, taking different routes to escape the road blocks, they reach a road blocked by a crowd of mourners. Veiled women and young men carry a Palestinian flag as a dead man (a martyr) lies on a stretcher. Khalil and his friend leave to get the registrar, telling Rana to wait in the car. But Rana gets out of the car and approaches the mourners. All mourners seem to be going in the opposite direction to Rana, whom they stare at while she stares back at them, alienated from the scene of death as she attempts to start a new life with Khalil. She goes back to the car, and a fantasy sequence shows Rana behind the car wheel but going nowhere, as

Figure 12   Rana awaits her wedding—*Rana's Wedding* (photo courtesy of Arab Film Distribution)

if trapped in the car. She bangs on the windows of the car but cannot escape. Later Rana tries to force her way through a road block, physically struggling with the male Israeli soldiers. In one of the most powerful scenes in the film, Rana expresses her fear to her friend Mary as Israeli soldiers destroy a house next door to Rana's. Rana looks out the window. Her point of view reveals soldiers standing in line facing her, all harmoniously carrying guns leaning to the right, with a bulldozer behind them. Holding her wedding dress, Rana says "They're destroying a house the day I'm trying to build one." Mary reassures her: "Don't worry; we'll rebuild it once more." Rana finally manages to hold the wedding in the street, where she dances in her white gown. Rana's wedding thus becomes a life-affirming act. This is parallel to the use of the wedding in *Wedding in Galilee*, which is also presented as an act of defiance to Israeli restrictions on Palestinian life.

The Algerian film *Rachida* uses women both to mirror the oppression of Islamic fundamentalism and to resist it. The film revolves around the story of a young female teacher, Rachida, living in Algiers. Rachida's *joie de vivre* is established at the beginning of the film, where our first glimpse of her is the reflection of her face in a mirror as she puts on her lipstick in preparation for a school photograph, and later where she listens to music on her headphones on her way to work. This peace is soon shattered as teenage fundamentalists try to force her to carry a bag of explosives to the school, and shoot her in the stomach when she refuses. The film presents a vivid portrayal of the fear engulfing Rachida and her mother as a result of this horrific incident. Even after moving to a remote village, they are still haunted by the Islamic fundamentalist terrorists. Rachida gets startled when she sees a man carrying a gun around his waist in a shop. Sitting in the living room with her mother, Rachida watches the television announcing the assassination of seven Christian monks by the fundamentalists and the news of four girls kidnapped and others killed in another terrorist attack. The terror follows her to the village school where she has found another teaching job; a veiled teacher reprimands Rachida for not wearing a veil, saying "God commanded us to cover our heads." Her female doctor admits that she is afraid of being murdered in front of her children by the terrorists. Eventually the terror becomes concrete, and the terrorists attack the village, stealing money from a café and killing Rachida's elderly neighbor while the villagers watch helplessly. She and her mother seek refuge in each other, with

Rachida announcing "I'm in exile in my own country . . . I'm afraid of my own shadow." Rachida is not the only female measure of fundamentalist terror in the film. Halfway through the film, we see a girl with torn clothes and uncombed hair walking through a forest. The camera follows her through bushes and among trees as she periodically glances behind her and runs barefoot. Rachida sees her from the school gates. Another teacher points out that that is the girl the fundamentalists kidnapped. The girl collapses in the middle of the village. Scared and startled, she is embraced by the village women who gather around her and cover her with their multi-colored veils. But despite this embrace, the girl is denounced by her father and is referred to as "the disgraced one." In a scene set in a women's *hammam*, the girl, now pregnant as a result of being raped by her captors, is seen in close-up as she rubs herself so hard with the exfoliating mitt that she starts bleeding. Rachida in turn refuses to go to the *hammam*, fearing other women might mistake her scar for a caesarian. Though unable to break the chains of patriarchy, Rachida eventually decides to defy the fundamen-talists after they attack the village and loot it. The film ends with Rachida picking up her walkman and bag and walking defiantly in the village, alone. A high angle shot reveals Rachida surrounded by destruction. Then slowly,

Figure 13   Rachida after being attacked by Islamic fundamentalists—*Rachida*

children begin to emerge from behind the trees in the forest, carrying their school bags and following Rachida to the destroyed school. Another high angle shot sees Rachida entering the smashed classroom, with its broken door and upturned chairs. The final shot in the film is of Rachida writing "today's lesson" on the board and looking into the distance as she imagines the sound of children singing in a playground.

Women under patriarchy

However, as Kandiyoti argues, activities of women participating in nationalist movements

> could most easily be legitimised as natural extensions of their womanly nature and as a duty rather than a right. Modernity was invested with different meanings for men, who were relatively free to adopt new styles of conduct, and women, who, in Najmabadi's terms, had to be "modern-yet-modest".
>
> (1994, p. 379)

Kandiyoti's point can be found in the Palestinian film *In the Ninth Month*. The film seems to demark the woman's role in resistance and her more traditional role in society. The film introduces us to Sana', a political activist whom we first see wearing a *kaffiyya* around her neck and denouncing Israel as "a terrorist state led by the United States," as she stands on a platform giving a speech to an anti-Gulf War rally. In Sana's bedroom hangs a Palestinian flag, and the words "revolution till victory" are written on the wall. Yet Sana's role is mainly to mirror the struggle her fiancé Ahmad is going through in trying to conceal the presence of his brother Khalil in their village, the latter being wanted by the Israelis. A fantasy sequence in the film reveals a nightmare by Ahmad, who is wrongly accused by the villagers of kidnapping a small boy, Hassan, and selling him to Israelis. The sequence shows a crowd of people carrying pictures of Hassan and marching on a narrow path surrounded by bubbling, boiling water and flames. Sana' leads in her wedding dress and falls into the boiling water, as the haunting sound of violins is heard. Ahmad watches Sana's fall helplessly. The sequence symbolizes Judgment Day, where Ahmad has to pay for Sana's suffering by not being able to rescue her from the flames of hell. Despite Sana's support of Ahmad, their relationship eventually cracks under the pressure, and towards the end of the film we see Sana' again, this time marching in a demonstration, but with tears running down her cheeks when she sees Ahmad in the distance. Thus political activism and relationships seem to be mutually exclusive in the film.

Franco argues that, even "when a woman managed to become a militant, she was often forced into a traditional gender role and classified as either butch or seductress" (1994, p. 366). Franco's argument is illustrated in the Egyptian films depicting politically active women or women who perform limited acts of resistance: *Road to Eilat* (a film about an Arab coalition under the command of the Egyptian marines on a secret mission to Israel), *48 Hours in Israel* and *Mission in Tel Aviv* (also about a mission to Israel before the 1973 War, this time using Egyptian spies), and *Naji al-Ali*, a biographic film on the life of the late Palestinian political cartoonist of the same name. *Road to Eilat*, *48 Hours in Israel*, and *Mission in Tel Aviv* present female fighters going undercover to Israel in order to accomplish missions that would aid in the preparation for the 1973 October War against Israel. All three women use seduction to achieve their aim of entering Israel and gathering intelligence information, the first by alluring Israeli men (*Road to Eilat*), the second by working as a showgirl (*48 Hours in Israel*), and the third by posing as a pro-Israeli spy (*Mission in Tel Aviv*). All the films use elaborate shots of the women's bodies in action, with whole dance sequences in *48 Hours in Israel* and *Mission in Tel Aviv*, and a scene of Maryam's body being caressed by an Israeli man in *Road to Eilat*.

Mulvey and MacCabe (1989) argue that women's sexuality is the condition that makes them visible in a male-dominated world. It is this sexuality that makes those women visible in a male-dominated resistance movement. The display of the women's bodies means that they no longer become sex objects for foreign men only (Enloe 1990); in this "nationalist movement," "the native continues to retain the same essential characteristics depicted in Orientalism, but nevertheless imagines himself [*sic*] as autonomous, active and sovereign" (Yegenoglu 1998, p. 123). As Yegenoglu (1998) argues, this nationalist movement sustains the legacy of Orientalism and its view of Oriental women as objects of men's gaze.

But Maryam's role is not confined to seduction. The film explains her participation in the struggle by reciting her story. The time line of the film is 1969, during which Palestinians were seeking refuge in Jordan as a result of the harsh conditions of being under occupation. These conditions resulted in several traumas ranging from illiteracy to lack of hygiene, and consequently "heightened political consciousness among [Palestinian] women" (Dajani 1993, p. 114). Some of these women "have broken through traditional prejudices to become fighters" (Holt 1996, p. 190). *Road to Eilat* follows Sayigh's explanation that at the end of the 1960s there was a "'revolutionary tide' generated by the defeat of the Arab armies in 1967" (1993, p. 176). Sayigh points out how Palestinian women underwent military training as members of the Resistance Movement, something which Maryam exemplifies. She is shown carrying a gun, wearing military uniform just like her male counterparts, and actively participating in missions for the Egyptian marines (hers is to go undercover to Eilat as an Israeli). A similar depiction is that of Shams in *The Door to the Sun*. Living under the tight Jordanian control in Amman, Shams's husband used to beat her up, which she argues was a compensation for his inability to carry a gun. Shams tells how she wore jeans for the first time after Tal az-Zaatar. The massacre motivated her to join the *feda'yeen* herself. Her resilience forced her husband to let her go with the *feda'yeen*, and she joined the PLO in Tripoli. Sayigh (1993) explains that a number of women had joined the Resistance Movement due to the encouragement of male kin, but Maryam in *Road to Eilat*, rather romantically, explains that she joined after her brother died for the Resistance. This invocation of equality resonates Majid's point that "it was the national struggle . . . that brought women out of their confined, privatized social spaces into the public sphere" (1998, p. 351). Palestinian resistance has generated the slogan *al-ard qabl al-ird*, meaning "land (or national freedom) before honour" (Abdo 1994, p. 162).

However, as Wilford argues, "fighting alongside men to achieve independence does not provide a guarantee of women's inclusion as equal citizens" (1998, p. 3). Shams is executed by the leaders in her refugee camp after she murders one of their men, her actions being regarded as bringing shame on their community. *Road to Eilat*'s presentation of the brother's death as the incident that caused Maryam to become a fighter serves as a justification of her actions, and as a reassertion of her femininity as well (Tasker 1993). Moreover, the film ensures that Maryam does not stray "too far from socially acceptable roles for women" (Inness 1999, p. 46). Maryam's role in the Egyptian marines' operation, for most of the film, tends to be complementary to that of her male colleagues. She spends most of the time encouraging her male colleagues and taking care of them in a sisterly way (for example, she pulls out a photograph of her deceased brother and shows it to one of the men, emphasizing the resemblance between him and her brother, and they strike up a quasi-sibling relationship). When Maryam is in a military uniform she does not fight, and when she is carrying a gun she does not shoot. Thus the film follows Anthias and Yuval-Davis's explanation that "in national liberation struggles . . . generally [women] are seen to be in a supportive and nurturing relation to men even where they take most risks" (1989, p. 10). Maryam's display of emotions serves to tone down her toughness and to "reassure the audience that . . . [she] is a 'normal' woman" (Inness 1999, p. 98). Looking at how Maryam's character is portrayed, we find that she generally acts in reaction to men's schemes: we do not see her planning, but executing her male leaders' strategies (Tasker 1993, 1998). Thus she can be said to be a sidekick, and not a central character, despite the length of time she spends on screen.

The journalist Suad in *Naji al-Ali* is another woman "fighter." Suad is perhaps the closest we can get to what Doane calls "woman's film" (1999, p. 71), whereby the woman is a central protagonist, instead of an object to be looked at. Resisting the proposals of her ex-fiancé, who offers to "protect" her from the perils of her job as a journalist during the Lebanese War, and dedicating herself to the cause of anti-Israeli Palestinian/Lebanese/Syrian resistance, running fearlessly along battlefields, and engaging actively in political debate, she epitomizes female power and confidence. Stacey explains that such a character serves to "[offer] women fantasies of resistance" (1999, p. 201). However, after an assassination attempt on Naji's life, we see Suad helpless in the hospital, staring at Naji who is lying in a coma. Tasker argues that the woman's role in this representation is merely to provide "an audience for the hero's suffering, his powerlessness emphasised by her gaze" (1993, p. 26).

Both Maryam and Suad are single women, which might be seen as a rejection of "the responsibilities of adult womanhood" (Tasker 1993, p. 14), or as strengthening their tough image (Inness 1999). This is emphasized in the character Suad, who is not only single, but has left her fiancé for her political involvement. She is also a "tomboy" sometimes in the way she acts (and sometimes dresses) (Inness 1999). Maryam also fluctuates between being "feminine" in her swimming suit and "masculine" in her military uniform. Such cross-dressing can be seen as a way of negotiating the portrayal of women's fighting bodies, as atypical, even deviant, with women's traditional non-fighting role (Tasker 1998). It can also be seen as emphasizing their toughness yet reaffirming their femininity. Suad and Maryam are both the only women in all-male environments. While this can be seen as highlighting their strength, their contrast with the other women in the films, who assume more traditional roles, emphasizes their portrayal as being exceptional women, and hence "their toughness is understood not to be a common trait of women" (Inness 1999, p. 97).

Thus, despite Suad and Maryam being strong characters at face value, they are a "revised stereotype" (Tasker 1993, p. 19) of women in cinema, strong but with their toughness undermined (Inness 1999). Perhaps because *Naji al-Ali* does not want to transgress patriarchy totally, in a scene where a party is held to celebrate Naji's safety, it is Suad, the only woman present, who makes the cake. This not only reaffirms Suad's femininity, but also undermines her toughness. The same can be said about Nadia El-Guindi's character in *48 Hours in Israel*, where she disguises as a dancer. Inness explains this use of disguise by saying that the woman's "toughness can be seen as only another example of her play with disguises; we need not fear her if we can believe that underneath the tough exterior a 'true' woman resides" (1999, p. 35). As Enloe (1990) argues, this depiction of women in nationalist movements descends from nationalism being masculine and patriarchal to start with. Schulze (1998) explains that nationalist movements do not erase the view of women as inferior to men: "when they are needed they may carry arms and fight, but ultimately they are still seen as 'other'" (p. 159).

Conclusion

"Nations are contested systems of cultural representation" (McClintock 1997, p. 89). Gender is one of the most powerful tools by which nations define themselves and others. In cinema, the way masculinity or femininity is represented can dictate political statements. In Hollywood, as we have seen in the context of Middle Eastern politics, gender has been used to exclude Arab Others from the American national identity and to vilify them. Whatever the political situation, from the Arab–Israeli conflict to the association between Gulf Arab states and oil as power, gender has been used to legitimize the actions of the United States while demonizing the Arabs. In this context, the male stands in for the nation, whether American or Other.

Women, on the other hand, are used in the cultural construction of the Arab nations, and as instruments of demarcation between the Self and the Other. As demonstrated by the representation of Tahiyya and the Egyptian virgins in *Girl from Israel*, "idealized images and real bodies of women serve as national boundaries" (Ranchod-Nilsson and Tetreault 2000, p. 5). This is contrasted with the image of the whore who epitomizes the Otherness of the enemy, namely Israel and the United States. Lying between the virgin and the whore are the silent, veiled woman who signifies the oppression of Islamic fundamentalism, and the politically active female who embodies the modern face of Egypt, Algeria, and Palestine.

Orientalism exists strongly in both sets of films. Most of the American films belong to the action genre. This genre is built upon issues of mastery, whether over objects or over others. The films do not deviate from this current, and they all conclude with the American hero's control over the situation and over Others. The films' political purpose is to illuminate a fantasy odyssey fought against primordial enemies. They operate within this general Orientalist perspective, depicting the Arab men as ultimate, essential Others.

The Egyptian films also employ sexist slants when portraying women. We have seen how, despite their casting of some women in "fighting" roles, the films rely on the display of the women's bodies. The women are thus objects of the gaze of the men in the film and of the audience. They are simultaneously used as the tool by which the "immorality" of Others is measured (in the case of the fundamentalists and the Israelis) and as validators of the patriarchal nation. This is epitomized in the representation of Tahiyya, who confines herself to her private sphere while leaving all the political work to her husband.

Thus it is important to pay attention to the way the nation is configured in the cinemas. The female nations of Arab cinemas and the male nation of Hollywood represent clashing political and cultural stances. The American focus on individuality and consequently individual freedom is absent from the Arab agenda. The latter's agenda is more consumed with issues of familial/national morality that are manifested in the feminine subservience to this larger-than-one's-life cause. The American nationalist agenda focuses on the other extreme, the masculine crusade for freedom. Hollywood thus has both created and appropriated what can be seen as global narrative transparency, setting its individualism stories as a striking, more resonant contrast to the Arab cinemas' apparent totalitarianism.

In all those representations, we find that men and women are embedded in good-versus-evil struggles around the authenticity of the American and Arab national identities (Moghadam 1994). The face of this struggle has changed throughout history. In the case of Hollywood, it has moved from representing the United States as an infallible hero to a new (caring but killing) man. But this has not completely eliminated essentialist notions of the Self. Hollywood films of the 1990s have presented a shift from the focus on the white hero to representing black heroes as well, as seen in Childers (Samuel L. Jackson) in *Rules of Engagement*, Sirling (Denzel Washington) in *Courage under Fire*, and Chief Elgin (Ice Cube) in *Three Kings*. The black body is used as a sign for American democracy (Willis 1997). But at the same time, despite the initial "subversion" of the system practiced by the three men, the character of the black man does not transgress the rules irreversibly. As bell hooks argues,

> part of what makes his character "acceptable" is that he is not threatening to change the system; he is working hard to uphold the values of the existing social structure. There is an underlying insistence throughout the film that no other system could be as good . . . The underlying assumption is that he commits to this because he worships, admires, and loves white patriarchal power.
>
> (1992, p. 101)

In the case of Arab cinemas, the struggle over authenticity has moved from representing the nation as a virtuous mother to representing it as a modern woman. However, the films send conflicting messages about modern, tough women. On one hand, their toughness is acceptable. On the other hand, this toughness is presented as such only in the sense that it is circumstantial. This emphasizes how, as McClintock argues, women "are typically constructed as the symbolic bearers of the nation but are denied any direct relation to national agency" (1997, p. 90). However, through showing how women play different, often conflicting, roles, the films challenge the Orientalist treatment of women in the "Third World" as a homogeneous entity. At the same time, they challenge resistant discourses that "elevate the racially female voice into a metaphor for 'the good'" (Suleri 1995, p. 273).

In this sense, the cinemas converge. Despite their generic differences, they utilize gender in the same way, strengthening their own national identities and constructing enemies as outsiders to those identities. The generic slant of each cinema has predisposed the construction of the nation as male in the American action films, and as female in the Arab melodramas and dramas. However, women in those cinemas remain outsiders who are at best sidekicks. And while the representations of the enemies in the cinemas may differ, with the American films portraying primordial yet submissive Others and the Egyptian films portraying essential materialist and sexually permissive ones, the cinemas rely on gender to convey those messages in a similar manner. Thus, the list of Others in the films grows. Not only is the "Orient" an Other according to Hollywood; the Orient itself has its own Others, signified by either indulgent women (the West) or repressed ones (Islamic fundamentalists).

III

Conflicts Within and Without: The Arab–Israeli Conflict (and the Gulf War)

The Arab–Israeli conflict and the Gulf War are two of the most controversial issues of the politics of the Middle East. Much has been written about those conflicts—the first one being one of the longest and most complicated on-going problems in this area, the second being a direct challenge to the romanticism of pan-Arabism. American cinema has only engaged in "us and them" narratives of the Gulf War, as analyzed in Chapters 1 and 2 of this book, and therefore will not be examined in this chapter in this context. The Arab cinemas have only touched upon the Gulf War in a series of short films made by directors from Tunisia, Morocco, Lebanon, and Palestine, published under the umbrella title *The Gulf War . . . What Next?* In addition, Egyptian cinema has produced only one film about the Gulf War, *The Tempest*. On the other hand, Palestinian cinema has been prolific in tackling the Arab–Israeli conflict, as have Egyptian cinema and Syrian cinema. In their representations of the Arab–Israeli conflict, the American, Egyptian, and Syrian films engage in a similar discourse of difference, and advocate subjective nationalisms that form part of an on-going cultural battle over the same "homeland" and that complicate the mythical form of the nation.

The relationship between the cinemas and nationalism belongs to a tradition of overlapping between nationalism and art. On one hand, art is influenced by nationalist movements. This can be seen, for example, in the Egyptian films about Nasser (like *Nasser 56*). The point can also be applied to Hollywood, with, for example, the several films glorifying the American nation and its allies produced during the Cold War (perhaps the most famous being the James Bond series). On the other hand, the Egyptian and Palestinian films about the Arab–Israeli conflict show how art can be seen as directing nationalism. This has led to the declaration that "[t]he nation . . . is an abstraction, an allegory, a myth that does not correspond to a reality that can be scientifically defined" (Mariategui 1971, quoted in Brennan 1995, p. 172). In this sense, we can look at nations as being invented (Brennan 1995) or imagined (Anderson 1983); the role of the films is to take part in this invention or imagination. However, we still have to remember, as Brennan points out, that not all art work about nations is nationalistic. Moreover, not all nationalist cultural practices are essentially progressive or regressive. Aijaz Ahmad argues:

> Whether or not a nationalism will produce a progressive cultural practice depends, to put it in Gramscian terms, upon the political character of the power bloc which takes hold of it and utilizes it, as a material force, in the process of constituting its own hegemony.
>
> (1995, p. 79)

On another level, looking at the representation of the Arab–Israeli conflict reveals the difficulty of applying traditional cultural theories to the conflict. The conflict is problematic in that, although it has often been referred to as an "ethnic conflict," it consists of various other factors that complicate notions of ethnicity. The conflict is mainly nationalist, but not in the sense that one nation is fighting another. It is in the sense that diasporic peoples are aiming at reclaiming the nation. This is not the case however in the Hollywood films, which construct the conflict between Palestinians and Israelis as an ethnic conflict. The films therefore do not go "so far as to question the basic assumptions of the dominant 'official' interpretations of the conflict" (Safty 1992, p. 145). This "official" discourse encompasses, first, the presentation of the conflict as one between ethnic groups, which distorts the position of the Palestinians. Second, the conflict is represented with sympathy to Zionism and the assumption of the legitimacy of the State of Israel. The American films invoke historical and religious notions to strengthen Israel's claim to Palestinian land. Third, this carries with it the representation of Arab acts of violence as terrorism, while showing those by Israel as "reprisals . . . directed at 'guerrilla bases'" (Safty 1992, p. 149) as seen in *The Little Drummer Girl*. And finally, there is the association of Palestinians with terrorism in general, which undermines their claims (Safty 1992).

The United States' position within this conflict is far from neutral; it has often been perceived as a supporter of Israel, which has alienated the Arab masses (Saikal 2000). It has been argued therefore that, in representing this conflict, the American media in general have been informed by a dominant Zionist discourse. The American films dealing with the conflict take a more sympathetic side towards Israel; yet the United States is represented in the films as a godfather, superior to both the Israelis and the Palestinians, and mediating for peace between the two warring sides. This representation forms part of the American national and global agenda, exhibiting sympathy to American Jews while at the same time confirming the position of the United States as a world policeman.

The Egyptian films, on the other hand, engage in a similar process of glorifying the Self and vilifying the Other. Yet vilifying Israel is complicated by Egypt's political stance towards Israel from the time of Sadat onwards, where, although normalization between Egypt and Israel has not been established, the two countries have signed a peace treaty. The Egyptian films choose to vilify Israel as an essential evil enemy that allows no space for negotiation or co-existence, and, more recently, the United States for ignoring conflicts in the Middle East. The Egyptian films then ignore Egypt's official discourse in order to satisfy both Egyptian populist discourse and wider Arab anti-Israel sentiment. Egypt is imagined in the films as a crucial Arab player, and therefore the films both resurrect and lament a golden age of pan-Arab nationalism that had reached its climax under Nasser. Syrian films, meanwhile, manage to present a degree of self-criticism, yet they also follow the Egyptian films' lead in presenting Arab (here Syrian) support to Palestinians.

The unity of Arabs in the Egyptian and Syrian films is not presented as being the same as that of Jews in the American ones. This is because, while Hollywood unifies Jews not only by using a myth of common culture, language, and religion, but also by using a myth of common ancestry, transforming the Jews from a religious to an ethnic group and therefore downplaying Israel as a political project, Egyptian and Syrian cinemas make no claim for common ancestry. Pan-Arabism can thus be seen as portrayed as a form of nationalism rather than ethnicity, i.e. it is a political project that utilizes common cultural aspects, language, and religion while recognizing and maintaining the ethnic diversity of the Arab world.

The Arab–Israeli conflict in the Palestinian films complicates notions of post-colonialism. This is demonstrated through the focus on the oppression of Palestinians compared to the transferring of Jews from the position of the subordinate to a dominant one with the building of the State of Israel. As Clifford (1997a) argues, "such 'homecomings' are, by definition, the negation of diaspora" (p. 287). By narrating the experiences of the Palestinians, the films construct themselves as a means of resistance. The films take a populist stance by praising the loyalty of ordinary people (or the masses) to the Palestinian cause while criticizing the Arab elites' indifference.

In the case of the Gulf War, the Arab films present different points of view on the conflict, oscillating between direct opposition to American policy that is seen to break the Arab world apart, and severe criticism of self-inflicted Arab divisions. The Arab films, viewed together, thus contradict notions of homogeneity of the Arab world implied by Hollywood.

Hollywood's America: world police

Hollywood's representation of the Arab–Israeli conflict revolves around three major themes: the construction of the conflict between Israelis and Palestinians as an ethnic conflict; the establishment of physical and ideological borders between Israelis and Palestinians, which entails the construction of each side as a predominantly homogeneous group; and the representation of the United States as a godfather whose role infantilizes both Israel and Palestine.

An ethnic conflict?

Brown defines ethnic conflict as "a dispute about important political, economic, social, cultural or territorial issues between two or more ethnic communities" (1997, p. 82). Anthony Smith defines ethnic community as "a named human population with a common ancestry, shared memories, and cultural elements; a link with a historic territory or homeland; and a measure of solidarity" (quoted in Brown 1997, p. 81). On one hand, Israelis and Palestinians share most characteristics of an ethnic community. They each have shared memories and cultures and a defined name, each is linked with (the same) homeland, and they both share a measure of solidarity. For both, their community structure is more authoritative than their economic and political structures (Rex 1997b). However, the complication comes when considering common ancestry. While Palestinians do not usually allude to notions of common ancestry, Israelis invoke that through religious tales and claims to one place of descent. Anthony Smith (1999) argues that common ancestry is one factor that constitutes ethnic myths. There are four other factors. The first is having a myth of spatial origins. Israelis and Palestinians both believe in belonging to the land of Palestine. The second is implicating a myth of a heroic, golden age. For the Palestinians, this is the pre-Zionist immigration phase, when they still lived in the whole of Palestinian land. For the Israelis, it is before the Jewish diaspora. The third is including a myth of decline, and finally there is a myth of regeneration, aiming at restoring the golden age. Both sides allude to such myths (for the Israelis, starting with the diaspora and then the Holocaust, establishing regeneration through the establishment of the State of Israel; for the Palestinians, decline starts with the establishment of Israel and the Palestinian diaspora, and regeneration in several nation-building activities, culminating in the *intifada* in 1987). Thus, both aim at restoring what they see as their golden age through their current struggle.

We can therefore see that neither Israelis nor Palestinians satisfy the full requirements of ethnic myths. The crucial factor here is the myth of descent. Smith (1999) explains that, in the quest for recognition and independence, ethnic spokesmen have "drawn on, or in some cases invented, a 'myth of origins and descent'" (p. 60). Smith (2000) argues that Israelis have "invented traditions serving the immediate needs of Zionist pioneering elites in the 1920s and 1930s as they sought to portray an activist, heroic 'new Jew' in Palestine—in contrast to the burdened and victimized 'old Jew' of the diasporic exile" (p. 56). This partly explains how Jews—racially, ethnically, linguistically, and nationally diverse—have mobilized themselves to establish Israel. In doing so, they have also drawn on a common ideology (Zionism) and a common history. The ethnic myth here is used as a nationalist tool (Jenkins 1997), as a means of "destroying local, and regional ties in the interests of the centre and the whole community" (Smith 1999, p. 61). The ethnic myth, in other words, has moved beyond culture and into politics. It no longer aims at just preserving an existing community, but also at creating a new one. In this sense, the present is placed in the context of the past, and Judaism is used as both a source and a vehicle of Israel's shared memories.

In light of this background, Hollywood constructs the conflict between Israelis and Palestinians as an ethnic conflict relying on the use of ethnic myth in the representation of Israel. Not only do Israelis in the films share a common ethnic myth, but Jews worldwide are portrayed as sharing this common sentiment and history and even origin, with no distinction between Zionist and non-Zionist Jews. *The Delta Force*, for example, represents an American Jewish couple who are devoted to Israel. This ethnic conflict then is constructed as one between two groups over the same territory who both claim it as their homeland. This struggle over landscape can be seen in an argument between Israeli students and a PLO figure in *The Ambassador*. The PLO figure, Mustafa, says he has "fought and killed for my homeland," to which Israelis reply they will "never give it back." Mustafa compares Palestinian refugee camps to concentration camps, saying Palestinians can never go back to them. He talks about "Palestinians thrown out of their homeland" while the Israeli students argue "We'll give back the land when America gives back occupied territories, like Texas to Mexico! Are you asking us to return land that we have conquered?" This echoes Shohat's (1997a) argument that the metaphor of the virgin land is shared by Zionism and American pioneer discourses. As she puts it, "Assumed to lack owners, [the land] . . . becomes the property of its 'discoverers' and cultivators who transform the wilderness into a garden, those who 'make the desert bloom'" (p. 100).

Another way in which the conflict between Israelis and Palestinians is "ethnified" is through presenting Palestinian resistance as a "revolution," as seen in *The Little Drummer Girl*. The film does not refer to the PLO by its name, but simply calls it "the revolution." The conflict is thus changed from being about Palestinian resistance to Israeli occupation to being about Palestinians revolting against an already-established order. The emphasis on an already-established order is one way in which Israeli claims to Palestinian land are naturalized in the films, and where Israel is constructed as driven by an ethnic nationalism. Smith (1999) and Kellas (1998) define ethnic nationalism as one where the nation is conceived of as a community where common ancestry is the prime condition of belonging to the nation. They argue that this nationalism is different from, though not necessarily mutually exclusive to, what they call territorial (Smith) or social/civil (Kellas) nationalism, where a nation is conceived of around a definite homeland, but where the individual can choose which nation to belong to. Kellas argues that this nationalism is individualist, in that anyone can join. Ethnic nationalism, by comparison, is problematic because it means that this nationalism is by definition exclusive and collectivist. Israel, as represented in the films and in reality, includes characteristics from the territorial model; however, the problem is that it emphasizes the ethnic one, making it an exclusive nation. This is due to Israeli claims to an "original," "natural" identity. Clifford (1997a) explains that "claims of a primary link with 'the homeland' usually must override conflicting rights and the history of others in the land" (p. 288). But how far back does one have to go in order to prove this primary link? Moreover, such a claim denies the heterogeneity of societies in history, in "ancient homelands." Clifford warns that such a claim risks ahistoricism by drawing a border between the "originals" and the "newcomers." In this sense, how far back in history should one go to have a claim to belonging? As Clifford (1997a) puts it, "How long does it take to become 'indigenous'?" (p. 288).

Homogenizing Israelis and Palestinians

The films construct ideological and physical borders between Israelis and Palestinians that place each group in essential opposition to the other.

The borders constructed by Hollywood are not abstractions; they are metaphorical and arbitrary constructions that form part of "the discursive materiality of power relations" (Brah 1996, p. 198). The way Palestinians and Israelis in the films are separated not only geographically, but also ideologically, necessitates the importance of looking at "psychic territories demarcated" (Brah 1996, p. 198). This exclusionary discourse constructs Palestinians as a threat to Israel from the outside. In *The Little Drummer Girl*, for example, no Palestinians are shown as living in Israel. In *The Ambassador*, Israeli students declare "There is no Palestine." This invokes notions of "a land without people for the people without a land" as stated by Golda Meir. As Safty explains, this slogan

> strips a people of its land, denies and annihilates its existence, rejects the assimilation of the Jews in their respective European societies, establishes the concept of the Jewish people as a distinct entity despite opposition from assimilated European Jewry, and creates in the collective consciousness of European audiences the image of Palestine as an empty heaven ready to perceive a homeless people.
>
> (1992, p. 139)

The ideological borders constructed by the films also serve to homogenize each side in the conflict. We can trace three major steps in the process of homogenization of Jews and Israelis employed by the films. First, we witness a redefinition of the Jewish communities around the world as a unified group with a single political culture as seen in *The Delta Force*. In the film the American Jewish couple on board the hijacked plane reminisce about their honeymoon in Jerusalem and invoke the Holocaust after the hijack. The couple, along with another American man of Russian origin on board the plane also express their belonging to the United States. This emphasizes the psychological similarities between the United States and Israel as immigrant nations (Kellas 1998).

Second, there is a re-education of the potential members about the nation's "true culture." The Israeli true culture according to Zionists can only be about establishing Israel in the land of Palestine. This "territorialization of memory" (Smith 1999, p. 152) results from regarding the land as sacred. *The Ambassador* opens with the American ambassador to Israel, Hacker, driving into Jerusalem, along the way pointing out "Moses' tomb" to his companion. Thus, while the nation is often argued to be a cultural system with religious characteristics providing meaning and continuity to people (Anderson 1983), this does not mean that nationalism has replaced religion. Rather, Israel and its representation in the films demonstrate how the two go together (Kellas 1998). But sacredness is not only applicable in the religious sense; it is also seen in how the Israeli/Palestinian land is imagined as a land free from oppression. In *The Little Drummer Girl*, Israel is portrayed as a safe haven, with a glistening sun and idyllic beaches, where Charlie retreats after her ordeals of being a spy.

Third, we witness a regeneration of that true culture, seen for example in the revival of Hebrew as the official language of Israel. The American Jewish woman in *The Delta Force* wears a wedding ring engraved in Hebrew. Israeli discourse thus has often invoked the past as a bedrock from which the present has emerged. The films show how religious, historical, and political experiences are used as accounting for the present. The Israeli nation thus is represented as a "deposit of the ages, . . . the outcome . . . of all its members' past experiences and expressions" (Smith 1999, p. 171). In other words, this is a determinist view of the Israeli nation, where the nation is determined by ethnic heritage. Ethnic heritage also plays a role in invoking the injustices of the past which justify the present. The Jewish exodus from Egypt at the time of the Old Testament and the marginalization of Jews in Europe at the beginning of the twentieth century and before, for example, are evoked in *The Little Drummer Girl*: when Charlie questions Israeli head of operations Marty on why the presence of the State of Israel is so crucial, he answers by saying "Maybe you would prefer us to take a piece of Central Africa or Uruguay? Not Egypt, thank you. We tried it once and it wasn't a success. Or back to the ghettos?"

Perhaps the most salient factor in how this ethnic heritage invokes injustices of the past to make sense of the present is the Holocaust. The films use the Holocaust not only to strengthen the Jewish/Israeli identity, but also to mirror contemporary Palestinian "terrorist" activities. Shohat (1997a) argues that this "idea of the unique, common victimization of all Jews at all times provides a crucial underpinning of official Israeli discourse" (p. 94); this discourse uses the Holocaust "as a stage for demonstrating (Euro) Israeli nationalism as the only possible logical answer to horrific events in the history of Jews" (p. 93). The Holocaust thus is part of Israel's social memory (Collard 1989) that endows it with a definite identity (Smith 1986) and that outlines its conflict with the Arab outsiders.

In *The Ambassador*, Hacker is taken by an Israeli man to visit a Holocaust exhibition, where still images of Holocaust victims are projected as slides. Later in the film, Hacker brings together Israeli and Palestinian students to meet at a Roman archeological site in Jerusalem in order to discuss ways of reaching peace. As the students squat on the ground, the Israelis on one side, the Palestinians on the other, with Hacker in the middle, they light candles, and then get up chanting "Peace." However, a Saika (a Palestinian-Syrian group portrayed as rejecting peace with Israel) man in a *kaffiyya* emerges from the ruins and shoots at the students. Close-ups of faces exploding with blood and heads being blown up are followed by shots of bodies lying on the ground, as Hacker is crushed in the middle. The images of the students' dead bodies mirror the images of Holocaust victims seen in the slide exhibition earlier, establishing Palestinian terrorism as a new Holocaust. This is also invoked in *The Delta Force*. Abdo Rifa'i, the hijacker of a flight on a Greece–Rome–New York route, summons the German hostess to pick passenger passports that have Jewish names. When she refuses, saying being German invokes the Nazis, and advising Abdo that he wouldn't want to be associated with "Nazis who killed 6 million Jews," he replies by saying "Not enough." A female Jewish passenger reacts by saying "No, this can't be happening, not again," to which her husband replies, "We survived once; we can do it again."

The films often regiment Palestinians and Arabs vis-à-vis Israelis and Jews, but at the same time present Palestinians in conflict. The films thus homogenize Arabs in general and Palestinians in particular in ascribing them a tribal status that invokes Orientalist discourses, where the Orient is uncivilized and unable to rule itself, thereby necessitating control by the Occident. This is portrayed through numerous terrorist activities conducted by Arabs against Israelis and Americans. Examples can be seen in *The Ambassador*, where Hacker survives an assassination attempt by the Saika group (described in the film as an extreme Syria-based terrorist PLO faction that threatens the establishment of peace in the Middle East). In reality Saika, created in 1968, was part of Syrian president Assad's regime, and engaged in attacks against Palestinians in Lebanon in 1967 despite belonging to the

PLO, and became anti-PLO after the Israeli invasion of Lebanon in 1982 because of a clash of interests over Lebanon (Nasr 1997). Therefore, on one hand, the films merge conflicting parties under a barbaric Arab/Palestinian umbrella. This also mythologizes the Arab Other as an abstract threat, as seen in *Executive Decision*, where an unidentified suicide bomber in London declares his support for Palestinians and Bosnians before blowing himself up. The film presents this at its beginning, as a context for a plane hijacking by Arab terrorists later. However, the bomber's Arabic, un-subtitled declaration makes it difficult for non-Arabic speakers to establish this context, leaving the hijacking and the American rescue it entails as a mere classic battle between good and evil.

On the other hand, the films present conflict among Palestinians, ascribing the Palestinians a primitive status that is contrasted with that of modern Israelis and Americans (Wilmer 1997). This is an illustration of how "group identities must always be defined in relation to what they are not" (Eriksen 1997, p. 37). *The Ambassador* presents a PLO member, Mustafa, who tells Israelis and Americans "You must recognize that Palestine is a nation, and not a tribe." Yet his statement is undermined when he declares that the PLO wants peace while it is extremists who want revenge, which the film follows by an attack by Saika on Mustafa and the group he is addressing. Thus, Mustafa remains a mere token in a sea of Arab protagonists, his discourse drowning in theirs. As Spivak argues, tokenism does not allow the subaltern to speak: "when you are perceived as a token, you are also silenced" (1990, p. 61).

Both the homogenization of Israelis and Jews, on the one hand, and of Palestinians and Arabs, on the other hand, and the presentation of the Arab–Israeli conflict as an ethnic one are problematic. Homogenization is problematic because it essentializes Israelis and Arabs. Much has been written on the essentialism of Arabs in Hollywood (for example, Jack Shaheen's [2001] book *Reel Bad Arabs*). A similar statement can be made on the essentialism of Israelis, namely through the work of Ella Shohat and Robert Paine. Paine (1989) points out the complexity of the allocation of identity (as Zionist, Jewish, or Israeli) to a land of immigrants with different cultural and social backgrounds. He also points out that the unifying discourse disregards how Zionism has changed over time. Shohat (1997a) argues that Zionism presents a "'proof' of a single Jewish experience"

(p. 95) that does not allow overlappings with other religious or ethnic communities. She then challenges the presentation of Israelis as a homogeneous group by invoking the differences and inequalities between Sephardic and Ashkenazi Jews (which are ignored in the films). Paine and Shohat differ in their interpretation of Israel. While Paine sees Israel as a master identity encompassing "*intra*-ethnic components" (1989, p. 129), Shohat (1997a) argues that Israel is a case of a state creating a nation. This is seen in how "Israel is a European strategy, conceived, organized, and blessed by Europeans (whether Jewish or Gentile), adopted and secured by the United States, which has been actualized by Western/Northern implants depending upon a mass of Eastern/Southern labor and military draftees" (Downing 1991, p. 263). Shohat thus highlights the ambivalence towards the East and the West experienced by Israel, which is again ignored in the films. This is seen in how Israel's claim to the land is part of a myth of origins located in the East, while the Holocaust invokes the West as a "place of oppression to be liberated from" (Shohat 1997a, p. 98), yet, at the same time, Israel's claim to be "a secular, western democracy and Jewish" (Paine 1989, p. 128) means that it looks at the West as an "object of desire to form a 'normal' part of it" (Shohat 1997a, p. 98), while looking at the East as backward and underdeveloped.

Presenting the Arab–Israeli conflict as an ethnic one is problematic because of the many complexities such a presentation entails. First, Israel assumes an ethnic character, where the nation is constructed on the basis of ethnic heritage. The main criticism of this view is that, though useful for its account of the importance of history, it ignores how the present also "shapes and filters out the ethnic past" (Smith 1999, p. 171). This entails looking at the nation as a cultural artifact. As such, a nation is the product of the accumulation and interaction of the collective myths and symbolic representations existing within it. The Israeli nation becomes an imagined, invented community. It is a nation still in the making, with continuous immigration by ethnically and socially diverse groups. Add to that the fact that the inhabitants of Israel are also heterogeneous in the same way. This emphasizes the importance of symbolic representation of the nation of Israel as a binding factor. The Holocaust is one of the major symbolic elements of the Israeli nation's psyche; today it is often invoked to strengthen Israeli unity. The conflict with Palestinians, especially with the various acts of

Palestinian resistance (whether political, cultural, or military), has now been presented as a new holocaust, creating the myth of the Arab who wants to drive Israelis into the sea (as stated by the characters Marty and Joseph in *The Little Drummer Girl*). Smith (1999) calls this process national archeology, whereby the past is not excavated as historical remains, but reconstructed to be related to the present.

Another complication in referring to the Israeli–Palestinian conflict as ethnic is the fact that Israelis are largely a settler community. Kellas (1998) describes Israeli nationalism as a hybrid of what he calls "colonial" and "integral" nationalisms. Colonial nationalism is an example of Hechter's theory of internal colonialism. Hechter argues that inequalities between regions in a country inhabited by different ethnic groups eventuate in consigning those on the periphery to an inferior position, while the core remains dominant, resulting in hostility between periphery and core. This is intensified by what Hechter calls the cultural division of labor, whereby the core group occupy the best positions and the periphery is left with inferior roles. Arab-Israelis in Israel are second-class citizens, and for example are not allowed to serve in the army (Kellas 1998). In this sense, the Israelis become "colonizers" and Arabs become "colonized." Kellas adds to Hechter's theory by marking how Zionist Jews in Israel are settlers; he compares the condition of Palestinians in Israel to that of blacks in South Africa under apartheid. However, he points out that the difference between Israel as a settler nation and other settler nations is that "the Jewish settlers ... claim that they have 'come home'" (Kellas 1998, p. 171). Integral nationalism applies to Kellas's description of an exclusive nationalism that is based on an absolutist ideology whereby the "own" nationalism is deemed superior to any other nationalism. In this sense, Palestinian nationalism is seen by Kellas as anti-colonialist nationalism, which complicates discourses that place the condition of Palestine within a post-colonial framework.

The United States as godfather

The position the United States has taken within the Arab–Israeli conflict historically has fluctuated between predominantly regarding Israel as a diplomatic liability under Eisenhower and Carter and regarding it as a strategic asset under Truman, Kennedy, Johnson, Nixon, and Reagan, or regarding it as a combination of both under Bush, Clinton, and George W. Bush. Yet throughout the twentieth century and beyond, Israel has maintained a special relationship with the United States, nourished not only by influential pro-Israeli Jewish lobbying in Washington, but also by the American view of Israel, with its geographical location and military prowess, as a strategic ally in the Middle East (Little 2003). This was perhaps most clearly seen during the Cold War, when the Middle East was a battlefield for the superpowers and their interests. Moreover, it has been argued that the United States' support for Israel emanates from American discomfort with Arab unity, which would undermine its influence in the Middle East (Idris 1991; Mansour 1991). This special relationship has continued until today, and is reflected in the films, some of which have been produced by pro-Israeli Jewish companies (like *The Delta Force*, in which it is declared that "Israel is America's best friend in the Middle East," after which the hijacked American plane is flown to Israel from Beirut by American rescuers).

This special relationship has cast the United States in the role of godfather to and protector of Israel, whose relationship with its Arab neighbors is a David and Goliath situation. The exaggeration of the Arab side is seen in three films: *The Little Drummer Girl*, where a journalist states that the Palestinian "revolution" is "the richest in history"; *The Delta Force*, where Chuck Norris's character enters Beirut and declares that there are 2 million people in Beirut—"Beirut is a goddamn big city" (in reality, the population of Beirut is 1 million, and was even less in the 1980s when the film is set); and *The Ambassador*, which opens with the (erroneous) statement that the Israeli population is 4 million and that Israel is surrounded by eight Arab countries with a total population of 80 million.

Israel's special relationship with the Unites States has also undermined the Palestinian claims to resistance by portraying it as terrorism, while representing Israel in a more favorable light. *The Little Drummer Girl* presents a masked Palestinian man giving a speech in Dorset, England, claiming: "They call us terrorists. Why? Because we deliver our bombs with our hands. We have no American planes to drop them from, no tanks to shell their towns. This Israeli tank commander who fires his cannon into our camps so that our women and children have their flesh burned from their bones, this Israeli is called a hero. But when we strike back, the only way we can, with our hands, we are called terrorists. If Israelis give us their airplanes, we'll give them our suitcases . . . What we ask is the return of what was taken from us, by force and by terror. We ask for justice." However, the film later depicts the same man as being a terrorist, planting a bomb at an Israeli diplomat's house in Germany that kills an innocent child and his mother. In contrast, the film presents Israel as more reasonable and willing to stop the bloodshed. Israeli secret agent Joseph in the film declares to Charlie: "Both sides [Israelis and Palestinians] have their madmen, their extremists. They have some who would drive us into the sea. We have some who would wipe them out and have the weapons to do it. But some, some on both sides, want to come together, Charlie, want the Palestinians to have their homeland beside us." Not only does this statement establish Israel as peace-seeking, but its blaming of "extremists" for causing Palestinian dispossession absolves Israel from any responsibility for anti-Palestinian violence (Safty 1992).

Throughout history, however, the United States, as a superpower, has maintained a superior position to both Israel and Arab countries. While the films present anti-American terrorist attacks by Arabs within the context of the conflict with Israel which the United States is shown to successfully overcome (as in *The Delta Force*, *Programmed to Kill*, *The Ambassador*, and *The Siege*), the main role the United States plays in the films is not that of fighting back. The United States in the films is ascribed a position seemingly higher than that of the conflicting parties, thereby constructing it as a godfather mediating between Israelis and Palestinians in order to arrive at peace not only in the Middle East but also worldwide.

The films reflect this through presenting the United States as orchestrating peace talks in the Middle East. The American superior position has simultaneously cast Israel and Palestinians an inferior position, almost as immature children fighting in a playground. This is most clearly seen in *The Ambassador*, where Israelis and Palestinians engage in mutual ideological attacks (though military attacks are confined to Palestinians) that are only resolved by the intervention of American ambassador Hacker. On one hand, the film depicts Israelis who regard Palestinians as untrustworthy, wondering why Hacker would doubt "why we're so suspicious of our enemies who have sworn to destroy us so many times." On the other hand, the film depicts Palestinians who shout "We don't talk with Jews; we kill them!" Hacker's efforts at achieving peace are hampered by an attempt on his life by Palestinian "extremists," and the Israeli Mossad who try to prevent him from arranging a meeting between Israelis and Palestinians. As a result, Hacker almost gives up on his peace mission, and decides to go back to the United States. The film uses this pretext to cast an Orientalist light on Israel, as Hacker is begged to stay by Israelis who state that they need him there.

Despite its advocacy of dialogue, the film does not make it clear exactly what the United States wants to establish in the area. Is it partition? Or is it a multicultural society? At best, the film portrays the area as a plural society, where each group exists almost totally independently, and where each group's private and communal worlds are separate from the working world. In other words, Palestine/Israel is represented with both groups operating separately in their private (moral education, primary socialization, religion) and public spheres (economics, law, politics) (Rex 1997a), but with Palestinians perceived more as residents than as citizens (Safty 1992). The film also emphasizes the United States' role in the region as crucial, while at the same time maintaining American superiority. Hacker is careful to tell the Israelis that "the superpowers will not let you win a decisive victory." In this sense, Hollywood represents the United States in a similar manner to the way the country is portrayed in the films about the Gulf War as discussed earlier: as a world policeman, rescuer, and carer.

Arab cinemas: nostalgia and resistance

The Gulf War and the Arab–Israeli conflict are two separate political issues in the Arab world that are nevertheless linked. While the Arab–Israeli conflict can be more easily constructed under an us/them umbrella, the Gulf War presents a challenge to the Arab concept of "us." However, American intervention after Iraq's invasion of Kuwait transformed the conflict into an Arab versus Western one in the eyes of many. At the same time, the complexity of the conflict placed several Arab countries in an ambivalent position, on one hand heightening their sense of Arabness, but on the other hand reminding them of division among Arabs. This ambivalence has been reflected in the Arab films representing the Gulf War.

The Arab–Israeli conflict is more easily tackled by the Arab cinemas that have represented it, namely Palestinian cinema and Syrian cinema, with both Palestine and Syria seeing themselves as direct victims of Israeli aggression. But the relationship between Egypt and Israel is not typical of the Arab world as a whole. In contrast to most Arab countries, Egypt has signed a peace treaty with Israel. This act initially alienated Egypt from most of its Arab neighbors. However, cultural ties between Egypt and the rest of the Arab world remain strong, especially popular culture. Egyptian popular music is the most widely listened to Arabic music across the Middle East; however, Egyptian cinema remains Egypt's most successful cultural export. The Arab–Israeli conflict has proven to be a delicate issue for Egyptian cinema. In detaching itself from the rest of the Arab world through the Camp David Accords, Egypt has sought to establish a separate national identity that is emphasized more than its Arab identity. Yet at the same time, Egypt relies on the Arab market for its cinematic products. Add to this the fact that popular sentiment in Egypt remains anti-Israel. Those three conflicting factors have meant that Egyptian cinema has largely refrained from representing the Arab–Israeli conflict for most of the duration of Egypt's peace process with Israel. Yet after peace with Israel was established, Egyptian cinema turned its attention once again to this conflict, constructing Israel as an essential enemy, thereby largely ignoring Egypt's political position in reality in favor of wider Arab/populist appeal. But Egyptian cinema converges with the cinemas of Syria and Tunisia in using the Arab–Israeli conflict to resurrect yet at the same lament a lost pan-Arab identity. Thus, the Arab films representing the Arab–Israeli conflict can be seen as nostalgic towards pan-Arabism (with the exception of Palestinian films), but at the same time they are sympathetic to the plight of Palestinians, and therefore celebrate Arab resistance to Israel. In the case of Egypt, the films' stance towards the Arab–Israeli conflict can be seen as an attempt at redeeming Egypt from its peace treaty with Israel.

Israel as villain

The Arab films construct Israeli nationalism as imperialist; in general, Israelis are depicted as a homogeneous group poised against the wellbeing of the

Arab world. In the face of this, the films construct Palestinian nationalism as anti-imperialist, attempting at reclaiming the nation and replacing the existing Israeli power (Lazarus 1997). It is therefore interesting to see that most Egyptian films about Israel do not give much screen time to Israeli characters. *Road to Eilat*, for example, represents only one Israeli man whose time on screen is limited to less than three minutes, and *Trap of Spies* also gives little screen time to its only Israeli Mossad character. The films also do not depict Israeli landscape, leaving it to the imagination of the audience. One reason behind this virtual absence is economic, in that the films do not have enough funding to always shoot on location (not only in Israel, but also in Egypt, as most of the films are limited in their outdoors scenes). Another reason is that the focus of the films is not on Israel itself, but on Egypt's and the Arabs' stance towards Israel. In accordance with a populist Arab stance, the films portray Israel as an essential villain, ascribed a similar set of characteristics to that bestowed on Arab terrorists in Hollywood.

Israel is thus associated with drugs, rape, deceit, murder, and disease in *Love in Taba* and *Girl from Israel*. The latter employs a set of visual signifiers to highlight Israel's pathology, like dressing the main Israeli character (played by Egyptian actor Farouk al-Fishawi, whose blonde hair and fair complexion often land him roles as a "foreigner" in Egyptian cinema) in a black suit. This is contrasted with the pale suit worn by the nationalist Egyptian father in the film (played by the black-haired and dark-skinned actor Mahmoud Yassin). Egypt and Israel are thus juxtaposed as good versus evil. *Love in Taba* and *Girl from Israel* are the only films dealing directly with Egypt's post-treaty relationship with Israel, and both send an anti-normalization message that is resonant with public opinion in the Arab world. The films show that normalization would only serve Israel, and would be a mark of disrespect for all of Israel's victims during the 1967 War and other atrocities. The young Egyptian man Wael's seduction by the permissive lifestyle of drugs, alcohol, and sex offered by Israel is condemned by his nationalist peers in *Girl from Israel*. The film emphasizes the artifice of Israel's embrace of Wael by showing how one of Wael's Israeli friends rapes an Egyptian girl holidaying with Wael and his friends and family. Wael hears the girl's screams coming out of a cave by the sea, and rushes to rescue her, only to be killed by his Israeli "friend." The film thus presents the complication carried in how Israel as "colonizer" tries to convince some of the "colonized" that they are in fact different from the rest of the colonized, hence being "one of us." This echoes Fanon's notion of black skin, white masks, whereby "the White man's artifice [is] inscribed on the Black man's body" (Bhabha 1994, p. 117). Bhabha argues that this process depersonalizes the colonized and dislocates them from their own culture. The film uses Wael's death as a wake-up call to those who are misguided by Israel's intentions in advocating normalization with Egypt. In this sense, the films seem to take an apologetic stance towards Egypt's peace treaty with Israel, which is mostly condemned by the rest of the Arab world.

Palestinian films deal more directly with the atrocities conducted by Israel against Arabs. *Canticle of the Stones* portrays Israeli intrusion into Palestinian everyday life. The film presents several examples of this, from Israeli soldiers closing a school after accusing the students of throwing a stone at them, to a shepherd who has to use another route to get his sheep back to his village after Israelis block the way home, to a young man who has stopped eating after losing his intestines as a result of being shot by Israelis. But Israel's intrusion is also one into the Palestinians' psyche. The room where the young man lies is decorated with photos of martyrs on the wall. The young man recites who they are, how old they were when they died, and how they died. His mother, at his bedside, says that, before his injury, her son had gone to a photographer and asked him to have his picture taken as he felt he was going to be a martyr. Violence becomes part of daily life for Palestinians. The film confirms this with a scene where children play with empty bullet shells as they would with marbles, explaining to the camera the difference between plastic bullets and iron ones.

The Door to the Sun starts with a detailed depiction of the events of 1948. The story begins in 1943—five years before the establishment of the State of Israel—in Galilee, shown as a traditional Palestinian town. Shadows of the future loom as the townspeople fight against the British selling their land to Jews. The start of the events of 1948 is symbolized in a scene depicting Younes's twelve-year-old bride Nahila working in the fields of the village Ain az-Zaitouna in 1943, which is cut to a scene of her doing the same as a young woman five years later, only this time under Israeli surveillance. The film then quickly moves to a depiction of Israel's seizing of Palestinian land. As the villagers harvest their olives, they are interrupted by armed Israelis carrying Israeli flags. The Israelis attack the village, saying they will kill the men and rape the women and declaring the area an Arab-free zone. We see Nahila standing outside her burning home as Israelis round up the villagers, killing one local man who tries to defy them. A woman drags her paralyzed husband on the ground in the background as two Israeli soldiers point guns at Palestinians squatting in a circle. The soldiers round up all the men in the circle and shoot them.

Israeli oppression of Palestinians is also portrayed in *Wedding in Galilee*. Israel in the film prevents Palestinians from going about their everyday lives, as well as from celebrating their special occasions. Abu Adel, the village mayor, has to wait outside the Israeli military governor's office to get a permit to hold his son's wedding. Israeli jeeps pass through the village liberally, the soldiers ordering Palestinian women who are ululating at the news of the wedding to shut up. A military patrol passes through the village and announces through loudspeakers that the day's curfew is going to start one hour earlier by the order of the governor. As the patrol jeeps skirt through the yellow brick houses, moving towards the screen, women close their windows and the village ends up in total silence. The villagers complain that the curfew prevents them from harvesting their crops. At nightfall, a woman is heard singing; sounds of gunshot are heard and an Israeli soldier's voice shouts "Quiet!" The Israeli oppression extends to verbal statements. At Adel's wedding, to which the governor invited himself and his assistants, the governor praises Abu Adel for the wedding celebrations, saying "In these conditions, we can stay with you for hundreds of years." The Israelis' not-so-subtle provocation continues when the soldiers are offered food during the wedding. A panning shot reveals the soldiers sitting around the banquet, the camera going to the left and then to the right showing them surrounding the governor. The soldiers start comparing Palestinian food with Lebanese food. The governor declares that he prefers the cooking in Aleppo as "They make real Oriental kebabs. Pray to God that He will soon let you taste the food in Aleppo." The governor's arrogance had been established at the beginning of the film, where he at first dismisses Abu Adel's request to hold the wedding by saying, in his accented classical Arabic, "You come from an extremist village that doesn't recognize the favors we have done for you."

In the Ninth Month differs from the above films by not concentrating on the depiction of Israeli aggression—though this is mentioned (Khalil,

for instance, states that Israel has built settlements on his land)—but by
showing how this aggression has resulted in tension and suspicion among
Palestinians themselves. The film twists an old myth from the days of
Ottoman rule, when tales of Turks kidnapping young men and drafting them
into the army circulated, into a modern one of a mysterious kidnapper who
steals children and sells them to Israelis, to allegorize this tension. The story
revolves around Ahmad, who has to protect the secret of the return of his
brother Khalil from Lebanon after ten years of exile, to smuggle his wife
Samira back with him. Having to go out at night dressed in black any time
he needs to see Khalil, and behaving secretly, Ahmad is accused by the
villagers of being a child kidnapper, and is subjected to an endless chain of
inquisition and psychological torture that he has to endure to protect not
only his brother, but also his brother's pregnant wife. Ahmad is often shot
from above or in long shot, rendering him small and giving him an air of
helplessness. A flashback in the film depicts Ahmad at night, surrounded
by men carrying torches and rotating around him, asking him about the
missing boy Hassan, and casting giant shadows on the wall, dwarfing
Ahmad. Children run scared when they see Ahmad, *kaffiyya* around his
head, and he is attacked by Hassan's father as he walks home one day. The
pressure on Ahmad rises, and he is summoned to Abu Saleh's house to
be judged. Men sit in a semi-circle on the floor, saying they saw Ahmad
wearing black at night; then they take him to a mosque and make him swear
on the Qur'an to tell the truth. When he says he is not the child kidnapper,
the men accuse him of lying and of not being a believer and abandon him,
kneeling on the floor in front of the Qur'an. Ahmad's despair reaches its
peak as he finds himself meeting an Israeli man to arrange Khalil's public
return to the village. The man asks Ahmad to work for him; disgusted at
himself for contemplating collaborating with Israelis, Ahmad leaves the
meeting and, in one of the most disturbing scenes in the film, we see Ahmad
lying in a grave-like hole in the ground, hurling soil on himself, lamenting
his inability to burn himself alive. The film then shows another of Ahmad's
nightmares in a fantasy sequence. This time, we are presented with a high
angle shot of men carrying black umbrellas in the dark as rain pours down.
All we see are the umbrella tops. The camera then penetrates the umbrellas
and zooms on Ahmad in his underwear, surrounded by three men on either
side. The camera moves back to reveal the umbrellas again. The umbrellas

part and Ahmad is led in the middle, and then hung on a cross. Ahmad's suffering becomes an allegory for the nightmarish life Palestinians have to bear under Israeli occupation and terror.

Palestinian response

Palestinian cinema balances the villainess of Israel with the depiction of various acts of resistance by the Palestinians. Palestinian films present strong statements against oppression, and give Palestine a voice against a dominant discourse that has constructed it as either aberrant or merely victimized. Palestine in its cinema is not weak. It is a witness to the cruelty of history, but it is also a place of hope and resilience. *Wedding in Galilee* is a film regarded as anticipating the *intifada*. The Palestinians in the film have to undergo the humiliation of being under the whim of the Israeli governor, but they use the wedding as an opportunity to fight back. When violence proves to be futile—with a halted attempt at attacking the governor and his assistant—the villagers resort to an even stronger method. As the groom makes his way from the bath to his wedding, his friends salute him through song and clapping. The song is carefully chosen to include a reference to landmines. The men sing "The handsome man emerged from the bath under the explosion of mines." The men later dance and continue singing "The pride of a country is its men; I'm Palestinian and I'm not afraid" in front of the governor and his assistants, which leads the female soldier Tali to faint. Palestinian women also participate in the dancing, singing "God punish those who destroyed Beirut." The mounting tension between Palestinians and Israelis in the village is symbolized by the wedding music getting louder and faster, and culminates in the governor and his soldiers leaving the village as they are pelted with household objects by the villagers in a scene mirroring the stone throwing of the *intifada* that followed.

Resistance in Palestinian cinema has moved historically from being realistically represented in the 1980s and 1990s to a more metaphorical representation in the twenty-first century. Films like *Rana's Wedding*, *Tale of Three Jewels*, *Chronicle of a Disappearance*, and *Divine Intervention* use symbolism and surrealism to depict Palestinian defiance. One way in which this is done is through depicting Israelis as lacking individualism. In *Rana's*

Wedding, Rana tries to call her fiancé but her mobile phone's battery is dead. She almost throws the phone in frustration at a row of Israeli soldiers sitting next to each other against a wall. The wall behind them is ironically graffitied with the sentence "May every year see you well" in Arabic. The camera pans on their faces from the left to the right, revealing that they almost look identical. We never hear the Israeli soldiers speak in the film.

Another method of resistance is done through the use of humor. A sequence in *Chronicle of a Disappearance* titled "APPOINTMENT with the Priest" subtly comments on the profanity of the tense situation in Palestine through filming a priest interviewed about life in Gaza. The camera presents a wide shot of a man on a jet ski in the sea as we hear the priest say "That's where Jesus is supposed to have walked on water." A scene in *Rana's Wedding* sees Rana and Khalil cuddling on a bench outdoors, watched by a CCTV camera. Khalil defiantly dances in front of the camera. Through the square, black-and-white CCTV view, we see Khalil picking his nose, performing a Chaplinesque sequence where he pretends to be slapped and beaten by an imaginary person, and raising his index finger as if threatening the camera in an exaggerated manner. The CCTV camera's response, symbolizing the anger of the Israelis, is depicted through the sound of the camera as it moves its lens, pans from left to right, and goes up and down and observes people from above. A wide shot reveals Al-Aqsa mosque and the Jerusalem markets and cityscapes. We are reminded that Israel is watching the Palestinians' every move. But Rana and Khalil manage to marry despite the restrictions. Although the marriage registrar gets stuck in a road block after the Israelis seize his ID, he still manages to marry the couple in a car in the street.

Three Palestinian films stand out in their representation of Palestinian resistance. What links the three films is their use of fantasy as opposed to realism in representing Palestine under occupation. *Tale of Three Jewels* is a fairy-tale-like story of dreams of escape. Youssef, a twelve-year-old boy, often escapes from the reality of living in a refugee camp in Gaza into a world of fantasy, occupied by knights and white horses and disembodied voices. When not in his fantasy world, Youssef is seen playing in the countryside or by the sea. But Youssef's world is far from enchanted: his brother is in the *feda'yeen*, who have to hide from the Israelis at all times, his father emerges from Israeli prison a broken man, and his mother

Figure 14　The jewels turn to blood drops—*Tale of Three Jewels*

struggles to make ends meet. When Youssef meets Aida, a gypsy girl, she convinces him that, if he finds three missing jewels from her grandmother's necklace, he will be able to marry her when they grow up. Believing that the jewels are in South America, Youssef starts planning his trip overseas, but eventually finds out that the jewels were not lost in South America, but in Palestine, when the grandmother had to flee her hometown of Jaffa to Gaza in 1948. The film ends with another fantasy sequence where the three jewels are transformed into three drops of blood. Youssef realizes that he is bound by history, time, space, and his own flesh to the land around him. The treasure he had been seeking is destined to be in his homeland. And thus the film relays a subtle message of resistance, communicated as simply adhering to the land of Palestine.

Elia Suleiman's two films *Chronicle of a Disappearance* and *Divine Intervention* stand out among all the Arab films analyzed in that the Palestine they create is one mediated almost completely through fantasy. Both films do not present classical narratives and are not plot-driven. Instead, with a focus on images and with very little dialogue, the films create a surreal world, where the life of Palestinians is presented with a focus on the banal and the whimsical, highlighting the absurdity of living under occupation. The films convey a sense of boredom and vacuous existence, yet this is underlined with a subtle political statement. In *Divine Intervention*, a man waits at a bus stop although he knows that no bus will appear, Waiting for Godot-style. Another man argues with his female neighbor over rubbish that they both claim the other has thrown into their yard. Two men sit on a stool watching a boy kick a football in an otherwise empty street. But underneath the boredom lie small acts of resistance. The director's father in the film is shown driving through the streets of Nazareth, greeted by people in the street whom he replies to by swearing at them, knowing they are unable to hear him behind the closed car windows. We soon find out that the people are collaborators with Israel. We then see the father collecting glass bottles on his roof which he throws at Israelis, and later walking down an empty street and proceeding to smash an Israeli-constructed road divider.

Chronicle of a Disappearance takes the shape of a film diary, with short episodes depicting daily life in Palestine separated with title cards informing us that another day has passed. Yet the intricacies of everyday life remain the same. Families gossip, fishermen go out to sea, and bored salesmen wait for non-existent customers. The film introduces us to the director, as himself, seen as a silent figure who does not choose silence, but one whom silence is imposed on. Towards the end of the film, the director is introduced to an audience in a theater as making a film about peace in Palestine, having returned from New York. Suleiman stands behind the lectern, but his microphone makes noise as soon as he is about to give his speech. This is followed by the sound of audience mobile phones ringing, and one audience member even answering the call while Suleiman stands silent, alone, surrounded by Palestinian flags.

Palestine is not only silent; it is also reduced to a represented space detached from its own reality. Some of the most evocative features in the film are the scenes representing a souvenir shop. Named "The Holy Land," the shop stands alone in an otherwise barren space. Its shopkeeper amuses himself by counting money and making sand bottles that no one seems to buy. The shop sells postcards, but the tourists who pass in front of the shop choose to take photographs of the shop itself instead. This sequence presents a sharp message on the history of Palestine. Close-ups of the postcards reveal pictures of traditional Palestinian dancing, mosaics, camels with al-Aqsa and the cityscape of Jerusalem in the background, and of men in *kaffiyyas*. The idyllic Palestine represented in the postcards could not have been further from the "real" Palestine of today. The film goes back to The Holy Land every now and then, emphasizing the sense of detachment, disillusion, and emptiness with shots or sounds of the round rack of postcards outside the shop, twisting on its own in the wind, ignored by the shopkeeper.

Both films rely on visual gags to challenge the audience's expectations of both Palestinian and Israeli actions, thereby commenting on our own prejudices towards both sides. In *Chronicle of a Disappearance*, two fast sequences emphasize this: the first depicts an Israeli police car driving really fast, with the siren on. Our expectations that the policemen are about to arrest someone are challenged, as they simply get out of the car and line up against a wall with their guns, urinate, and then drive back. The second depicts the director looking on as Palestinian men converse about connecting wires. Our expectations that the conversation is about planting a bomb are shattered when we find out they are talking about fireworks. In *Divine Intervention*, men seen behind pillars seem to be beating up someone on the ground with sticks, and then another man shoots the beaten target three times. But it turns out the target is a snake. Later in the film, three Israeli soldiers hurriedly emerge from a small military jeep, our expectations leading us to believe that they will shoot at three men standing with their hands up against the jeep. But the soldiers simply check the soles of their boots, in sync, and get back in the car. Suleiman therefore highlights and challenges the dominant discourse on Israel and Palestine in the media. However, this challenge is political: the Israeli soldiers seen in both films are mostly represented as a group, and often engage in synchronized movements, which serves not only to dehumanize them, but also to deny them any sense of individualism.

The films' playfulness is underlined with an important comment on Palestinian oppression. *Divine Intervention* presents examples of Israeli control over Palestinian life. From car passengers at the whim of Israeli checkpoint soldiers, to lovers who cannot cross the Ramallah checkpoint to meet each other and who have to resort to silent meetings in a car on the "border," Palestinians are represented as being under the power of

Israel. In *Chronicle of a Disappearance*, a sequence, "APPOINTMENT with Estate Agent," shows a Palestinian woman trying to rent an apartment. An estate agent tells her to marry first and study second, as opposed to get a flat on her own. She resorts to looking for a place in a Jewish area, but her fluent Hebrew is let down by her Arabic name, Adan, and no Israeli is prepared to have her as a tenant.

But Adan, like other Palestinians in the two films, has her revenge in a fantasy sequence. We see Adan sitting on a chair that later turns out to bear the shape of the Palestinian map and colors of the Palestinian flag. What seems like a gun on the table in front of her turns out to be a lighter used by Adan to light a cigarette. Adan uses a walkie-talkie to intercept communication by the Israeli police. She sits in her dark apartment, and talks into her walkie-talkie, instructing the police to attend a fictional incident in an area of Jerusalem. Police cars arrive quickly, in the dark, and circle around comically as Adan gives them conflicting information. She orders them to withdraw from Jerusalem: "Jerusalem is no longer united. Jerusalem is nothing special. Oslo is not coming. Oslo is not even calling." She sings them a song about gazing towards Zion and the hope of 2,000 years. Adan's song is superimposed on black-and-white footage of Arab men dancing traditional *dabke* in a theater. The men's slow movements are in sync with the song, transforming the sequence into a powerful statement on shared culture between Arabs and Israelis. But any shared culture is overshadowed by Israeli irrationality and paranoia. The film shows another fantasy sequence where Israeli soldiers raid the house of the director. As he sits at home in his khaki pajamas drinking coffee, visible through his glass front door, two Israeli soldiers appear behind the front door and break in without seeing him, as he looks at them, bewildered. Waltzy music ironically plays as they look around the place theatrically; then they leave suddenly, describing the contents of his place on a walkie-talkie: they report finding chairs, Japanese notebooks, Samira Said tapes and other banal details.

Divine Intervention goes further in its use of fantasy, presenting a number of memorable sequences of fantasies of resistance. Those start with one of the director driving a car, eating an apricot. He throws the pit out the window, and it hits a parked tank. The scene is cut to one of the tank exploding, and then back to the director seemingly oblivious in his car, and back again to the tank, now reduced to shattered parts. This is followed by another sequence of a woman in a tight pink dress and pink shoes, parking her car near a checkpoint and walking towards the other side. The camera zooms on her legs that she deliberately places one in front of the other, and then shows us a shot of her head through the viewfinder of an Israeli soldier's gun as he and others point their guns at her. She takes off her sunglasses to glance at them, puts the sunglasses back on, and continues walking. Suddenly, the checkpoint booth to her right collapses as the soldiers run away to the left and she continues walking in the middle of the road defiantly. Those sequences of wishful thinking are followed by two more featuring the director and the woman. The first one shows the director staring determinedly at a Jewish settler (with an Israeli flag on his radio antenna) as both their cars stop at a traffic light, and they both refuse to move even when the light turns green. The staring game occurs in front of a huge billboard depicting a sword-carrying bomber hiding his/her face behind a black and white *kaffiyya*, with only the eyes showing. The words "Come shoot if you're ready" are written next to the picture in red Hebrew letters. The second sequence moves beyond all the others into transforming the woman into a ninja fighter, clad in black, who fights five Israeli armed men. As the men shoot at the woman, she lifts up in the air, twisting and dodging the bullets in a scene reminiscent of some of the sequences in *The Matrix*. The camera freezes as the woman is in mid-air, and the bullets stop just before they hit her head, forming a crown. The woman performs ninja-like movements, throwing an arrow with a star and crescent attached at one of the men, killing him, and a heavy metal chain at another as she stands on a mountain cliff. She then emits several fast-moving stones from her fist, eliminating the men one by one. She finally uses a metal shield shaped like the map of Palestine as a boomerang to counter-attack an Israeli helicopter. But perhaps the most evocative sequence in the film is one where, at a checkpoint, the director pulls his car next to that of the woman he loves but cannot reach, as they live on either side of the Ramallah–Nazareth border. His car window displays the words "I'm crazy because I love you." He blows up a red balloon, which turns out to have a picture of Yasser Arafat on it. He raises the balloon from the car and lets it float. The red balloon floats towards the checkpoint, the Israeli soldiers looking at it through binoculars: One wants to shoot it down while the other calls for instructions. The balloon passes over the checkpoint and floats over the city, the olive trees,

Figure 15 The Arafat balloon—*Divine Intervention* (photo courtesy of Arab Film Distribution)

Figure 16 *Divine Intervention*'s ninja fighter

the ancient buildings, a church, towards al-Aqsa mosque, its shadow cast on al-Aqsa's golden dome. It then sticks to the top of the dome, next to the crescent. The balloon's free movement represents a flight of fantasy for Palestinians who are unable to move in their own land, its floatation in the air transcending Israeli restrictions.

But despite this use of humor, the endings of both films serve to remind us of the graveness of the Palestinian situation. *Chronicle of a Disappearance* ends with a shot of an elderly Palestinian couple sleeping on a sofa in front of the television as a channel closes late at night. The television screen shows a close-up of an Israeli flag as the Israeli national anthem is played. The camera then zooms out to reveal two more flags lined up, rustling in the wind. The television transmission stops, and the film ends with a black screen. *Divine Intervention* ends with a shot of a pressure cooker whistling and steaming as the director and his mother sit watching it. The mother utters the last words heard in the film, which summarize Suleiman's take on Palestinian oppression: "That's enough."

Pan-Arabism: the lost dream

Pan-Arab nostalgia

The representation of the Arab–Israeli conflict in Arab cinemas outside of Palestine has tended to emphasize the support of Arab countries to Palestine in times of crisis. This nostalgic pan-Arab nationalism is mainly advocated in the Egyptian and Syrian films. This nostalgia is also seen in the context of the Gulf War in Egyptian cinema, but is challenged in the Tunisian, Moroccan, Palestinian, and Lebanese films about the issue. Pan-Arabism is therefore marked as a political, rather than a cultural or ethnic, project, although it does carry elements of culture and ethnicity. The Egyptian films' resurrection of pan-Arabism focuses on two major political themes: the Arab victory in the 1973 October War, and the achievements of the late Nasser. Although both of those myths are linked to Western political activities in the region, they remain confined to the Arab world and therefore are not shared by Western discourse at large. The October War, which brought together Egyptian and Syrian troops as well as OPEC Arab members against

Israel, is recreated in the films as a golden, heroic age. The films thus sub-limate a fading, yet still present, Arab hope of eradicating the Israeli threat through reviving shared memories of the myth of Arab unity. In doing so the films represent Egypt as a strong, unified front, ignoring how its political behavior is in fact divided between acceptance of Israel and sympathy for Palestinians (Kellas 1998). The films revolving around the October War, *48 Hours in Israel*, *Mission in Tel Aviv*, *Trap of Spies*, *Execution of a Dead Man*, and *Road to Eilat* all mainly depict Egypt as a glorified leader whose acts have been essential for the Arab victory. It is as if the films seek redemption from Egypt's peace treaty with Israel through emphasizing Egypt's pan-Arab character.

All the Egyptian films on the October War represent fictional intelli-gence operations that are shown to be crucial for the 1973 victory. The film *48 Hours in Israel* depicts an Egyptian spy who goes to Israel and obtains information on Israeli settlement plans in the Sinai desert in the summer of 1973, which the film shows triggers the Arab attack in October that year. *Mission in Tel Aviv* presents an almost identical plot, with the Egyptian spy gathering information on Israel's weapon development prior to the war. *Execution of a Dead Man*, set in 1972, depicts another Egyptian pro-Israel spy, Mansour, who is captured by the Egyptian secret service, sentenced to death, and replaced with a look-alike whose mission is to find out whether Israel is manufacturing an atomic bomb, so that Egypt can make the neces-sary preparations to reclaim its territories that were occupied in the 1967 War. *Road to Eilat* is set in 1969, and depicts a marines operation by a Jordanian, Palestinian, and Egyptian coalition whose aim is to gather information pertinent to the subsequent 1973 attack. The film's careful choice of nationalities is paradoxical when analyzed in a historical context. September 22, 1970 marked the start of Black September, an operation where Jordan's King Hussein, with American and Israeli backing, drove out thousands of Palestinian militants and their families from Jordan (Little 2003). The film then can be seen as glossing over inter-Arab divisions, and as an attempt at rewriting history.

The marines in *Road to Eilat* are shown to be given the blessing of President Nasser (who communicates with them through an emotionally moving speech delivered by phone, and whose picture hangs on the wall of the marines' head office). This covert support of Nasser is also seen in

Trap of Spies. Set in 1971, the film depicts an Egyptian woman who betrays her country by acting as a spy for Israel. The film explains how the spy's father had been close to the exiled King Farouq (who had supported the colonial British), and how she resents Nasser's Revolution, which stripped her family of everything. She is lured by the prospects of being a spy for Israel, and keeps that role even after her arrest by the Egyptians, who ask her to become a double agent. The secret service eventually resorts to making her believe that she caused her brother's death, reminding her of all the others who died because of her actions. The secret service spies on the spy's life, and follows her to Athens where she regularly meets with Israelis. The film ends with a statement that President Sadat executed all spies in 1972, sending a message of morality, patriotism, and solidarity of vision that contradicts Sadat's stance towards Israel, as he initiated peace talks with Israel and eventually signed the Camp David Accords in 1978.

Cinematic support of Nasser's pan-Arabism is not confined to covert cases as mentioned above. Two films, *Nasser 56* and *Nasser*, focus entirely on Nasser and his good pan-Arab deeds. *Nasser 56* tells, in great detail, how Nasser succeeded in nationalizing the Suez Canal. The film constructs Nasser not just as an Egyptian, but also as an Arab leader and mythical figure whose aim is to unify the Arab world, and whose nationalization of the Suez Canal is the first step towards relieving the Arabs of foreign intervention and authority (namely American, French, and British intervention, as Nasser was inclined to the Soviet Union). One step towards this in the film is how Nasser saw the American decision to withdraw its plans to finance the Aswan Dam as a declaration of war against Egypt. This did not come as a surprise to Nasser in the film, who had always viewed the West, mainly the United States, as a force hindering the progress of Egypt and the rest of the Arab world (in his speech for the Revolution's fifth anniversary, Nasser is shown referring to the United States as a liar). Despite being told his decision to nationalize the Canal is risky, Nasser does extensive research on the matter and decides to go ahead, viewing the operation as a matter of honor and an act of triumph not just for Egypt, but also for the Arab world as a whole. The film emphasizes the West's antagonism toward Nasser and his (pan-Arab) nationalist plans. After Nasser announces the nationalization of the Canal, the film shows that he was referred to in a British newspaper as the "Hitler of the Nile." The film also glorifies Nasser by showing how he refuses to flee from Cairo during the consequent Israeli/ British/French attack on Egypt.

Nasser also focuses on the late Egyptian president, but this time on his life as a whole. The film focuses, among Nasser's many deeds, on his opinions and actions within the Arab–Israeli conflict. The film shows Nasser's skepticism in 1939 when everyone around him thought that, if Nazi Germany won World War II and defeated Britain (which had a mandate over Egypt), it would give Egypt its independence. At the same time, he is shown to believe that Britain will establish a Jewish state in Palestine. Nasser, as an army officer, is portrayed as fully participating in the 1948 War fought between Arabs and Israelis, where he is shown as meeting an Israeli general. Nasser's stance towards Israel is made clear in the film's portrayal of his disagreement with the general's statement that an Israeli state will bring prosperity to Palestine. The film does not only glamorize Arab support for Nasser, but shows that even his enemies have a high regard for him. After the 1952 Revolution, admiring Israelis in the film are shown

Figure 17 Ahmad Zaki as Nasser—*Nasser* (photo courtesy of Arab Film Distribution)

as saying "Nasser doesn't hate the Jews; he just hates Zionism." Nasser in the film is also an advocate of pan-Arabism, establishing Syrian/Egyptian unity in 1958, and mediating between Jordan and Yasser Arafat after Black September in 1971. The film conveniently omits Nasser's proposal (with Jordan's King Hussein) to recognize Israel in November 1967 on a land-for-peace basis, and his acceptance of the Rogers plan in 1969, put forward by the United States, which called for Israeli withdrawal and a negotiated settlement of the conflict (both proposals were rejected by Israel) (Safty 1992).

Selective presentation of history is also seen in *Days of Sadat*. The film is a biopic of the late Egyptian president, where Sadat is played by the same actor (Ahmad Zaki) who played Nasser in *Nasser 56*. A positive link between the two presidents is established with the film opening with a devastated Sadat after Nasser's untimely death. Sadat is shown as the one announcing the news of the 1952 Revolution to the Egyptian people on the radio. Nasser and Sadat are put on a par where Sadat is shown as receiving a threatening phone call after the assassination attempt on Nasser. The film is a long flashback of Sadat's ascendance to power and his presidency. Sadat is presented as an Egyptian nationalist who ends up in prison more than once after opposing the British presence in Egypt. In contrast to Nasser and his extraordinary stature, Sadat is presented as a man of humble origins, reading a book about Gandhi while in prison, leaving his food untouched on the prison floor, and working in construction and as a vegetable seller in a village after his release. Sadat's ordinariness is emphasized in a shot of him cutting up stones, looking small as he is dominated by the huge mountain he is carving. Even when he becomes president he does not forsake his roots, choosing to celebrate his birthday in the countryside on television while talking about the simple pleasures of country life. As with the representation of Nasser in *Nasser 56*, the film represents Sadat as canny, declaring that he is not convinced when the radio announces the destruction of 90 Israeli planes during the Six Day War, saying "Governments lie when there is a catastrophe." When Sadat decides to declare war on Israel in 1973, he is shown asking the *Ahram* newspaper to put on the front page a smoke-screen story about Egyptian officers going to Mecca on a religious visit. After the war, he declares in a speech that the operation was a "miracle. This nation has restored its honor." But it is Sadat's visit to Israel and the signing of the Camp David Accords that have made him a controversial figure in Arab politics. The film justifies Sadat's visit to Israel by depicting him saying "This is the only way of establishing peace. We [the Arabs] have spoken to everyone on this earth except the Israelis." The film emphasizes Sadat's speech in Israel where he asks for total withdrawal from all post-1967 occupied land including Jerusalem, total peace and the stopping of violence, and the establishment of a Palestinian authority. The documentary footage used in this sequence depicts an enthusiastic Sadat addressing a solemn Israeli audience that is then cut to footage of the audience clapping and cheering for Sadat. This sequence becomes ironic when compared with the Palestinian film *The Fertile Memory*, where Sahar writes in one of her novels "Israelis say Sadat licked our ass, so how dare you Palestinians lift your heads?" *Days of Sadat* mentions Sadat's protest against Begin's refusal to let Jerusalem be shared by all Jews, Christians, and Muslims, but glosses over the Camp David Accords, which are merely mentioned but not represented. The film in fact dedicates significant screen time to the early days of Sadat, while it rushes through the more memorable moments of his presidency.

A similar presentation of history can be found in *Hero from the South*, an Egyptian film about an Egyptian mother's search for her son who disappeared in Beirut at the outbreak of the Lebanese Civil War. Returning to Beirut 15 years later, Mona, a Christian, finds that her son has been raised by a Lebanese family as a Muslim. After being duped into joining an anti-Christian Muslim militia, the seventeen-year-old man is reunited with his birth mother, and in a moment of clarity decides to abandon the militia for the anti-Israeli resistance in the south of Lebanon. Although the film touches upon the complexity of the Civil War conflict in Lebanon in two scenes—one showing Mona watching a documentary about the war on television, and another where Mona's son and his adoptive mother try to explain the conflict to Mona unsuccessfully (she eventually likens the "mess" to the Egyptian dish *koshari*)—it remains a sanitized, one-dimensional melo-drama reducing the Lebanese Civil War to a case of misguidance on the part of the warring Lebanese factions, and blaming the conflict on Israel primarily. Thus, the television documentary watched by Mona relates the war to the creation of Israel, and declares that Israeli forces "alone" committed the massacre of Sabra and Shatila, thereby avoiding the issue of the involvement of Lebanese militias in the incident. It then mentions the creation of Hizbullah and that "martyrs died to liberate Lebanon." The voice-over lists the names of famous male and female martyrs in Lebanon who conducted suicidal operations against Israel in the 1980s, but does not mention the different political parties that those martyrs belonged to. The film also condemns the militias by presenting the "Muslim" ones as profiteering from arms deals and the "Christian" ones as being pro-Israeli. The film ends with Mona's son declaring his embrace of both his Muslim identity and his Christian heritage, shortly before dying as a martyr himself in an anti-Israeli operation.

Thus, the Egyptian films disregard historical accuracy in favor of oversimplification, resurrecting pan-Arabism, and representing the conflict with Israel as one that goes beyond Palestine, where Egypt has taken an active, positive role, and where Arab countries eventually stand united in the face of the Israeli enemy. The films thus celebrate Arab nationalism, which is an example of regionalism as characterized by Stubbs and Underhill (1994), and thereby comprises three factors:

"First, there is a common historical experience and sense of shared problems among a geographically distinct group of countries or societies" (Smith 1997, pp. 70–71). This can be seen in how, historically, Arab countries have often shared collective fates, from Ottoman rule, to European mandates, to conflict with Israel, to the Gulf War. This is highlighted in the films, where the Arab–Israeli conflict is flagged as a common problem shared by the whole of the Arab world.

"Second, there are close linkages of a distinct kind between those countries and societies, in other words, there is a 'boundary' to the region within which interactions are more intense than those with the outside world" (ibid.). Linkages among Arab countries span geography, culture, religion, and language. However, with the exception of language, those factors are shared with neighboring non-Arab countries as well (like Iran), making the boundary of the Arab world based on political projects and the mapping of Europe. The films emphasize the political boundaries between the Arab world and the outside, constructing Israel as an external threat jeopardizing harmony between and within Arab countries.

"Finally, there is the emergence of organization, giving shape to the region in a legal and institutional sense" (ibid.). This can be seen, for example, in Nasser's attempt at establishing a gross Arab state (starting with Egypt, Syria, and Jordan), but, more successfully, in organizations such as the Arab League, which all Arab countries belong to. Nasser's failed United Arab Republic project is glossed over in the films, focusing instead on his successes. The resurrection of pan-Arabism can be seen as an act of remembering or, as Bhabha (1986) puts it, "a painful re-membering, a putting together of the dismembered past to make sense of the trauma of the present" (p. xxiii). Yet the complication is that, as Niranjana (1992) points out, the fragments that are now put together "were fragments to begin with" (p. 173).

Pan-Arab lament

The Syrian films depict Syria as an avid supporter of the Palestinian cause, but blame past governments for the failure of this support to manifest itself in measurable gains by the Palestinians, and thus mark a move from embracing pan-Arabism nostalgically to lamenting its loss. In *Refuge*, the plight of Palestinians at the time of al-Nakba in 1948 is merged with that of the Syrians. The film tells the story of a Syrian family, where the father Zaki (Abu Fahd) chooses to leave his job as a builder to join the ranks of anti-Israeli fighters in Palestine. The film is set in Hama, portrayed as an idyllic Syrian town that serves as the perfect host to a number of Palestinian refugees who had fled their homes after the Der Yassin massacre. The town is constructed as a harmonious place where Christians and Muslims live together in peace and fraternity. The opening scene sees a group of children carrying bunches of roses and running through the town streets in commemoration of Good Friday, who are then given more roses by a young Muslim girl. One of the Christian children, Fahd, is later shown offering to buy groceries for his Muslim neighbors.

The entrance of the Palestinian refugees to Hama is presented in the film in a celebratory manner. A train arriving in the town carrying the refugees is decorated with two Palestinian flags at the front. As the families step off the train, they are showered with greetings emphasizing Arab fraternity: "Welcome to the Palestinian brethren in Arab land." At the local school, a teacher, Mohamad Dib, is shown reciting to his students a poem on how the Zionists seized Palestine, and later asking the students to welcome an orphaned Palestinian child who was admitted to the school. The displaced Palestinian families begin to erect tents outside the mosque, their beige tents merging with the color of the land surrounding them. When a storm uproots one family again from their tent, with the heavy rain dampening the children's books and turning the ground to mud, the camera lingers on their young faces as they try to hold the tent up. A close-up of the tent plugs coming off the ground precedes a shot of the dramatic collapse of the tent. But the support of the local Syrians does not fail, and Mahasen, Abu Fahd's wife, gives shelter to the family in her own home.

The film illustrates a parallel suffering of Palestinian and Syrian families. The Good Friday commemorations are disturbed by the absence of Abu Fahd, who has not returned from Palestine. Good Friday's graveness allegorizes the solemn existence of a family without a father, just as it does a people without a land. In church, during the Good Friday ceremony, Mahasen is shown wearing a black veil, crying. The reciting of "Today he was hung on a piece of wood" links her suffering with that of Christ. Just as the trains carried the Palestinian refugees, they also symbolize the loss of the Syrians. Local town residents gather in the streets, eagerly awaiting the arrival of another train bringing the Syrian fighters in Palestine back home. The men descend from the train, guns in hand, and are embraced by their families as children call for the long-missed fathers. This ceremonial event further isolates Mahasen and her family, for Abu Fahd is not one of the returning fighters. The last train departs, leaving Mahasen and her children alone on the platform. A flashback shows us the idealist, Arab nationalist Abu Fahd trying to convince his wife that by going to Palestine he will make money so she will not have to weave rugs to make a living again. But Mahasen's isolation is reduced when she decides to visit the mosque where the Palestinian refugees have set up tents. Mahasen wanders from one refugee family to another, asking about her husband who was in Safad, her grief merging with that of other families who have also lost fathers and loved ones.

The compassion of the ordinary Syrian people is contrasted with the stance and actions of the government. Mahasen's attempt to ask a sergeant where her husband might be is dismissed. As she leaves his office we see a crowd of women outside the building with the same query. The film presents Syria as a turbulent place where the people are duped by a chain of corrupt governments. Shortly after Mahasen's unsuccessful attempt at locating her husband, a bloodless coup, led by Husni Az-Zaeem, to form a democratic state takes place. The people of Hama gather in the streets celebrating, the men dance, and flags decorate the alleys. The teacher gives a speech about Syria's greatness to the crowd: "The humiliation period is over! We'll be victorious." The old government is openly criticized, and Abu Fahd is finally able to return home. A journalist, Abu Ghazwan, speaks against the soldiers' failure in 1948, calling them traitors, and asks Abu Fahd to publish his memoirs in his newspaper, encouraging him to expose the soldiers and the bad weapons during the anti-Israeli resistance. Abu Fahd concurs that "previous leaders weren't better; they spent their time in women's laps and let us die in Palestine." The scene is cut to that of a public hanging in front of a white government building: a long shot displays the horrific image of three hanged men with white sacks covering three-quarters of their bodies. Shortly after Abu Fahd returns to his job, his family chooses to give shelter to a neighbor accused of anti-government sentiment. This act, coinciding with the publishing of Abu Fahd's memoirs, leads to his capture by the army, who seize him from the building site and send him to prison in Damascus. The scene cuts to a shot of the teacher Mohamad Dib being arrested too as children look on from behind window bars at the school.

A second coup takes place in August 1949, and an announcement is made that the army will cease interfering with politics. Abu Fahd is released from prison. Although Majid Bey, Abu Fahd's boss, reminds him, referring to Abu Fahd's newspaper account which led him to prison, that "you can't always tell the truth," Abu Fahd optimistically declares that the "new president is patriotic and cried in Palestine when the Israelis took Safad." A fellow builder agrees, saying that Syria is the only democracy in the Arab world at the time. But the conversation between the men is cut to a shot of the army arresting people. The idealist Abu Fahd is left with no option but to abandon Hama. He walks into empty land, leaving a half-built castle which he was constructing for a Bedouin behind. He crosses the Assi River and heads to Lebanon. At the next Easter, Abu Fahd's fellow refugee Ra'fat makes a paper boat on which he writes: "Happy Easter from Lebanon's Assi to Hama's Assi," and lets it float in the river. The film ends with Abu Fahd looking back at the camera, unable to return home, and disillusioned at his leaders who have abandoned him and the Palestinian cause.

Nights of the Jackal is another film tackling Syria's involvement in the Arab–Israeli conflict, and marks a bolder move from nostalgia to lament vis-à-vis pan-Arab nationalism. Set in 1967, the film uses radio announcements as an indicator of political change. At the beginning of the film, a radio announcement of the day's programs is heard as a Syrian family heads to work in a field. The radio listing hints at Syria's on-going engagement with the Palestine question. The listing consists of a mixture of socialist shows targeted at workers (a series: "Land Price," and "Workers' Program"), news, music (including the song "The Petrol of the Arabs is for Arabs"), and a program called "Voice of Palestine." When the Six Day War breaks out, love songs are no longer broadcast and the radio announcement changes to updates on Syria's preparation for defense, and a series of nationalist songs about Arab unity. The radio announcements follow actual announcements in 1967 which duped the Arab masses into believing that the Arab forces were winning the war. In the film the radio announces that the Syrian defense attacked and pulled down 23 Israeli planes. As another nationalist song is played, the head of the family joyfully announces that "Palestine is back!" A long shot sees the father standing on a roof carrying a big radio as he orders his family below to dig a trench in preparation for defense. The radio announces that Syria considers the attack on Egypt an attack on itself. The father is promptly summoned to join the army. The film here criticizes the government's waste of resources. The father is assigned the role of patrolling the village bridge when he is a trained telecommunications specialist. The film ends with the Arab defeat mirrored by the father's helpless flicking through radio stations, where the transmission presents news of a *coup d'état* in Syria, a song by Fairuz about Jerusalem, greetings sent by people to their families to inform them of their safety, and news of further Israeli aggression. With this message of impotence, *Nights of the Jackal* offers a subtle criticism of the failure of Arab unity in the presence of incompetent governments that deceive their own people.

This lament of the loss of Arab unity continues in the film *Borders*. *Borders* tells the story of an Everyman, Abd al-Wadoud, whose car is stopped at a checkpoint as he is about to cross the intersecting international borders of five fictional Arab countries, Northstan, Southstan, Eaststan, Weststan, and Middlestan. After losing his passport at the border of Weststan, and after a series of endless bureaucratic procedures going back and forth

Figure 18 The father's anger at his powerlessness – *Nights of the Jackal* (photo courtesy of Arab Film Distribution)

between the countries, Wadoud is not allowed in any of them, and is forced to live literally on the border. The film starts with a song by Lebanese singer Fairuz, 'Watani' (My Country). The lyrics "My country is as big as the universe" are heard as Wadoud is stopped by the first checkpoint. The song serves as an ironic statement on the demise of Arab solidarity. Wadoud finds himself stuck in between the clashing border officials of Eaststan and Weststan, with each side accusing him of collaborating with the other. Wadoud's solution is to build a camp across the border of the two countries, which he declares his home. And thus begins the film's critique of Arab politics during a turbulent time in the Middle East. Made in 1984, two years after the Israeli invasion of Lebanon, *Borders* laments the reduction of pan-Arab nationalism to banal expressions which the Arabs became occupied with. Wadoud's character stands alone in the film. Being on the border, literally nowhere, allows him a critical distance from which to examine the five Arab countries surrounding him. But the film does not focus on the citizens of those countries. Most of the characters that we see are border police, who are used as a metaphor for the tyranny of Arab governments. On the border of Weststan, when interrogated by a sergeant about his political affiliation, Wadoud stresses that he is non-aligned, to which the sergeant replies that this is the first time someone has come to his office and is found not to be guilty of anything, leading Wadoud to declare "I am the only innocent person in this country." When Abu Mazhar, a passing taxi driver, inquires about Wadoud's health, the reply he gets is "The government says I'm fine so I'm fine."

The Arab world created by *Borders* is a stagnant one obsessed with ceremony, routine, and ritual. The film's narrative structure is cyclical, involving endless repetitions of banal bureaucratic procedures that Wadoud has to endure to secure entry into any of the countries around him. Wadoud is told by the Weststan officials to go to Eaststan, where the official meeting him constantly asks him if he would like a drink, and showers him with verbal niceties, yet does not grant him permission to enter the country. Wadoud later decides to turn his camp into a traveler's inn. When a customer asks for a newspaper, Wadoud says he has "tomorrow's *Times* and last year's Arabic newspapers, because the Arab newspapers are all the same." Wadoud's camp is compared to those of Palestinian refugees, whose demise has been sidestepped as a result of inter-Arab division. An exchange between Wadoud and an officer hints at this, after the officer asks Wadoud whom the camp belongs to, and Wadoud says it belongs to "the nations":

Officer:	The United Nations?
Wadoud:	Who else builds camps?
Officer:	Why is either half of the camp in different countries?
Wadoud:	If you harass me, I'll go to them and if they harass me I'll come to you.
Officer:	And if we harass you together?
Wadoud:	You have never agreed, so you won't!

This is further emphasized in a sequence depicting a rally organized after a media frenzy in which vocal support for Wadoud arises. A speaker from Northstan gives a speech saying "No more borders . . . those were created by imperialism." But the speech is interrupted by a man in the audience who gets up and starts giving an impromptu speech at the same time, so no one can hear what the man on the platform is saying. The sequence transforms into a fast-edited series of shots of different speakers intercut with close-ups of farm animals. Wadoud jokes that he is going to apply to the UN to make his camp an independent country called Solidaritystan.

The lament of the loss of pan-Arab nationalism is also seen in the only Egyptian film about the Gulf War. *The Tempest*, set in 1989, opens with the image of a clapping crowd of university students in Cairo, who are attending a lecture criticizing the immobility of Arab nations against Israeli aggression. The students sing a song of resistance, and chant against Zionism and in support of the *intifada*. They leave the lecture hall and start a demonstration against Israel. One of the students, Nagi, is seen wearing a *kaffiyya* on his shoulders. But the popular support for Palestine is contrasted with the official stance in Egypt, which is caught between Egypt's treaty with Israel and its historical position in Arab politics. At a school, Nagi's mother, Hoda, is giving a geography lesson. One of her students wonders how it is that geography book maps use the word "Israel" to refer to the land adjacent to Egypt, while history book maps refer to it as "Palestine." The point made by the student is emphasized in a flashback where Hoda remembers her dead husband. The husband had sustained injuries after he fought in the Suez War. When he returned from the war, he said that the war against Israel and the United States was not over. The flashback shows him witnessing Sadat's visit to Israel on television, then images of the Camp David Accords, and later the opening of the Israeli embassy in Cairo with the raising of the Israeli flag. His anger led him to disappear, and he was subsequently pronounced dead, a victim of official politics.

The film moves to a direct criticism of inter-Arab divisions with its depiction of the Iraqi invasion of Kuwait. The film's main message here is a reminder of fraternity in the Arab world, which is symbolized through the stories of the brothers Nagi and Ali. Ali has chosen to travel to Iraq to work, while Nagi is drafted to military service in Egypt. Ali is tempted by the chance of making five times more money through working for the Iraqi army, and leaves his job in a garage to install petrol pipes in the desert. He is assured by the army that he will not have to engage in battle. However, he is made to undergo military training. When Iraq finally invades Kuwait, Ali learns that 120 Iraqi officers who refused to take part in the invasion were executed. But when Ali's division is ordered to attack a Kuwaiti one, he and a friend of his manage to refrain from killing the Kuwaitis. Ali, knowing that Nagi is in the Egyptian army, tries to further object to participating in the invasion when Egypt decides to send troops to the Gulf to counter the Iraqi army, but fails. As students demonstrate against American intervention in the Gulf, we see Nagi on the Kuwaiti side, and Ali on the Iraqi one, forced by their officers to launch tank missiles on each other, which they do with tears flowing down their faces. The film ends with the burning of Israeli and American flags in Egypt amidst demonstrations. The final shot is of a black screen while the slogan "One Arab nation against the American attack" is recited.

A similar stance is taken by two other Egyptian films, *Naji al-Ali* and *Hello America*, which abandon grand narratives of pan-Arabism in favor of mini-narratives of ordinary people, namely Naji in the first and Bikhit in the second. The stance those two films take towards pan-Arabism is as a promising yet unsuccessful project. In this context, mini-narratives of resistance can be seen in *Naji al-Ali* in the representation of the Palestinian diaspora. The Palestinian diaspora's collective identity in the film is represented as defined by its relationship to the homeland (Clifford 1997a). The film contextualizes the presence of Palestinians in the Ain al-Helweh refugee camp in the south of Lebanon by opening with the depiction of the eviction of Palestinians from their homes in 1948 at the onset of the declaration of the State of Israel. The Palestinian diaspora in the film is exemplified by the character Naji, who is represented as bravely expressing his uncompromising attitude towards regaining the whole of Palestine and as not being afraid to express his dismay at Arab internal differences and conflicts triggered by leaders. The real Naji in turn had used a caricature character, Hanzalah (meaning 'bitter'), as a representation of Palestine and of himself. Hanzalah is a small boy who stands barefoot, with his back to the viewer, arms crossed behind him, wearing rags, and with hair like a porcupine's. Naji said that he intended Hanzalah to be a child, because childhood is a symbol of truth, innocence, and reality. He also said that Hanzalah's appearance recreated Naji's own childhood in the refugee camp in Lebanon. As for his hair, Naji said that it was because porcupines use their thorns as a weapon; at the same time, they are creatures that look unbearable on the outside, but are good on the inside. Hanzalah, moreover, is a prisoner and captive. Hanzalah's arms were not always crossed behind his back; Naji explained that he decided to cross his arms after the 1973 October War, because Naji, who did not believe in compromise, felt that the Middle East then was going to become subject to an American solution that would be unjustly compromising. Hanzalah's crossed arms represent his refusal to participate in such a solution (Kallam 2001). The film's stance towards the Arab–Israeli conflict is based on Naji's characterization of Hanzalah. Naji in the film is shown as having created Hanzalah in 1969, two years after the Arab defeat in the Six Day War of 1967. The war triggered President Nasser's announcement of his resignation. The film shows that Naji was deeply disheartened by this announcement, this sentiment latently continuing within him until he creates Hanzalah and proclaims his date of birth to be June 5, 1967. Naji declares Hanzalah's nationality as just Arab, and explains that "Hanzalah seems to turn his back on the people, because he is looking at Palestine, and people have turned their backs on Palestine."

The elites' abandoning of Palestine is symbolized in the film in the stance taken by a rich Palestinian businessman, Abu'l'fawares, who, in contrast to the lay Palestinian people in the diaspora living in refugee camps, lives at the top of a ten-storey building in Beirut. Naji goes to a party held in Abu'l'fawares' roof garden. At the party, Abu'l'fawares reveals the garden, full of fruit trees, to his guests and declares that he calls his garden Palestine. As the guests drunkenly chant about sacrificing themselves for Palestine while sipping champagne, Naji turns his back to them and urinates on a tree, saying "He who takes trees from their land can never return people to their land." The next day, Naji creates a new caricature character of Abu'l'fawares, who epitomizes the economic elites who care more about money than about Palestine. Kellas (1998) argues that the economic elites are usually the least nationalist in a nation, mainly because of their links with markets beyond the nation.

Naji al-Ali's criticism of the economic elites is coupled with criticism of the political elites. In this context, it presents a similar stance to that of the Palestinian film *The Milky Way*, where the elites are represented as benefiting from Israel. The character of the village mayor (the *Mukhtar*) in the film summarizes this case. The *Mukhtar* is introduced as a ruthless man who lets his desires run free; when he sees Um Kamal carrying a rooster, he demands that she take it to his wife without paying her for it. The *Mukhtar*'s son Mohammad threatens the village metalsmith Mahmud because he wants to marry Suad, a teacher whom Mohammad wants for himself despite her love for Mahmud. And when the Israeli governor discovers people using forged work permits in the Galilee village, the *Mukhtar* does not hesitate to accuse the innocent teacher Ahmad of being the culprit, in order to divert attention from himself (ironically, he later discovers that his own daughter is the forger).

Naji al-Ali laments the demise of pan-Arabism through the representation of a nameless, drunken, homeless Egyptian man whom Naji encounters on the streets of Saida during the Israeli invasion of Lebanon in 1982. As the man roams the empty streets, he asks Naji "When will the Arab armies come?" to which Naji answers "They're busy." The Egyptian man is later shot by the invading Israeli army, his death signifying that of fading pan-Arab sentiment. Towards the end of the film, the PLO is shown being forced to leave Lebanon after the Israeli invasion. The film shows that lay people in Lebanon lament the exodus of the PLO and throw rice over the departing Palestinian tanks as a sign of blessing. Naji realizes Palestinian resistance might be ending, and punches a glass window while tracing the Palestinian resistance's exile route: "From Palestine to Jordan, from Jordan to Lebanon, from Lebanon to where, Hanzalah?"

Narratives of diaspora are "differently imagined under different historical circumstances" (Brah 1996, p. 183), and therefore diasporas are heterogeneous, contested spaces. Thus, there are many questions to consider in discussing diaspora: "Who is empowered and who is disempowered in a specific construction of the 'we'? How are social divisions negotiated in the construction of the 'we'? What is the relationship of this 'we' to its 'others'? Who are these others?" (Brah 1996, p. 184). The film addresses the first two questions through showing how, although the Palestinian diaspora "has a mass character, it is not uniform" (Cabral 1994, p. 56); it encompasses various configurations of power. The film thus contrasts the artificial nationalism of the political and economic elites with the representation of Naji, drawn from the creative arts world, as a "cultural nationalist" (Kellas 1998, p. 98). The film portrays how Israelis attempt to arrest Naji in order to silence his powerful cultural nationalism. Naji's uncompromising position on the necessity of returning to Palestine is contrasted with that of Abu'l'fawares, who has settled in Beirut and implicitly declared it his home. This way, the film problematizes the definition of diaspora. Abu'l'fawares' is an example of the argument that not all diasporas entail "an ideology of return" (Brah 1996, p. 197), while Naji's is an example of the argument that a diaspora exists when an ethnic group or a nation "suffers some kind of traumatic event which leads to the dispersal of its members, who, nonetheless, continue to aspire to return to the homeland" (Rex 1997b, p. 274), and thus that "home" is a singular place. The film's criticism of the political and the economic elites vis-à-vis the loyalty of the masses shows how each side's relationship with nationalism is different, and therefore their presence accounts for divisions within the nation (Cabral 1994). However, despite this criticism, the film's representation of the Palestinian diaspora remains romantic, essentializing Palestinians as resistance fighters (literally and figuratively), and largely ignoring the tensions among Palestinian factions as well as with Lebanese ones.

As for the third and fourth questions, Brah points out that it is usually assumed that one dominant Other exists against which the "we" is constructed. Constructing binaries as such denies the historical, cultural, and political complexities of a diaspora. In attacking both Israel and corrupt Arab leaders, *Naji al-Ali* complicates the us/them binary. The film depicts Naji's caricatures of Arab leaders being refused by censors in Beirut. Depressed, Naji leaves for Kuwait in 1983 to work for the *al-Qabas* newspaper. There he gets an anonymous threat asking him not to criticize internal conflict. He refuses. He goes to London in 1985 to work for the international branch of the newspaper, where he is assassinated by the PLO in 1987. The film ends with Naji's voice saying "I've never had a complaint about my drawings from the lay people. We'll continue." The last scene of the film celebrates the resistance of the masses by showing images of the Palestinian *intifada*.

Criticism of Arab leaders can also be found in *Hello America*. *Hello America* represents the experience of a naive Egyptian man who is lured out of Egypt by the chance to work in the United States. However, his experiences in the USA are so negative that he decides to go back home for good. The film criticizes the indifference of Arab leaders towards Palestine and the dominance of the United States in world politics, as well as criticizing the indifference of the United States itself towards Palestine. The film also blames the Arab leaders' indifference for the success of Islamic fundamentalists who attract and exploit the dismayed masses with statements such as "America is the great Satan; it lies to its people."

As the main character, Bikhit, embarks on his trip to America, he is reminded by his neighbors to "beware of imperialism" and to "tell the American president to keep his eye on the 'question.'" When he asks which question, they reply "The Palestine question! The Third World! Globalization." Bikhit gets involved in a hit-and-run car accident, where he pretends to fall victim to the driver, the daughter of the American president who is about to run for elections again. Not wanting to cause a scandal that would jeopardize her father's position, she tries to seduce Bikhit into dropping charges against her: "I want my dad to stay president. He can increase Egyptian aid." Bikhit replies "Let him also free Jerusalem. And tell him to unify the Arabs, for when we are unified we can destroy the hell out of you, God willing." Bikhit refuses her offer, and holds a press conference expressing that "We don't need American aid." The Egyptian government's swift response is "Bikhit's comments do not represent the Egyptian government; there is no Egyptian–American crisis." Bikhit succeeds in meeting the American president, but the encounter ends up being a mere photo opportunity for the president. As soon as the cameras go, he does too, leaving Bikhit with no chance to discuss anything. The film thus criticizes not only the United States, but also Arab leaders who are not doing anything about Palestine, who bow in front of the United States because of their great debt and political weakness, and who cannot even organize themselves, instead giving the United States free rein in the region and, in doing so, ignoring the interests of their own citizens.

Abandoning pan-Arabism

The rest of the Arab films dealing with the issue of Arab unity present a criticism of this concept. This is because there are many problems with pan-Arabism. The concept itself is idealist. It is hard to define what being Arab is actually about. Is it about the language? A common culture? A common descent? A common religion? Arab countries have elements of all of those factors, and at the same time lack others. Pan-Arabism tries to bring together countries as diverse as Egypt and Lebanon under one umbrella. The creation of the State of Israel is one factor that had strengthened the idealism of this concept. Pan-Arabism was strong from 1948 until the Six Day War in 1967 as Arab countries stood together in the face of Israel. Said

(1992) argues that, during that time, Palestinians embraced pan-Arabism because of the lack of alternative ideologies and also because Arabism was an inclusionary ideology, in contrast to Zionism. Arab leaders during that time regarded the liberation of Palestine as part of a bigger project aimed at reforming and transforming the Arab world's political and social landscape. However, this Arab solidarity was soon to fall apart as a result of political clashes between various Arab countries, as well as within them. Moreover, the failure of the United Arab Republic in 1961 catalyzed Palestinian skepticism towards pan-Arabism; this was intensified by the Arab defeat in 1967 (Mohamad 1999). Since then, pan-Arabism has been in decline. The Arab–Israeli conflict was slowly being overshadowed by growing Palestinian nationalist movements focusing on local Palestinian, rather than regional Arab, priorities (Moten 1980). Palestinian cinema is more critical of the Arab abandonment of the Palestinian cause. *Canticle of the Stones* criticizes the Arabs' stance towards Palestine through the story of a woman who laments the loss of her father's land in 1967. But the woman confirms that the "land lost in 1967 was only a quarter of what was lost in 1948," and wonders "Why haven't the Arab states remembered *this* land?"

In *The Door to the Sun*, the relationship between Palestine and the rest of the Arab world is presented as an ambivalent one. This relationship can be divided into three historical stages. The first one occurred in 1948, when the Arab countries surrounding Palestine first declared war on Israel. Arab forces were seen as a "rescue army" by the Palestinian people, and offered hope that the exiled would be able to return to their homes. In the first Palestinian refugee camp in the Chaab village in Galilee, the camera zooms on a rock with "Long live the Arab rescue army" written on it. But the rescue army is depicted as being impotent. Mahdy, the lieutenant in charge of the army in the area, is shown as being obsessed only with polishing his cannon, saying that the rescue army is under no orders to fight. Younes and his fellow resistance fighters try to protect the camp but fail, and the Ain az-Zaitouna refugees end up having to stay in tents. They decide to go back to their village in defiance. When Mahdy witnesses this, he decides to ignore orders and commands his troops to fire at the Israelis. When Galilee is taken over by the Israelis, Lieutenant Mahdy kills himself in shame. A shot of villagers emerging from behind a hill is dominated by the sound of orders by the Israelis to the women and children: "Go north! Go to Lebanon!" The rescue army is ordered to surrender and to pull out. The exodus to Lebanon marks the second stage of the Palestinian/Arab relationship, where cracks begin to occur between the two sides. Black-and-white images of villagers moving slowly in the derelict landscape depict the refugees arriving in Lebanon and Syria. Khalil's voice-over narrates how the fighters were captured by the Syrians and how the Lebanese scattered the refugees. The Lebanese army is shown pointing guns at refugees in a camp. But the army is still depicted as being supportive, with an officer, Haytham, ordering the release of Younes after his capture. Haytham winks and excuses Younes by claiming that he is "insane," and later allows Younes and his fellow fighters to take army guns and tells them how to get dynamite.

The third, and longest, stage is one of confrontation and avoidance. The film moves forward to Beirut in 1952. Younes is arrested and beaten by the Lebanese secret service after President Chamoun declares that he will allow no militias on Lebanese soil. The situation gets worse with the start of the Lebanese Civil War. Khalil recalls the siege of the Tal az-Zaatar camp in 1976, and laments the expulsion of the PLO from Beirut in 1982. The PLO is shown leaving under the throwing of rice and rose petals by the local camp residents. Fairuz's song 'Sanarja'u yawman' (We'll return one day) is heard as women ululate and the PLO fighters shoot in the air. Finally, the film moves forward in time to 1994. Khalil's Lebanese friend shows a French actress around the Mar Elias refugee camp in Beirut. He explains to her that "The camp is not recognized in Lebanon. Like all Arabs, we are for the Palestinian cause, but we hate Palestinians."

The film also criticizes the Palestinian resistance fighters. Khalil censures the Palestinian involvement in the Lebanese Civil War that distanced the Palestinian resistance fighters from their original cause. Khalil says "The Lebanese war turned us into criminals . . . Palestine was farther away; it became vague with the battles of Qarantina, Maarek al-Fanadeq [both were street-fighting events in the center of Beirut], and Sabra and Shatila." Khalil himself has fallen out with the PLO, and runs away from PLO security after his girlfriend, Shams, kills a PLO man, Sameh. A doctor working in a hospital in a refugee camp in Beirut, Khalil is angry that all the PLO money goes on police, prisons, and weapons, not hospitals. The PLO is depicted as almost tyrannical, with a flashback of Khalil during his training with the PLO showing him forced to crawl on the ground shouting "la ilah illa Allah" (There is no god but God [Allah]) after his trainers accused him of blasphemy. After Khalil is arrested by PLO security who are investigating Sameh's murder, a nurse, Um Hassan, confronts them by saying "Where were you during the invasion? You were hiding in Tripoli like cowards."

Iraq's invasion of Kuwait was a further confirmation of inter-Arab divisions. The absence of Arab solidarity is reflected in the series of short films about the Gulf War, *The Gulf War . . . What Next?* In particular, the Lebanese film *Eclipse of a Black Night* stands in direct opposition to the position taken by the Egyptian film *The Tempest.* The film portrays a Lebanese filmmaker, Mounir, looking for an idea for a film he is asked to direct about the Gulf War. He phones an Egyptian friend, Magda, for inspiration, and the plot she suggests to him is an almost exact replica of that of *The Tempest.* The ending of her "film" is that the two Egyptian army officers meet, hug and kiss, and erect a tent ("the tent of love") on which they place "white flags that flutter like doves," demonstrating Arab unity to the fighting Iraqis and Arab allies. Mounir's response to her absurd suggestion is a slow-building, manic laugh which forces her to hang up on him, after which he stands up and mocks her assertion to him that "The whole of Cairo will respect you. I swear that this will win you the Nobel Prize." Mounir stands with one hand on his hip, and almost belly dances as he imitates Magda's voice. On his left the television transmits images of the bombing of Baghdad. Mounir's mockery becomes a powerful comment against the empty idealism of Arab unity that has been reduced to no more than clichés, and which has little bearing on Arab reality.

Mounir's position is echoed by the character Kamal in the Tunisian film *It's Shehrazade They're Silencing.* Kamal comments on the Gulf War by saying that "We're used to bad luck. We are a defeated people. Every new leader lures us with bright prospects and big words. Suddenly we remember that we are Arabs. We cheer; we get proud; we feel a sense of relief. Then we take a few more blows and go back to sleep." The film depicts a Tunisian family arguing over their positions towards the Gulf War. The son regards Saddam Hussein as his own personal Rambo, and so does his aunt's fiancé, who regards Saddam's invasion of Kuwait as a simple mistake. Kamal, the uncle, on the other hand, is critical of Saddam's selfish actions, while the father, Mohsen, has just returned from Baghdad and is saddened by the American action against Iraq, which has left ordinary people suffering. The family members all agree that the Gulf War has heightened their sense of Arab belonging. But they differ in their interpretation of what being Arab means in this context. So while the fiancé stresses that "thinking Arab" means defying the West and Israel, the aunt is pessimistic about violence, even against Jews. Although she says that she has never felt so Arab before, she still criticizes how "Arabs go to war and then blame it on the 'Palestinian issue.'" Kamal laments the death of the Arab slogan "One united Arab nation from the ocean to the Gulf," and mocks Mohsen's optimism that the Gulf War might awaken the Arab masses into rejecting dictatorship. The family's division becomes an echo of that of the wider Arab world.

The theme of Arab division continues in the Moroccan film *The Silence*. The film uses a song performed by a female in a television studio to weave a critical comment on this subject. The song appears at regular intervals in the films, its lyrics presenting a clear stance: "Arabs, you'll go nowhere because you have no common vision. You should have reached an agreement. The day has come and you remain divided." The film's plot revolves around a film crew whose work is interrupted through their occupation with the Gulf War. The crew passionately deliver lines criticizing Arabs, with one actress questioning "What kind of Arabs are you? You have killed each other in blind ignorance . . . You have uprooted the great cedars of Lebanon to lay Gulf oil pipes" and an actor pondering "Who knows? One of these days Schwarzkopf or Bush will show us how to face Mecca." This is juxtaposed with the deadpan delivery by a female intellectual of her position on the Gulf War, which she constructs as a criticism of the West's use of the concepts of democracy and human rights to invade Iraq, and of the bias in the application of international law which condemned Iraq's invasion of Kuwait but not Israel's of Jerusalem and the Golan. Her blank stare at the camera as she makes her statement reminds the viewer of the endless occasions in which conflicts in the Middle East have been presented as incidents of absolute victimization, and how the Palestine question has become like the joker in a pack of cards, drawn whenever the Arabs need to justify their actions, righteous or not.

A similar stance is taken in the Palestinian film *Homage by Assassination*, which uses captions like "Occupied Land" to make a connection between inter- and intra-Arab divisions during the Gulf War and the Arab–Israeli conflict, critically ending with a shot of Robert Powell in his role as Jesus

Christ in *Jesus of Nazareth*, looking at the camera and stating "He among you who is without sin, let him throw the first stone," cut to that of Palestinian children throwing stones at the Israeli army. The connection between Palestine and Iraq is presented positively in the final film in the series, the Tunisian *The Search for Shaima*. The film offers a criticism of universal acts of aggression. This is done through a collage of footage of different atrocities conducted by Israel, the United States, and beyond, juxtaposing images of crying women in Iraq, Beirut after the Sabra and Shatila massacre, Chile (at the funeral of Pinochet), Cyprus after the Turkish invasion, and Vietnam (the famous footage of a napalm-burned female child wandering naked in the streets). The footage is preceded by that of American female soldiers in training, chanting "I wanna go to Iran, I wanna kill an Iranian," and of Bush Sr smiling as a man shouts at him "It's a crime for the rich to attack the poor," juxtaposed with the image of Martin Luther King as he delivers his "I have a dream" speech.

The dominant political stance in the films emphasizes how Arab unity today has been reduced to no more than an "emotional attachment" (Al-Ahsan 1992, p. 52). Pan-Arab nationalism is an example of how regionalism can undergo tensions between demands of the state and those of collective action (Smith 1997) as demonstrated by Egypt's and Jordan's peace treaties with Israel. Thus, pan-Arabism has proven to be both an integrative and a disintegrative force in the contexts of the Arab–Israeli conflict and the Gulf War. The Arab world is heterogeneous, constructed of post-colonial (or at least post-mandate) countries, whose borders have been created by European powers and not by their indigenous populations. Thus, they are fragile constructions where ethnic groups, languages, and religions merge among different states, but where internal and external politics have superseded elements of commonality to transform pan-Arabism from a hopeful ideal into a lost dream.

Conclusion

The representations of the Arab–Israeli conflict and the Gulf War in the films are based on a discourse of difference. Difference in this context is conceptualized in four ways. First is difference as experience. The films present different constructions of the various events marking the Arab and the Israeli national selves. They show how, culturally and historically, "Israel" and "Palestine" are constructed differently in the eyes of their nationals and the eyes of the films themselves. Second is difference as social relation. This concept refers both to everyday experiences in localized arenas such as the household, and to national or global economies, politics, and cultural institutions. As Brah (1996) defines it, difference as social relation refers to "the interweaving of shared collective narratives within feelings of community" (p. 118). The films articulate those narratives, emphasizing the oppression of Jews in Hollywood, and reciting the narratives of the Palestinian diaspora in the Arab films. Third is difference as subjectivity. Needless to say, the cinemas follow contrasting political paths, portraying incidents as seen through the eyes of groups or individuals who embody the experience of the whole community. Thus, the hijacked passengers in *The Delta Force* represent a renewed threat to Jews as a whole, while *Naji al-Ali* is an epitome of the suffering of Palestine. Finally is difference as a constituent in the construction of identity. While the Hollywood films homogenize the identity of Israelis and Jews on one hand, and Arabs and Palestinians on the other hand, the Arab films present a struggle over the expression of Palestinian nationalism, showing how this struggle over meaning is a struggle over the Palestinian identity. For example, the films' contrast between the identity of the political and economic elites and that of the lay Palestinian people in diaspora illustrates how the Palestinian identity is not fixed and not singular, and therefore complicates a simple us/them binary.

The Arab films thus distinguish between two kinds of nationalism stated by Fanon (1994): bourgeois nationalism and anti-imperialism nationalism. The first refers to a kind of nationalism appropriated from colonialist discourse, a nationalism constructed by the elites. Films like *Naji al-Ali* and *The Milky Way* criticize this nationalism as being fake. The second on the other hand refers to populist nationalism that aims at the "reconquest of identity" through anti-colonialism (Abdel-Malek 1981, quoted in Lazarus 1994, p. 266). Lazarus (1994) complicates Fanon's argument by pointing out Fanon's implied progressive nature of such anti-colonial resistance. History has shown that anti-colonial struggle does not necessarily lead to post-colonial progress, in that, while a people may succeed in evading colonial powers, they may still fail to do so vis-à-vis internal oppression

(Lazarus 1994). Lazarus argues that this is a result of the non-elites' formation of their identity as one that aims to recreate the past, and therefore such an identity would fail when faced by a changing present. The contradiction is that the films revolve around a discourse of authenticity that contrasts the artifice of the elites' affiliation to Palestine with the genuineness of the loyalty of the Palestinians in refugee camps.

Through Hollywood's representation of Israeli unity, and the Arab cinemas' resurrection and subsequent lament and criticism of pan-Arabism, the films represent how individual identities are mobilized to become part of a larger, collective experience that demands that the internal hetero-geneity of the group be overcome. The films are an example of Brah's argument that "power is performatively constituted in and through . . . cultural practices" (1996, p. 125). In a Foucauldian sense, "if *practice* is productive of power then *practice* is also the means of challenging the oppressive *practices* of power" (Brah 1996, p. 125, emphasis in original). The cinemas attempt to rewrite history with their subjective representations of political events. Despite American sympathy towards Israel, the Hollywood films' focus on the role of the United States as peace mediator serves to establish the USA as a world policeman. The Egyptian and Syrian films' portrayals of Egypt and Syria as loyal Palestinian affiliates also serve to establish them as salient Arab nationalist leaders. Thus those cinemas not only follow political agendas that are nationalist, serving the United States and Egypt and Syria respectively, but also present global (USA) and regional (Arab) political agendas that are crucial for the maintenance of each side's role within a wider political context.

All those films remain about strengthening contrasting nationalisms, celebrating golden ages, and sympathizing with political allies. Despite *Naji al-Ali*'s and *Hello America*'s criticism of internal differences, their criticism is directed at those in power, and not at the "lay people." The films thus still cling on to a notion of homogeneity of the Self. In Hollywood, Jews are denied their "multiple experiences of rediasporisation, which do not necessarily *succeed* each other in historical memory but echo back and forth" (Jonathan Boyarin, quoted in Clifford 1997a, pp. 284–285, emphasis in original). Clifford (1997a) argues that Jews have been a "multiply centered diaspora network" (p. 285). Indeed, some Zionist Jews had considered establishing a "homeland" away from the land of Palestine (after Britain offered the Jews Uganda in the early twentieth century), though the majority believe in one true Zion. The films silence the minority's voices and erase the multiplicity of ethnic pasts (Smith 2000) in the effort to affirm the existence of Israel. Moreover, the films ignore political differences among Jews; although a significant proportion of the Jewish diaspora is not necessarily separatist (with many Jews preferring to continue living in their "host" societies where they have "selectively accommodated" with the hosts' political, social, cultural, and economic and everyday life aspects [Clifford 1997a]), the films portray Jews as eventually yearning towards the Holy Land. In the Egyptian and Syrian films, Arabs stand united in the face of Israeli threat. This representation glosses over the many populist clashes between Palestinian refugees and citizens of their host nations, mainly in Lebanon. Lebanon in *Naji al-Ali*, for example, is presented as a selfless, sympathetic host. In this way, the films try to resurrect a dead pan-Arabism. The films can thus be seen as an example of Smith's (1986) argument that "it is not society or ethnicity that determines war, but conflict itself which determines the sense and shape of ethnicity. War may not create the original cultural differences, but it sharpens and politicizes them" (p. 39). The issues the films raise then change the question from how does the past shape the present into how did the present create the past? As Chapman, McDonald and Tonkin (1989) argue, "social, moral and political considerations can render people selective in their treatment of the past, and surprisingly indifferent or hostile to alternative accounts" (p. 5). The films become one of "the institutional uses of fiction in nationalist movements" (Brennan 1995, p. 170).

But most interestingly, the Palestinian films exemplify the difficulty of applying post-colonial discourse to the practices and representation of the Arab–Israeli conflict. As Shohat (1999b) argues, "the paradox of Israel is that it presumed to 'end a diaspora' characterized by ritualistic nostalgia for the East, only to found a state ideologically and geopolitically oriented almost exclusively toward the West" (p. 7). Shohat says that the Jews have moved from being victims of Orientalism to its perpetrators, which makes the conflict between Israel and Palestine difficult to place within any standard categories of national conflict (Shohat 1989a).

McClintock (1994) argues that the limitation of the term "post-colonial" lies in its implied linearity. This means that it invokes looking at history in terms of a series of stages marked by the colonial experience: pre-colonialism, colonialism, and post-colonialism. This also carries the danger of implying that the history of the subaltern here marks progress and development, reached with post-colonialism. The emphasis on the colonial experience thus suggests that the subaltern culture is defined only in relation to colonialism, which endows the subaltern with a fixed subordinate position. The Palestinian films challenge this linearity by demonstrating the Palestinians' continuing anti-colonial struggle against Israel, and using the Palestinian victimized position as a means of resistance.

Also, there is a danger in the implication of uniformity that the term brings. This is a complication of discourse on Orientalism, as it implies that Western discourse is continuous, unified, and uniform, and therefore fails to look at hegemony as process (Porter 1994). This refers to the practice of talking about *the* post-colonial experience, thereby denying various cultures their historical specificity. This is intensified when talking about *the* post-colonial Other, implying that the subaltern is the same unchanging Other to the same colonizing forces, and thus carries a danger of essentialism and overlooking power imbalances, within both the West and the non-West. Looking at the Other as such neglects the various differences between and within cultures that have undergone (or are still undergoing) colonialism in all its forms. They are all thus defined in relation to the "West." The Palestinian films challenge this in their representation of intra-Palestinian difference. Moreover, post-colonialism may deny that colonialism may be imposed by the non-West as well, as seen in the relationship of Israel with the Arab world in the films. McClintock (1994) also points out that the term "post-colonial" is "prematurely celebratory" (p. 294), in that it implies the absence of any experience of colonialism at present. She presents the case of Palestinians under Israeli occupation as an example. In general, McClintock's reservation regarding the term "post-colonial" revolves around the term's temporal, rather than power-focused, orientation. She also criticizes the term's glossing over of colonialism's continual influence, and its negligence of including more subtle "imperialism-without-colonies" (1994, p. 295) as seen in the United States and Israel.

In this sense, the Hollywood films themselves become part of colonialism. Fanon (1994) argues that colonialism not only imposes itself on the present and future of oppressed people, but also distorts and destroys their past. In doing so, colonialism negates a people's national reality. It also strives to make the people appropriate notions of their own inferiority and even the unreality of their own nation, as seen in the representation of Palestinians in *The Ambassador* and *The Little Drummer Girl*. In response to this oppression, the oppressed resort to various forms of combat, one of which is what Fanon calls the literature of combat. Fanon describes this as shaping national consciousness and fighting for the people's existence as a nation. Culture, in other words, becomes a resistance tool (Cabral 1994). In *Naji al-Ali*, Naji's attempted arrest by Israelis demonstrates Israel's attempt at paralyzing Palestine's cultural weapon. It is thus that Naji becomes a heroic figure who defies this oppression through drawing, using the most limited of resources. Naji's art becomes another step in a long process of national liberation that attempts to affirm the identity of the Palestinians in the face of Israeli oppression. Furthermore, the Palestinian representation of struggle makes the films a site of resistance vis-à-vis Hollywood's and America's dominant discourses. However, being the dominated group allows them to utilize what Spivak (1990) calls "strategic essentialism," in that appealing to common, unique historical/cultural experiences serves the purpose of creating new, resistant political identities (Blythe 1993; Brah 1996).

The Palestinian films thus complicate the application of nationalism theories, namely notions about the coercive nature of nations, through their celebration of the Palestinian national liberation movement (including the *intifada*) (Ahmad 1994). Moreover, the films converge in their approaches to the nature of the nation. The films' representation of Israel and Palestine is largely modernist, where nations are politically, economically, and socially determined. The films reveal each of the Israeli and Palestinian nations "as a 'narrative' to be recited, a 'discourse' to be interpreted and a 'text' to be deconstructed" (Smith 1999, p. 167). Like Israel in Hollywood, Palestine in its cinema becomes a matter of symbolic representation, constructed through "the images it casts, the symbols it uses and the fictions it evokes" (ibid.).

Despite generally resorting to fixed boundaries, the Arab films are an illustration of the changing cultural identity of Arabs and Palestinians. This identity is shaped by discourses of history, memory, fantasy, narrative, and myth. As Stuart Hall argues,

Cultural identity . . . is a matter of "becoming" as well as of "being". It belongs to the future as much as to the past. It is not something which already exists, transcending place, time, history and culture. Cultural identities come from somewhere, have histories. But, like everything which is historical, they undergo constant transformation. Far from being eternally fixed in some essentialised past, they are subject to the continuous "play" of history, culture and power. Far from being grounded in mere "recovery" of the past, which is waiting to be found, and which when found, will secure our sense of ourselves into eternity, identities are the names we give to the different ways we are positioned by, and position ourselves within, the narratives of the past.

(1994, p. 394; see also Hall 1989)

IV

From the Other Outside to the Other Within: Representing Islamic Fundamentalism

Why fundamentalism matters

The notion "Arab" has often become a synonym for Islamic fundamentalism in contemporary Western culture, from movies to news to social theory. The events of September 11, the war on Iraq, and the conflict in Palestine have all aided in linking Islamic fundamentalism with terrorism, and in turn in positioning fundamentalism as an essential anti-Western enemy. Islamic fundamentalism has been perceived and represented in the context of several myths based on an East/West binary. Perhaps most famously, Islamic fundamentalism has been invoked by theorists such as Samuel Huntington (1996) to indicate a clash between the cultures of the West and those of the East. In this sense, Islamic fundamentalism has been often conflated with Islam and with the Middle East in general. This stance has generated significant critiques of those perpetuating myths about Islam, fundamentalism, and the Middle East. Most notably, Fred Halliday (1995) has argued against the placing of Islam as a monolithic force poised against the West. He has also criticized the construction of the West itself as a homogeneous entity that is necessarily oppositional to a threatening Islam. Halliday argues against stereotypes of Muslims and Arabs, pointing out their contradiction: the Muslim/Arab Other is at once sensual and hedonistic, militant and passive.

One of the most fertile arenas for such myths is Hollywood. Surveying Hollywood films over the last two decades and a half, we find that several films often engage in representing Arabs as ruthless, faceless Islamic fundamentalist killers. Islamic fundamentalists are reduced to terrorists, and therefore dehumanized. There is often no distinction between the notions Arab, Muslim, and Islamic fundamentalist. This mythical Other is usually perceived as an "enemy" in a battle of good versus evil, us against them. Fundamentalism has thus been looked at as a symptom of the Otherness of the Arab world, rather than as a problem within it. The other side of this construction is that of the United States as a nation. In contrast to the degeneracy of the Arab/Muslim/fundamentalist Other, the United States in Hollywood stands superior, morally right, and unbeatable.

There have been attempts at addressing this cinematic essentialism of the Arab/Muslim world and its representation. The most well-known work in this area is that of Jack Shaheen (1984, 1997, 2001), whose books analyze the stereotyping of Arabs and Muslims in Hollywood as well as on American television. Shaheen's work is informed by a cultural imperialism perspective—as expressed by numerous scholars such as Schiller (1973), Tunstall (1977), Smith (1987), and Tomlinson (1991)—which locates the relationship of the West to the East as one of dominance. More recently Sardar and Davies (2003) have referred to the representation of Muslims in Hollywood and American television programs to discuss the position of the United States as a "hyperpower" (p. vi) whose narratives export stereotypes about Others worldwide but whose alternative cultural products are submerged in this mainstream discourse.

Said's (1978) work on Orientalism can be used in analyzing the Occident's view of the Orient as seen in Hollywood. In also analyzing how the "Orient" represents itself as seen in Egyptian and Algerian cinema, Said's views on Orientalism are complicated, in that, when the Orient itself takes part in the process of Othering (here, of Islamic fundamentalists), the Orient no longer becomes merely "a European invention" (Said 1978).

Islamic fundamentalism complicates the East/West dichotomy, in that it is by nature a global movement occurring both in the "East" and in the "West." While representations of Islamic fundamentalism in the three cinemas generally differ, they still converge in representing Islamic fundamentalism as an Other. Bhabha has argued that "[i]n order to understand the productivity of colonial power it is crucial to construct its regime of 'truth', not to subject its representations to a normalising judgement" (1983, p. 19). Hence, it is important to examine the different Truths created by each side in their representations of Islamic fundamentalism. Bhabha (1995) adds that the post-colonial perspective aims at undoing the view of the First and Third Worlds as a binary opposition. Following this point, the intricate political and cultural boundaries existing not only between but also within the American and Arab sides are highlighted.

Benedict Anderson (1983) has stressed the centrality of the role of communicative space in the process of nation formation. Hobsbawm (1990) adds to this argument that communication functions not only in the creation of a nation, but also in maintaining it. In this sense, cinema can be looked at as a space for the creation and maintenance of an imagined community whose members imagine themselves as a coherent community with a secure shared identity and sense of belonging (Anderson 1983). In the American, Egyptian, and Algerian films, Islamic fundamentalism is used in many ways to validate nationalist identities and agendas. Islamic fundamentalism is made to stand outside the imagined community, at the same time functioning to add to this community's sense of belonging by being a common threat. Islamic fundamentalism then is an example of the tension between the cultural singularity invoked by nationalism and the reality that the American, Egyptian, and Algerian nations are in fact plural and diverse (Hobsbawm 1990). The cinemas use fundamentalism to validate their respective national identities, identities that assume the superiority of the inside over the outside, the familiar over the different. As Balibar puts it, "the construction of identity is not an imaginary process but a *processing of the imaginary*" (1995: 187, italics in original). And the "idea of nation is inseparable from its narration" (Bennington 1990, p. 132). Cinema then is an example of what Hobsbawm (1990) calls "invented traditions," national myths and symbols that bind a nation together yet that are also an official, rather than a populist, creation. The analysis argues that the cinemas only narrate the "official" story of the nation, where the rise of Islamic fundamentalism as an oppositional force has necessitated the validation of "a felt need for a rooted, bounded, whole and authentic identity" (Morley and Robins 1990, p. 19). The analysis then highlights how Islamic fundamentalism is constructed as an artificial entity vis-à-vis the ideological construction of the nation as natural. Thus, the representation of Islamic fundamentalism in cinema seems to follow the classical view of Otherness as telling us more about "us" than it does about "them."

Characteristics of Islamic fundamentalism

There has been a considerable degree of disagreement over the term "Islamic fundamentalism." The term originated in the Christian tradition as referring to groups that regard the Bible as the literal word of God (Tehranian 2000). The term was later appropriated by the media to describe certain Muslim political groups, and thus the term has been seen as a Eurocentric label that has not originated from the peoples it is describing (Agha 2000). Moallem defines the term as "a regime of truth based on discourses identified with, or ordained by, God (taken metaphorically or literally) and binding its observants" (1999, p. 323).

Though the term is here used to refer to various groups and traditions, it has to be stressed that each should be looked at in a specific historical context (for example, there a difference between the "fundamentalism" of Saudi Arabia and that of Iran) (Tehranian 2000). The term has been defined from various angles, and to describe diverse and unrelated movements (Agha 2000). The term can refer to "the growth of Islam as a religious force and a political ideology and . . . to the desire to reinstate the Islamic legal code" (White, Little and Smith 1997, p. 7). The term can also refer to "the emotional, spiritual and political response of Muslims to an acute and continuing social, economic and political crisis that has gripped the Middle East" (Ehteshami 1997, p. 180). However, it has also been defined as a challenge to America's position as a global power and its hegemonic interests, a term used by the United States as a shorthand to discredit opponents as irrational and irresponsible (Saikal 2000). At the same time, it has been seen as a challenge to Western ideologies in general like secularism

(Mowlana 2000). It has also sometimes been defined as synonymous with terrorism (White, Little and Smith 1997). This has led the Organization of Islamic Conference in 1997 to explicitly condemn terrorism as being against the principles of Islam (Tehranian 2000). The term "fundamentalist" has also been used to describe someone who represents the essence of society, and thus Islamic fundamentalism has become a metaphor for a terrorist Arab society (Bleiker 2000). Islamic fundamentalism has also been seen as a branch in a general mode of fundamentalism, "defined as cultural intolerance and violence . . . secular as well as religious" (Tehranian 2000, p. 217). The term has caused such controversy that it has been proposed that it should be avoided altogether. This is because it "has become a psychological scapegoat for those who refuse to acknowledge and take responsibility for the real international and intercultural problems" (Tehranian 2000, p. 217). Here the term is used loosely to refer to "a diverse set of competing political opinions held within the Muslim community" (Ehteshami 1997, p. 179). In short, the use of the term emanates from the fact that other terms ("Islamists," "extremists," "fanatics," etc.) are no less damaging, and also carry their own complications. Thus, "Islamic fundamentalism" is used in the political sense, to refer to groups that use Islam as a basis to achieve political power.

Islamic fundamentalism is a combination of several movements and groups. These various Islamic fundamentalist groups (whether political or militant) are severely divided, to the extent that "each refuses to recognize the legitimacy of the others" (Karawan 1997, p. 25). There are "different tendencies and varieties of Islam" and fundamentalism (Sayyid 1997, p. 36). Therefore it is mistaken to talk about Islamic fundamentalist movements as one entity (Said 1981). However, as put by Sayyid, "the diversity of Islamic movements does not mean that . . . [Islamic fundamentalism] lacks coherence" (1997, p. 157). Moghissi explains that all fundamentalist movements "see Islam as a totalizing force that inspires and regulates all aspects of public and private life" (1999, p. 70). What links the various Islamic fundamentalisms is three characteristics, which are of importance when examining fundamentalism in the context of the cinemas' representation of politics. First, even if it is a religious movement, Islamic fundamentalism is also a political one that aims to establish a "polity of believers" (Hamzeh 1998). This conflicts with the idea of a secular nation-state, adopted in many countries, such as Egypt, where fundamentalism exists. For example, Sayyid Qutb—an Egyptian fundamentalist guru—has been quoted as saying that a "Muslim's nationality is his [*sic*] religion" (quoted in Faksh 1997, p. 10). Indeed, Qutb had himself engaged in an active opposition to Nasser's nationalist-secularist regime, which ended in Qutb's execution in 1966. Second, Islamic fundamentalists believe in Islamic authenticity, juxtaposed with what is seen as Western hegemony, which in turn is believed to threaten this authenticity. Western hegemony is not confined to Western countries; it also applies to secular people in the Muslim world who are seen as even worse than the "foreign infidels" (Faksh 1997, p. 9). They are seen as "representing the interests of the . . . formerly . . . colonial powers" (Taheri 1987, p. 16). Again this has resulted in conflict between secular governments such as in Egypt and fundamentalist groups. Finally, fundamentalist groups seem to agree on the necessity of Jihad (holy war) in order to preserve the Muslim community. However, the groups differ in their interpretation and application of Jihad. While some see Jihad as non-violent, others like the Islamic Jihad Organization view Jihad as being military.

Castells sees the Islamic fundamentalist identity as a resistant one, and describes it as an expression of "*the exclusion of the excluders by the excluded*" (1997, p. 9). He sees the Islamic fundamentalist identity as being defensive against the dominant institutions/ideologies. Indeed, Islamic fundamentalism may have been a reaction to the state in countries like Egypt, but Castells's description excludes cases like pro-Western Saudi Arabia where Islamic fundamentalism is itself the dominant ideology. However Castells's view of fundamentalism is useful, as he points out the construction of the Islamic fundamentalist identity as opposing "failing ideologies of the post-colonial order" (1997, p. 17), like nationalism, capitalism, and socialism. Yet what Castells misses is the cooperation between fundamentalism and these ideologies themselves, as, for example, fundamentalism was used in Egypt to support the nationalist project in the 1920s and 1930s. It was a means to rally the masses against British rule. A similar case is seen in the activities of the FLN (National Liberation Front) in Algeria against French colonialism. In the case of Saudi Arabia, we can also see no conflict between fundamentalist ideology and capitalist business ventures. Thus, Castells's supposed net/self binary is challenged.

The controversy of Islamic fundamentalism

Most of the films analyzed represent Islamic fundamentalism from different angles. In contrast with other political issues covered in the films (like the Arab–Israeli conflict or the Gulf War), the representation of Islamic fundamentalism is a prime example of the complex nature of power. The controversy of Islamic fundamentalism lies in how it challenges the East/West divide, as this "local" force in itself becomes a globalizing force. Therefore, Islamic fundamentalism complicates theories of globalization and nationalism. At the same time, Islamic fundamentalism is Othered by the West as well as the East, and therefore is a strong case for complicating Orientalism. The struggle over the representation of fundamentalism shows how it is a contingent form of power that cannot be reduced to a simple us/them dichotomy.

The West and the East have both claimed to have the Truth about Islamic fundamentalism. These Truths are not necessarily always contradictory. One way in which these Truths converge is how both the West and the East see fundamentalism as an attempt not at modernizing Islam, but at "Islamizing modernity" (Kepel 1994, p. 2). Islamic fundamentalism is presented as seeing the modern world as corrupt and "Satanic" because it does not adhere to Islamic ways, whether in morality, politics, government, or social state. Modernity is exemplified not only in the West, but also in secular (and non-Muslim) Eastern states. Islamic fundamentalism condemns how modernity has meant that the state has not just undermined the role of religion, but has replaced religion altogether (Abaza and Stauth 1990). On another level, while this common Truth suggests that fundamentalism opposes the West and its manifestation in the East, a closer scrutiny challenges this Truth. Fundamentalists may have opposed the secular ideological aspect of modernity, but they have "adopted the most sophisticated techniques of modernity and tried to dissociate them from the secular culture, to show that there is no necessary connection between the two" (Kepel 1997, p. 5). An example is how Islamic fundamentalists used their American weapons and guerrilla training to expel the Soviets from Afghanistan. The United States excuses its support of these militants by saying that it could not directly confront the Soviets (Karawan 1997). This example is one of many that complicate the idea of fundamentalism as being totally oppositional to the West.

Another example can be derived from an argument by Sayyid. Sayyid presents the West's Truth about fundamentalism by observing that one "way of describing the discourse on 'Islamic fundamentalism' is to call it 'orientalism' . . . This allows the 'abnormality and extremism' of fundamentalism to be contrasted with the moderation and reasonableness of western hegemony" (1997, p. 31). Thus, fundamentalism becomes "a means of establishing and reinforcing the identity of the West" (Sayyid 1997, p. 33). It is clear from this argument that the West tends to equate the East with fundamentalism (Moallem 1999). Needless to say, the East itself is divided into a pro-fundamentalism minority and an anti-fundamentalism majority. The latter category uses fundamentalism to define its identity too. For example, in the Egyptian film *The Terrorist* and the Algerian film *Bab el-Oued City*, while the "moral" woman is seen by fundamentalists as being veiled and home-bound, for non-fundamentalists she is not veiled and enjoys a far higher level of freedom. The non-fundamentalist East thus uses the same "abnormality and extremism" of fundamentalism that the West uses to define the Eastern identity as its opposite. At the same time, what adds to the controversy of fundamentalism is that Islam is constructed by fundamentalists themselves as "a master signifier, the point to which all other discourses must refer" (Sayyid 1997, p. 47). Hence we can establish an interesting connection: fundamentalists use Islam to affirm their identity the way the West and the East use fundamentalism to affirm their identities —only that the first is a positive affirmation, while the second is a negative one.

However, in the cases of the West and fundamentalists there is "an attempt . . . to hegemonize the general field of discursivity" (Sayyid 1997, p. 46). Just as, in Said's words, "the Islamic Orientalist expressed ideas about Islam in such a way as to emphasize his, as well as putatively the Muslim's, resistance to change, to mutual comprehension between East and West, to the development . . . out of archaic, primitive classical institutions and into modernity" (1978, p. 263), so do Islamic fundamentalists when they talk about the modern world, with their call for preservation of tradition, their denial of any comprehension between East and West (instead, some justify brutal action against the West), and their emphasis on the *return* to an ideal past (Moghissi 1999). In doing so, Islamists refer to Islam as an "incarnation of goodness" (Sayyid 1997, p. 48), while Orientalists see Islam as "a degraded, dangerous representative of the Orient" (Said 1978, p. 260). At the same time, Islamic fundamentalists see non-Muslims (whether Western or not) as Others (Moghissi 1999). As put by Moallem, "[f]unda-mentalist discourse . . . is dependent on 'otherness' to organize an ideological 'we'" (1999, p. 335). Fundamentalists then have also used the West to construct their identity.

So where does the non-fundamentalist East stand? From analyzing the Egyptian and Algerian films, we see that this East occupies a position somewhere in the middle. It sees Islam as good, but so does it see other religions; it does not necessarily argue for East/West harmony but it calls for the appropriation of "good" elements from the West; and it supports modernity and condemns extremism, while remaining in the realm of tradition. Here it is important not to romanticize this non-fundamentalist East. Condemning fundamentalism does not give any country the status of absolute "goodness"; such a condemnation can be a means to an end on the country's political agenda. Often, in countries like Egypt and Algeria, opposing fundamentalism serves as part of a nationalist project. Neverthe-less, the argument moves beyond that of an East/West dichotomy and into a tripartite situation where every side is attempting to have a claim over the Truth. According to Sayyid,

> [t]he truth is one way of describing statements which we consider to be good or useful . . . Politics . . . is the process by which societies arrive at a new vision of the truth, a new way of describing the good or the useful. To paraphrase Michel Foucault, "[t]he political question . . . is truth itself". As such, truth and politics cannot be separated.
>
> (1997, p. 12)

Hollywood's fundamentalist terrorists

Against this backdrop, Hollywood has equated Islamic fundamentalism with terrorism. The Arab Islamic fundamentalist terrorist Other is constituted as possessing a fixed identity that poses a threat to the existing social order

(Bleiker 2000). Connolly (1989) argues that terrorism is an Other which is essential for any state's self-definition. Bhabha argues that this is a feature of the ideological construction of Otherness in colonial discourse. He points to the contradictory nature of this "fixity," connoting "rigidity and an unchanging order as well as disorder, degeneracy and daemonic repetition" (1983, p. 18). In its reliance on terrorist images, Hollywood's portrayal of fundamentalists justifies "ruthlessness against the other by concealing points of similarity between the other and itself" (Connolly 1989, p. 334). While Hollywood condemns the intolerance of the fundamentalists towards Jews, for example, it ignores how the "West" it is defending can itself be intolerant towards marginal groups. In *The Delta Force*, the fundamentalist terrorists hijacking an American plane segregate the Jews (and those who they think are Jews) from the rest of the passengers in what is compared to another Holocaust, whereas *The Siege* portrays Muslim American citizens being locked up in cages by the American army as a means to arrest fundamentalist terrorists. In this sense,

> [t]errorism becomes a monstrous evil . . . because it threatens to expose self-subverting characteristics in the global system unless it itself is defined to be the monstrous source of that subversion . . . Terrorism functions as a sign whose power of signification must be inverted to preserve the identity of sovereignty.
>
> (Connolly 1989, pp. 334–335)

Fundamentalism as an essentialized Arabia

Hollywood's portrayal of Islamic fundamentalism is part of a national project that idealizes the American nation while essentializing the Other. There is a tendency in the West in general to refer to Arab countries as "Arabia." While this term has been generally accepted, it invokes images of a unified Arab world. The myth of Arabia has in part been created through the pan-Arab ideal, advocated by Nasser. Smith (1991) points out that, despite the failure of the pan-Arab project (with inter-Arab wars such as the Gulf War and the lack of political consensus, especially regarding the Arab–Israeli conflict), the concept has emerged from and forged cultural links across the Arab world. However, Hollywood tends to blur not only Arab countries, but also Islamic fundamentalism and Islam as a religion with those countries and others in the Middle East region (namely Iran, as seen in *The Delta Force*). This is problematic because Islam is not parallel to the nation-state; its community is both smaller and wider than the nation-state (Worsley 1990). In fact, most of the world's Muslims (a population of 1.1 billion) live outside the Middle East (Ehteshami 1997). But Hollywood also portrays "terrorists" speaking Arabic (*The Delta Force, Hostage, Executive Decision*), associates Islamic prayer ritual handwashing with preparation for terrorist acts (*The Siege*), and gives the terrorist groups names such as "The Holy Freedom Party of Allah" (*Hostage*). Thus, even though Islam, both in the religious and in the political sense, is not a monolithic force, but rather subject to various interpretations and practices, Hollywood has constructed the myth of a unified Islamic fundamentalist Arab world "represented as a monolithic bloc poised against the West" (Esposito 1999, p. 225). A characteristic of this bloc in Hollywood is how it is state-supported (Crenshaw 1990). The governments of the fundamentalist terrorists in Hollywood either do not interfere with or openly support the terrorist acts (*The Delta Force, Executive Decision, The Siege, Hostage, Programmed to Kill*).

This utilization of a generalized Iranian/Islamic/fundamentalist/Arab identity is linked to an exclusionary visual imaginary as illustrated in Hollywood. While the films romanticize American nationalism, they vividly portray its ideology of exclusion. Cinema as a narrative of collectivity emphasizes not only the commonality of a nation's history, but also its difference from other nations (Preston 1997). The United States is often used as a classic example of nations emerging from the reconstitution of ethnic cores (white Protestants) and their integration with other ethnic groups (blacks, Chinese, Latinos/as, etc.). However, the films analyzed show a reluctance to reconstruct the American nation to fit in the Arab minorities represented (*The Siege*). The American nation thus becomes a fortress society, with the American nationality becoming an exclusive one.

Richard Slotkin (1998) gives an interesting account of this situation by arguing that this exclusiveness is a result of a resurgence of the Myth of the Frontier, whereby the white hero is idealized in his fight against savages. Slotkin argues that the perceived threat posed by other peoples, namely through the various acts of terrorism against the United States in the

Figure 19 An Arab terrorist about to blow himself up in *Executive Decision*

twentieth century (and beyond), has started an extreme reaction against not just threat from abroad, but also cultural heterogeneity, so that the threat of the Other has been displaced upon immigrants as well (as seen in *The Siege*). As Slotkin puts it, the perception is that "the civilized world [is] threatened with subjugation to or colonization by the forces of darkness" (1998, p. 635). Tracing the political context of the resurgence of this myth, Slotkin argues that the beginning of the 1980s added to the American nation's feeling of malaise (heightened as a result of the defeat in Vietnam) with events like the 1979–1981 Iran hostage crisis. The Reagan administration, however, regenerated the nation's morale through the resurrection of war against savage enemies (such as Libya). The Gulf War continued this tradition, with Bush declaring the war a "symbolic victory" regenerating the nation's spirit after Vietnam. The events of September 11, 2001 further emphasized the myth, although Hollywood has been reluctant to represent this incident cinematically (despite the existence of a number of independent

American films about September 11, like *The Guys* and Sean Penn's contribution to *11'09"01—September 11*). In the four years following September
11, the Arab terrorist has generally disappeared from Hollywood, replaced
by more symbolic Others. However, at the time of writing, Oliver Stone has
been preparing for a film about September 11, to be released in 2006. The
film is based on the real story of two police officers caught in the World
Trade Center during the attack. One of the men whom the film is based on,
Sergeant John McLoughlin, has been quoted as saying "It needs to be told
how this horrific tragedy brought Americans and the world together to help
those in need" (BBC News 2005). The film therefore seems to be following
a similar trajectory to those preceding it in strengthening American national
identity in the face of Others.

William McNeill (1982) refers to such national ideologies as public
myths. He argues that public myths serve to sustain a society in the face of
crisis, unifying the nation and holding it together. Public myths are not only
given, but also made. Throughout the twentieth century and beyond, we
can see that America's public myths have been used, read, and rewritten
selectively, according to political projects. For example, Iraq's position has
shifted from an ally during the conflict with Iran to an enemy with the Gulf
War—shifting with it the myth of the Gulf friend to that of an all-threatening
essential evil embodied in Saddam Hussein—and again to a country in need
of "our" help with the war on Iraq in 2003. In the case of the representation
of Islamic fundamentalism, Hollywood has acted as a generator and
enforcer of the new Frontier Myth, thus acting as an important factor in
strengthening an exclusive American national identity (Scott 2000). Being
part of mass culture, cinema usually expresses "official memory" (Preston
1997, p. 65). With films like *The Siege* denying a part of the community
(Arab-Americans) their say in the United States' official memory, we can
see that a nation's historical memory is contested, representing a conflict
between the powerful and the subordinates over the possession of history
(Preston 1997). Thus Hollywood's representation of national memory implies
a "selective interpretation of history" (J.W. LaPierre, quoted in Schlesinger
1991, p. 153). The only exception seems to be the Gulf War, which has
challenged the myth of the existence of a unified Arab world. Esposito
argues that the "greatest incongruity, perhaps, was that Saddam Hussein,
the head of a secularist regime who had ruthlessly suppressed Islamic

movements at home and abroad, would cloak himself in the mantle of Islam and call for a jihad" (1999, p. 252). *Three Kings* explicitly recognizes the separation between the notion Arab and the notion Iraqi in the Gulf War context, as well as, implicitly, the separation between Muslim and Islamic fundamentalist in its sympathetic depiction of Islam.

A characteristic of the fundamentalists belonging to the unified "Arabia" in Hollywood is their collectivism. Individualism (along with other ideals such as equality, democracy, and liberty) is one of the major elements in the ideology of Americanism. This ideology is conceived of as a model to be emulated by other nations, and hence is essentialized as both unique and superior (Preston 1997). While the Americans in the films are portrayed as being individualized through the focus on the ego-oriented hero who destroys the enemy single-handedly (*Executive Decision*, *The Delta Force*, *Programmed to Kill*, *Into the Sun*), the fundamentalists seem to operate in clusters or "collective social networks" (Shapiro 1999, p. 115) where the individual seems to be submerged in a larger system—that of the terrorist group. This "closed" identity is assigned to the fundamentalists in the films in a dogmatic way whereby non-conformists are punished. When the terrorists try to rebel or act outside of the group's cause, they are killed (*Hostage*, *Executive Decision*). This severe punishment is contrasted with that of the conforming fundamentalists, who are merely arrested by the individual heroes (*Executive Decision*, *The Delta Force*).

This contrast can be traced to a misunderstanding by the individualist United States of the collectivism of Islam. This is because each case presents a different configuration of selfhood. Individualism is characterized by three main elements: an internally driven goal orientation; the construction of the individual as an ideal type of or miniature society; and the individual's disembodiment from social relations. Collectivism, on the other hand, is characterized by the group member's constraint by external forces; having a group, rather than an individual, identity; and the absence of true personal authority (Friedman 1994). Under this collectivism, the group shares a common fate and common norms and goals (Triandis, McCusker and Hui 2001).This collectivism has been utilized by Islamic fundamentalists to challenge the responsibility of citizens to the state, by arguing that affiliation should be to a collective Muslim *umma*, where sovereignty lies with God and not the people (Ehteshami 1997).

Fundamentalism as barbarity

Hollywood equates fundamentalism with killing, kidnapping, and torture (*Executive Decision, Hostage, Programmed to Kill, The Siege, The Delta Force*). In doing so, "[d]eath . . . is called forth to secure the commitment" of the viewer to the films' supposed antiterrorist argument (Fortin 1989, p. 193). In particular, Hollywood represents fundamentalists executing their terrorist attacks against (American) civilians, including children (*Programmed to Kill, Hostage*), the elderly (*The Delta Force, The Siege*), and women (*Hostage, Programmed to Kill*). This "language of antiterrorism," as Fortin calls it, problematizes "issues of world order and conflict . . . as issues of everyday life. The threats are universal and localized" (1989, p. 189). The fundamentalist terrorist threat then becomes more than an abstract threat to the world; it becomes a threat to "us" and "our" children. Perhaps the best illustration of this is the attack on the World Trade Center on September 11, 2001. In such circumstances, whether "real" or represented, the local is embodied with a specific, national ideology. In a globalized world, the local and the global are two sides of the same coin; in this way a "global" threat such as Islamic fundamentalism becomes a localized threat. As Massey argues, "in the historical and geographical construction of places, the 'other' in general terms is already within. The global is everywhere and already, in one way or another, implicated in the local" (1994, p. 120).

Another thing that the films seem to be doing is victimizing political leaders in the same way as children and the elderly. In *Executive Decision*, the fundamentalist terrorists kill a senator on board the plane they hijacked, with their leader declaring "We are the true soldiers of Islam." This, on the one hand, portrays fundamentalist terrorists as undiscriminating between who their targets are. On the other hand, Fortin argues that this serves to create "a strategic contagion of innocence among the subjects" (in this case, the American politicians) (1989, p. 195). This "innocence" is then juxtaposed with the representation of the terrorist as a dehumanized monster. Two of the films also use religious figures as victims. Nuns and priests are among the passengers kidnapped in *The Delta Force* and *Hostage*. The films thus introduce a "diabolical reference" (Fortin 1989, p. 196) that evokes the classical myth of holy good versus unholy evil.

Hollywood has also constructed the figure of the primordial, Oriental Other who is at the same time despotic, rich, degenerate, and primitive (*Hostage, The Siege, Three Kings*). The iconic version of this mythical Other (Karim 2000) can be seen in *The Siege*. The opening sequence of the film sees a terrorist sheikh riding in the desert. The old, bearded man in a Mercedes recalls the Saudi international terrorist millionaire Osama bin Laden, who has been linked with terrorist activities such as the bombing of the World Trade Center in 1993 and its destruction in 2001, and attacks on tourists in Luxor in 1997, and who has blatantly "threatened attacks against Americans who remain on Saudi soil," as well as declaring in 1998 "the creation of a transnational coalition of extremist groups, the Islamic Front for Jihad against Jews and Crusaders" (Esposito 1999, p. 278). In *The Siege*, the image of the sheikh in his traditional dress riding in the desert is juxtaposed with that of American intelligence agents in Western clothing monitoring his journey via radars. The desert is thus used to signify Arabia or the Orient; the sheikh's traditional dress signifies primitiveness; and the Mercedes indicates the vulgar materialism often associated with, for example, the classical Orientalist representation of African tribal kings with leopard skins and Rolexes (*Coming to America*)—all contrasted with the "civilized us." The film continues a tradition of representing Arab materialist terrorists seen in 1980s films like *Iron Eagle*, where the mustachioed Arab villain is seen smoking a cigar and wearing a white, gold-embroidered military uniform.

Even *Team America: World Police*, the only Hollywood film to date to tackle the subject of September 11, does not deviate from this representation of Islamic fundamentalism as barbarity. The film is a parody of Hollywood action movies set against an allegorical representation of the United States' war on Iraq that began in 2003. It satirizes Hollywood's essentialism of Arab terrorists: they are represented speaking a non-language that is supposed to be Arabic and uttering the terms "Mohammad" and "Jihad" at every occasion; physically, they all look like Osama bin Laden clones; and they are occupied with executing terrorist attacks. It also parodies the war on Iraq with the construction of an attack by Team America—American "world police"—on Cairo that results in further Islamist terror attacks and anti-war rallies in America. But despite the film's deconstruction of the representation of fundamentalism in Hollywood, with its parody of the depiction of

Figure 20 Iron Eagle's materialist Arab leader in gold-embroidered uniform

American heroism, and its criticism of both the right and the left (Team America are criticized as much as the left-wing, anti-war "Film Actors' Guild"), the film still adheres to the familiar depiction of Islamic fundamentalist terrorists who pose a world threat. In this sense, the film follows earlier parodies of American action films like *Hot Shots* and *Hot Shots! Part Deux* (two post-Gulf War films depicting Iraqi villains), where the mere existence of the films, with their parody of the representation of Middle Eastern villains, confirms the central space that this representation occupies in the Hollywood imagination of the region.

Fundamentalism and political space in history

The representation of Islamic fundamentalist terrorists in the films implies a reconfiguration of political space. The terrorists in the films are not given a particular political agenda. Hence, "they represent nothing beyond themselves" (Fortin 1989, p. 196) and seem to remain outside politics. Even when they do have demands, the demands seem to be limited to "25 million dollars in gold" (*Hostage*). The films thus attempt to silence any legitimate claim the Other may have. The labeling of all Arabs as Islamic fundamentalists, and associating that label with negative connotations (mainly terrorism) is a process by which images are used as a means of cultural defense. In other words, cinematic space becomes a "political metaphor" (Schlesinger 1991, p. 144) whereby only one discourse (American foreign policy) is dominant.

It is interesting to compare this with the political/historical context: Ehteshami (1997) argues that, post-colonialism, many Muslim states have been faced with economic and social problems that have required them to "withdraw from the public sphere and in doing so" to create "a political space that the Islamists have been quick to exploit and occupy" (p. 188) (for example, through providing welfare services). Thus, political space is no longer defined by national territorial boundaries. Rather, it is contested by global forces outside the state's realm. So in addition to the influence exerted by the United States, for example, there is a growing influence by Islamic fundamentalist groups which may be disparate but which are forming a kind of imagined community that transcends national borders (Beeley 1995; McGrew 1995). The films, as mentioned above, however, deny the fundamentalists that political space.

Yet the films also seem to rely on historical facts in their portrayal of fundamentalist terrorist acts. *The Delta Force* opens with an account of the 1979–1981 siege of the American embassy in Tehran. It—along with *Hostage* and *Executive Decision*—also uses the TWA flight hijacking in 1985 as a basis. Fortin argues that such a use of history puts the films "within the familiar" in order to gain credibility; the films seek "to comfort the initiated and signal a challenge to the unbeliever" (1989, p. 194). Moreover, the films make extensive use of proper names of places: Beirut (*Navy Seals*), Algeria (*The Delta Force*), Libya (*In the Army Now*), Tehran (*The Delta Force*). Barthes argues that such use also serves to gain credibility (Fortin 1989). At the same time, the names of places usually associated with terrorism in "real" life function as a connotation that projects actual horrific experiences on to the characters in the films. This also applies to the films' use of certain historical incidents. *The Delta Force*'s description of the fundamentalist terrorists' abuse of Jews as another Holocaust invokes ready imagery of horror. As Shapiro argues, "the issue becomes not one of the fidelity of the representation to the real, but the kind of meaning and value a representation produces" (1989, p. 73).

The films also rely on portraying plane hijacking (*The Delta Force*, *Hostage*, *Executive Decision*) by the Islamic fundamentalist terrorists. Fortin argues that this terrorist disruption of travel and communication "affects precisely those interests that are dependent on the regularity of exchange" (1989, p. 195), namely capitalism. Thus, the films indirectly send a message that the terrorists pose not only a localized threat but one targeted against Western ideals as a whole. This reliance on the portrayal of a "'fortress community' . . . drawing lines between the West and the rest" (Shapiro 1999, p. 117) recalls Samuel Huntington's (1996) argument about the existence of a clash of civilizations in which Islam is the greatest challenge to civilizational coherence. Islam in this sense is seen as a totalitarian force. This is projected on to the films that also represent Islamic fundamentalism as a totalitarian force seeking to replace "Western" ways of life.

Shapiro counter-argues by saying that "Huntington denies the interdependencies involved in producing and reproducing the West and the rest, as well as the ambiguities of the cultural orientations within the various groupings" (1999, p. 117). As mentioned earlier, Islamic fundamentalists do not exist in isolation from the "West," as Islamic fundamentalism is a global phenomenon that also depends on the West for its economic subsistence. One can even argue that fundamentalism needs the West for its existence just as the "West" needs it. It is the "West" that is blamed for the "evils" that fundamentalism is supposed to overtly oppose: liberation of women, secular governments, colonialism. And the complex existence of fundamentalism as an Other within the "rest" also challenges this East/West dichotomy which assumes the uniformity of both the "West" and the "rest."

Islamic fundamentalism in Egyptian and Algerian cinemas: the Other within

The two Arab cinemas that have concerned themselves with the representation of Islamic fundamentalism are Egypt's and Algeria's. This is not surprising considering that those two countries have been suffering from conflict with Islamic fundamentalist dissonants for decades. Cinema in Egypt and Algeria is one way in which the countries are disseminating antifundamentalist messages. One of the most prominent figures in this context is the Egyptian actor Adel Imam, whose films *Terrorism and Barbecue*, *The Terrorist*, *Birds of Darkness*, and *Hello America* all oppose Islamic fundamentalists. This has led to his receiving death threats from fundamentalist groups who declared him an enemy of Islam (Faksh 1997). His 1994 movie *The Terrorist* even witnessed intense security outside the cinemas showing it (Sackur 1994). The film has also been alleged to have been released as part of a wider government-controlled anti-fundamentalism campaign (Armbrust 2002).

In contrast with the monolithic way Islamic fundamentalism is represented in Hollywood (as terrorism), Egyptian and Algerian cinemas portray Islamic fundamentalism from several angles that are generally more complex than Hollywood's. The cinemas look at both the internal (psychological distress, sexual repression) and external (corruption, terrorism) characteristics of the fundamentalist. What links those angles is how fundamentalism in those cinemas is portrayed as an Other. The portrayal of Islamic fundamentalists in those cinemas is in line with the way Islamic fundamentalism is viewed by the Egyptian and Algerian governments as a threat to nationalism and to democracy. The Egyptian films explicitly portray the government jailing Islamic fundamentalists. *Nasser* depicts the way President Nasser imprisoned his Islamic fundamentalist opponents in the 1950s after they conspired against him. The way fundamentalists are treated at present is also represented in the films, with *Birds of Darkness* depicting the government's arrest and imprisonment of an Islamic fundamentalist political activist. In such films fundamentalists are contrasted with the image of the government, which is portrayed as being "good." However, this does not negate the existence of government criticism. *Bab el-Oued City* hints at cooperation between the fundamentalists and corrupt government officials, and *Terrorism and Barbecue* criticizes the malfunctioning of government services. But the latter, at the same time, subtly blames Islamic fundamentalists for this malfunctioning through the depiction of an Islamic fundamentalist man who spends his day in the office praying instead of working.

Fundamentalism as artifice: moral and political corruption

One way in which fundamentalists are portrayed is as being corrupt and hypocritical. This hypocrisy can be seen on several levels. First, fundamentalists are portrayed as being hypocritical in relation to the West. While they preach against it, we see them buying weapons from it in *The Other*. The film portrays the fundamentalist Fat'hallah objecting to his sister's marriage to an American man while he buys weapons from the same man's mother. Youssef Chahine continues his stance against Islamic fundamentalism and its relationship with the United States in his segment in the film *11'09"01— September 11*. Chahine casts the actor Noor El-Sharif as his alter ego, playing an Egyptian director contemplating the attacks on the World Trade Center in 2001. A fantasy encounter between the director and a dead American marine who has come back to life starts a conversation about America's role in the Middle East, in which Chahine criticizes both the United States and Arab countries. When the marine tells the director "Arabs did this [the September 11 attacks]," the director responds "But the bin Laden people were trained by Americans. I am angry that you have never tried to understand the Other." The marine promptly replies by saying "Did you [Arabs] ever try to tell us something and we did not listen?" But Chahine then moves to placing the blame for the attacks on the United States. He portrays a Palestinian mother and father whose son was a suicide bomber talking about Israeli atrocities against them saying "Americans decide who the terrorist is. Have you ever seen them destroying your house? Have you ever seen your ancestors' olive trees destroyed by a bulldozer? Have you seen an 18-year-old humiliating a father in front of his children? And you ask where violence comes from?" This leads the director to count the millions who have died in the world because of American violence, wondering "Why does America have to defend its interests at the expense of others?" Islamic fundamentalists then become a tool in the hands of the United States, their partnership resulting in nothing but destruction.

Second, fundamentalists are shown to be hypocrites in the context of charity and morality. Thus while fundamentalists emphasize family values, *The Other* sees the fundamentalist Fat'hallah setting a trap for his sister in order to separate her from her husband and "sell" her to one of his friends. While they supposedly collect money from people for charity, we see them using this money to pay for their personal lawsuits in *Birds of Darkness*. The film shows the fundamentalists using zakat (Muslim charity) money in order to bail one fundamentalist man convicted of corruption. While the fundamentalists preach morals and values, they steal money in *The Terrorist*. Ali, the fundamentalist terrorist, raids his host's office with the justification that the host is an "infidel," and takes a sum of money, which the host—a medical doctor—had been saving to build a hospital in a needy village.

Third, fundamentalists are hypocritical about sexuality. In *The Terrorist* and *The Closed Doors*, while the fundamentalists on a surface level practice Islamic ways, they use "infidel" women and hence are portrayed as contradicting Muslim sexual mores. In the first film, Ali prays and reads Islamic books but sexually harasses his host's daughter. In the second, the teenager Hamada is torn between his sexual desires and his fundamentalist preachers' warnings against women. One of the preachers, Sheikh Khaled, addresses a group of young men, including Hamada, in a mosque, saying "We live in a sinful society. Women walk around half naked. The female anatomy causes intense sexual desire in man's brain, causing him to harm himself and others," and later promises the boys a reward in heaven, where they will marry/own "4,000 virgins, 8,000 concubines and 100 slaves." But Hamada excuses his attempt at having sex with his neighbor Zainab and his visiting a prostitute as not being a sin as the women are "infidels." The fundamentalist man Rashad in *Terrorism and Barbecue* also stares at and tries to seduce a call girl. In *Rachida*, fundamentalists preach morals but rape an innocent village girl and attempt to do the same to the teacher Rachida.

Fourth, fundamentalism is hypocritical in its participation in national politics (parliamentary elections). Islamic fundamentalists in *Birds of Darkness* are not living on the edge of society when it comes to politics. Since they cannot run for parliamentary elections themselves, they back certain "secular" candidates and exchange favors. The fundamentalist lawyer Ali supports the politician Rushdie Khayyal in his campaign and the latter wins only after this fundamentalist support. The film shows how Rushdie is not a religious man: he indulges in parties and women, and marries his mistress in order to "appear" moral in front of his fundamentalist supporters. We later find out that Ali turned to fundamentalism after being a Communist because he realized the former would make him more money. This is similar

to a line said by Sadat in *Days of Sadat*, where—just before his assassination—Sadat declares that "fundamentalists are cooperating with the
Communists against me."

Moreover, fundamentalists in this political context are at the same
time confused and manipulative. Said in *Bab el-Oued City* works for corrupt
government officials who at the end of the film shoot him on the beach.
Several scenes in *Birds of Darkness* play on these themes. The film is critical
of the government. When the lawyer Fat'hi is talking to his fundamentalist
colleague Ali, he tells him "The government is smart. It has left you mosques.
Lets you publish books. Hold interviews. All this to prove it is democratic."
However, the film starts with a disclaimer saying that the film is entirely
fiction. This self-censorship is linked with Egypt's reliance on a 30-year-
long emergency law that allows the president to censor any form of
expression prior to publication in the interest of "national security," and
also for arousing religious sensitivities (*Silence in the Nile* 1998).

The major fundamentalist figure in *Birds of Darkness* is the lawyer Ali.
The film mentions how Ali once tried to sue the Minister of Culture for
allowing "immoral" film posters to be posted in the streets. Fat'hi, the liberal
lawyer, explains how Ali's stunt is merely to advertise the Muslim Brothers.
Ali's character is smart, manipulative, and calculating, in contrast to the
fundamentalist majority in the film who are portrayed as being stupid and
having no will of their own. Fat'hi walks into a fundamentalist gathering,
walking in between two rows of bearded men dressed in white skullcaps
and white *gallabiyyas*. He repeats, "May God separate you," to which they
respond "Amen" parrot fashion. The film thus demarcates two kinds of
fundamentalists who are nevertheless equally condemned: "true" fundamentalists who are mere blind followers who cannot tell right from wrong,
and "fake" fundamentalists who are in charge but who are there merely for
economic and political power.

The ones in charge are thus portrayed as putting on an act and not
genuinely believing or practicing what they overtly do. When Fat'hi first
talks to Ali in the film, Ali speaks to him in classical Arabic. Fat'hi tells him
to save that for lawsuits, after which Ali speaks in colloquial Arabic. When
Fat'hi's client Samira, a prostitute found innocent after Ali defends her case
(a favor done for Fat'hi, who chose Ali for the defense because the judge
was pro-fundamentalist), tries to kiss Ali on the cheek and offers him food

to thank him, he quickly responds by "I take refuge in God" and refusing to eat "*haram*" food. Fat'hi sarcastically reminds him she is innocent in the eyes of the law. Ali has put his "beliefs" on hold in his defense of Samira. Thus, the world of fundamentalism is one of deceit and contradiction. The Egyptian films tend to make claims about the fundamentalists which, though they might be based on Egypt's experience of fundamentalists, tend to essentialize the identity of fundamentalists as an extreme Other. At the same time, the films essentialize the identity of Egypt as a homogeneous anti-fundamentalist monolith. This raises the question of whose experience of fundamentalism is being depicted. The exclusionary stance that the films adopt suggests that the Egypt we see is the one constructed by the Egyptian government. Thus, despite the existence of government criticism, the film, like *Terrorism and Barbecue*, in the end presents the government's "national story."

Psychologizing fundamentalism: internal and external oppression

Fundamentalism is portrayed as one way of dealing with personal psychological crisis. *The Other* reveals how Fat'hi—who is now the fundamentalist Sheikh Fat'hallah—had slept with his sister while they were teenagers, and how fundamentalism was the only way in which he could cope with his guilt (she on the other hand seems undisturbed). *The Closed Doors* also presents fundamentalism as the route Hamada is led to after sensing the developing of a relationship between his widowed mother and his school teacher, which subsequently results in his killing of them both. The films thus psychologize fundamentalism as a kind of post-traumatic stress disorder. At the same time, the films tend to portray fundamentalism as an unreasonable way of dealing with crisis. The Egyptian films differ from Hollywood's again here, as Hollywood represents fundamentalism as emanating from the nature of the Oriental primitive Other. The Egyptian films, on the other hand, tend to represent fundamentalism as a state of "becoming" as opposed to one into which one is born.

Fundamentalists are sometimes also individuals with moral dilemmas. They are shown to struggle with their own desires. They are portrayed as fantasizing about women. In *The Other*, the fundamentalist Fat'hallah fantasizes about "loose" Parisian women whom he cannot get to except in his imagination; at the same time, he tries to separate his sister from her Christian husband. In *The Terrorist*, Ali fantasizes about his host's daughter. In *The Closed Doors*, Hamada peers at female students from a hole in the wall separating his all-male classroom from theirs, and stares at the thighs of a woman wearing a short skirt, later asking God for forgiveness for this. They also struggle with their desire for personal freedom. In *Destiny*, fundamentalists kill a singer and try to ban dancing, but they are also seen trying to repress the desire to participate in a party by performing Sufi rituals. In *The Terrorist*, Ali eventually sets his desires free, smoking cigarettes, drinking alcohol, and flirting with women. The fundamentalists thus are represented as being highly contradictory, while "we" are portrayed as having no such psychological conflicts. In addition to the contrast with Hollywood's fixation of the fundamentalist identity as collective, Egyptian cinema differs from Hollywood in how it gives room for reform. Ali regrets his terrorist deeds at the end of *The Terrorist*. Yet his leader shoots him dead at the discovery. The message remains that hard-core fundamentalists are

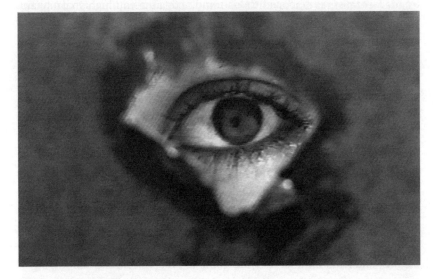

Figure 21 Hamada peering at female students through a hole in the classroom wall—*The Closed Doors*

unforgiving and "evil," and that, once one becomes one of them, there is no way out.

Terrorism in the films is linked with how the fundamentalists themselves are repressed and thus find refuge in killing. In contrast with the lawyer Ali in *Birds of Darkness*, who has clear political interests, the terrorists in *The Other* and *The Terrorist* have no clear political cause and act on mere personal interest. In *The Other* the fundamentalists are anarchists who do not hesitate to shoot at the Egyptian army or to plant bombs in Cairo killing innocent people. *The Terrorist* goes deeper into portraying all aspects of the Islamic fundamentalist terrorist's life. After Ali burns a video shop, the film traces his footsteps into his dark, barren apartment where he sits on a chest full of grenades reading a book about "the torture and bliss of the grave." Ali tries his best to cut himself off from worldly pleasures but finds himself fantasizing about his sexy neighbor whom he peeps at from his window while she sings and laughs. Later, Ali's leader, Ahmad, who uses Ali's fantasies and promises him a wife if he completes the task successfully, lures Ali into conducting a terrorist act. Ahmad does not deliver his promise but guarantees Ali a wife if he assassinates an anti-fundamentalist liberal government official. Ali's character is thus portrayed as being driven by his fantasies, as opposed to his mind, and as being highly compliant to his leader. This is the major difference between the Egyptian films' and Hollywood's portrayal of Islamic fundamentalist terrorists—being portrayed almost exclusively as killing and terrorizing people in the latter. Thus Egyptian cinema portrays everyday life aspects in its representation of the terrorists, though it is just as condemning as Hollywood.

Islamic fundamentalism is also portrayed as a threat to basic freedoms, such as freedom of expression and religion. The opening sequences of three films illustrate the first case. The opening sequence of *The Terrorist* sees fundamentalists destroying and burning the contents of a video shop. *Hysteria* briefly introduces us to a group of Islamic fundamentalists led by a man with disheveled hair and wearing a *gallabiyya* that is too short. The man runs down the stairs of a subway station in Cairo, calling the singer Zein and his musician friends who are performing on one of the platforms infidels, and shouting that they are going to hell ("music is a sin, singing is a sin"). When Zein and the musicians continue their singing on the platform some days later, they are faced with another group of fundamentalists who suddenly appear, the camera introducing them by showing an extreme close-up of one of the men's hands clutching a chain. Four men carrying sticks and chains stare at Zein and his friends, and then attack them, with a silent, slow-motion sequence depicting the musicians running away from their attackers. *Destiny* also begins with the image of a man being tortured and then burned at the stake and hailed a heretic for translating the work of Averroes. The film then moves to directly accusing Islamic fundamentalists for the act, and later portrays them burning Averroes's books. *The Terrorist*'s burning of the video shop and *Destiny*'s burning of Averroes's books remind us of Egyptian fundamentalists succeeding in continuing the ban on some of Naguib Mahfouz's books (namely *Awlad Haritna* [Children of our Neighborhood]) (Moussalli 1998). The book had been banned under Nasser's regime in 1959 for its allegorical suggestion that God is dead (Allen 1994), while other works continue to be banned for themes considered offensive to the religious authorities.

Islamic fundamentalists also attacked Naguib Mahfouz and stabbed him in the neck in 1994 after Sheikh Omar Abdul Rahman, leader of the Islamic Group (al-Gama'a al-Islamiyya), issued a fatwa excommunicating him (*Silence in the Nile* 1998). *Destiny* allegorically portrays the fundamentalists killing the singer Marwan and succeeding in converting the caliph's son Abdullah into fundamentalism and away from the scenes of songs and dance. Chahine has used Averroes as a portrayal of himself, as Chahine was attacked by fundamentalists after they accused his earlier film *The Emigrant* of being blasphemous. Chahine's message against the oppression to freedom of expression exerted by fundamentalists is made even more evident in a sentence that appears on the screen just after the film ends: "Ideas have wings, no one can stop their flight" (Privett 1999, p. 7).

Regarding products and people who are not strict Muslims as infidel and corrupt is a common stance taken by fundamentalists in the films (*Terrorism and Barbecue, Birds of Darkness, The Other, The Closed Doors, Bab el-Oued City*). Smith (1991) points out that nations are usually not invented (i.e. they do not just "happen" ahistorically), but are a matter of reconstructing existing and arriving ethnic and religious groups. These factors complicate the existence of a modern Egyptian nation, pointing out the need to integrate minorities into the core. However, the films seem to prefer a selective integration, celebrating the nationalism of the Copts while portraying Islamic fundamentalists as intolerant of people from other religions. Egypt's regime, though nationalist, is not entirely secular, as it relies on Islam as one source of jurisdiction, despite its large non-Muslim minority (Al-Ahsan 1992). This use of Islam is an "attempt to use traditional regulations as markers of communal identity, and not as part of a broader program for instruments for the totalistic reconstruction of society" (Eisenstadt 1999, p. 151). Eisenstadt sees this as one of the reasons behind the clashes between Islamic fundamentalists and the government. This is expressed in *The Terrorist*, where Ali's dream is to establish a purely funda-mentalist state, excluding any Christians or non-fundamentalist Muslim "infidels." The fundamentalists' view of "infidels" is essentialized around their being inherently evil. *The Terrorist* puts this point across in a conver-sation between Ali and the Christian Hani. Unknowing of Hani's religion, Ali expresses his utopian views to Hani. When Ali later finds out that Hani is a Christian, he is shown to be shocked as he had always perceived Hani as a "good" person. The film also emphasizes the difference between Islam and fundamentalism through the portrayal of the tolerant Muslim family that hosts Ali. This is similar to *Rachida*, where, in a conversation with Yamina in the latter's village house, Rachida wonders about the cruelty of fundamentalists and how they raped women and slaughtered babies. Yamina's answer is "God is innocent of all the crimes committed in his name." The imam in *Bab el-Oued City* is also used as an indicator of Muslim tolerance. In a conversation with Said, the imam declares "Our city needs peace and serenity. Think of what happened in October, the dead, the wounded. This must give us a cause for reflection. Violence begets violence. Islam is a religion of tolerance, against violence." The films thus try to deconstruct the fundamentalist ideal world, and even collapse it.

Essentializing fundamentalism: fundamentalism and nationalism

Egyptian and Algerian cinemas depict Islamic fundamentalists as an Other. In a classical Orientalist way, this Other is assigned everything the national identity is not meant to be. The films also focus on how the fundamentalists themselves construct "boundaries between the 'pure' inside and the 'polluted' outside, as well as their self-perception as the 'elect'"; this is described by Eisenstadt as "utopian sectarianism" (1999, p. 90). In this light, the fundamentalist identity can be seen as intolerant towards those who are different, and thus fundamentalists are a threat to national unity. Eisenstadt points out how this drawing of boundaries necessitates the assignment of an "ontological enemy," such as "the USA, Israel, and Zionism" (1999, p. 90). While this is the list of "enemies" the fundamentalists are shown declaring their opposition to (if any) in Hollywood, the Egyptian and Algerian films add to that list all non-fundamentalists. This mainly includes Christians and non-fundamentalist "loose" women (as discussed earlier in the cases of The Other and The Terrorist). In Bab el-Oued City, fundamentalists object to the presence of the ex-revolutionary woman Ouardiya in the neighborhood. Ouardiya, who lives on her own and who drinks alcohol, is threatened by fundamentalist leader Said who enters her apartment and terrorizes her with a gun, giving her a week to leave the city. In this light, the fundamentalist identity is portrayed as being intolerant towards those who are different, and thus fundamentalists are a threat to national unity.

Days of Sadat is another example of this, affirming Sadat's religious-ness by depicting him as a young man reciting Qur'anic verses in his village kuttab, and later, as the president, granting Islamic fundamentalists freedom, and cooperating with them against the Communists after demonstrations against the raising of flour and sugar prices take place in Egypt. The film emphasizes Sadat's identity as the "believer president," but represents the fundamentalists in dismay after Sadat's visit to Israel in 1977—an event presented by the film as inevitable if peace in the Middle East was to be achieved. The fundamentalists are shown to disapprove of Sadat's hosting of the shah of Iran after his expulsion, which is depicted as the final straw leading to their assassination of the president.

West (1995) argues that the propagation of essentialist notions of "homogeneous national communities" and "positive images" (p. 161) is a means by which the authoritarian elites repress their heterogeneous populations. Thus, nationalism as advocated in the films is a form of hegemony. Balibar (1995) sees this hegemony as creating a conflict for the "nonnational," forcing them to make a choice between their competing belongings, thereby implying that those belongings cannot co-exist. Balibar (1991) argues that nationalism is an ideology built on the symbolic difference between ourselves and foreigners—an ideology based on the concept of frontiers. According to Balibar,

> the "external frontiers" of the state have to become "internal frontiers" or . . . external frontiers have to be imagined constantly as a projection and protection of an internal collective personality, which each of us carries within ourselves and enables us to inhabit the space of the state as a place where we have always been—and always will be— "at home".
>
> (1991, p. 95)

Balibar uses the term "fictive ethnicity" to refer to the idea that nations produce ethnicity, in the sense that

> no nation possesses an ethnic base naturally, but as social formations are nationalized, the populations included within them, divided up among them or dominated by them are ethnicized—that is, represented in the past or in the future *as if* they formed a natural community, possessing of itself an identity or origins, culture and interests which transcends individuals and social conditions.
>
> (1991, p. 96)

The problem here is that Islamic fundamentalists are not an ethnic group or a religious minority, but are constructed in a similar manner. The concept of nation as such is therefore problematic, for it threatens to erase the pasts of those within it, forcing them to cling on to those pasts. The films, acting as vehicles to strengthen national identities (besides other such vehicles, such as race, language, and religion), add to that threat by naturalizing the nations they represent or, in other words, essentializing them.

The naturalized nation is represented in the films by non-fundamentalist ordinary people engaging in various daily activities, from going to work to fighting with their spouses, while at the same time enjoying the pleasures of life such as music and alcohol. This norm is then contrasted with the lives of fundamentalists. We do see the fundamentalists performing everyday activities, but even these activities tend to be "different." While the "normal" Egyptian man has dinner with his wife and children (*Terrorism and Barbecue*), the fundamentalist man eats dinner with his four wives whom he communicates with the way he would with animals, not speaking to them but shouting and gesturing at them (*The Terrorist*). While the "normal" Arab woman goes to work freely, her fundamentalist sister is confined to working as a secretary or a messenger (*The Terrorist, Birds of Darkness, Rachida*). In other words, while the modern Arab woman is portrayed as being active in her choices, the fundamentalist woman is confined to executing orders made by her male superiors. The use of women here falls into the general view of women as symbols of the nation and the gauge that measures the nation's morality and modernity. By portraying Egyptian and Algerian women as modern and independent (and not silent, the way Islamic fundamentalist women are portrayed), yet respectful of values, the message sent by the films is that the Egyptian and Algerian identities are like this. Islamic fundamentalists are used as tools to emphasize this moderate, non-corrupt identity.

This parallels Shapiro's view of films as "identity stories" which form "the basis for a nation's coherence" (1989, p. 47). Shapiro argues that identity stories by nature must create a boundary between "us" and "them" and "impose a model of identity/difference" (1989, p. 48). In other words, this post-structuralist formulation, with its insistence on margins against centers, constructs difference as a prior condition of identity (Bennington 1990). A complication of the above model occurs when the Other shares some of the characteristics of "us." In the case of Egyptian and Algerian fundamentalists, the fact that they are Egyptian or Algerian and Muslim, living in the same society as "us," perplexes their projected difference. Nationalism implies the existence of a social unit that governs itself; however, it is difficult to define this social unit, who is included in it and who is not (Birch 1989). This is why national integration is a complex concept, namely when nations contain ethnic or other minorities. In this case, there is a danger that national integration becomes a form of totalitarianism. This takes us to the point that, what with the potential conflicts in the name of national integration, nationalism is in the end an ideal (Kedourie 1961). Kedourie cites the Middle East as an example of governments oppressing their minorities post-imperialism even more than they were oppressed under the Ottoman Empire or under the British mandate. As he puts it, "nationalism and liberalism, far from being twins, are really antagonistic principles" (Kedourie 1961, p. 109).

Thus, the films continue to try to demarcate the two sides, the "national" and the "fundamentalist." This is done in a variety of ways. Fundamentalists are portrayed as living on the edge of society as opposed to participating in it fully. The films make use of space to emphasize this point. While fundamentalists in Hollywood always operate outdoors (deserts [*The Siege*], planes [*Executive Decision*], destroyed cityscapes [*Navy Seals*]), in Egyptian cinema they are mostly confined to interior spaces, staying in a dark room while a joyful neighbor laughs and sings outside (*The Terrorist*), and talking about the outside world with ambivalence while spending all their time indoors (*The Other*), while in Algerian cinema they pose a danger to the national space (*Rachida, Bab el-Oued City*).

The way the fundamentalists communicate is also portrayed as being alien. Not only do fundamentalists speak in classical as opposed to colloquial Arabic, but they also have their own system of greetings (involving mutual shoulder kissing) and their own greeting phrases (elaborate "Islamic" greetings). They also have a distinctive way of dress (long, white *gallabiyyas* and white skullcaps) and a distinctive appearance (with all the men growing beards) (*Terrorism and Barbecue, The Terrorist, Destiny, The Other, Bab el-Oued City*). The only way in which this appearance is altered to look like "ours" is when the fundamentalists want to blend into society in order either to execute a terrorist attack or to achieve a political aim. The fundamentalist lawyer Ali in *Birds of Darkness* is bearded but wears a suit, which serves to add to his credibility in his political campaign. The terrorist Ali in *The Terrorist* goes further in shedding his beard and white *gallabiyya* (much to his dismay) in order to disappear in society so that he can assassinate an anti-fundamentalist government official.

The films' attempt at showing that the fundamentalists are utterly different recalls Shapiro's argument that "the claim to distinctiveness has required an energetic denial of otherness within" (1989, p. 54). This denial is part of the effort to preserve a national identity that simply does not recognize the fundamentalist's right to be represented. Still, the representation of Islamic fundamentalists in Egyptian and Algerian cinemas— from a nationalist point of view—remains heavily reliant on "metaphors" which attempt at "fixing" the Egyptian and Algerian cultures as essentially anti-fundamentalist, thereby denying the dynamic nature of culture itself

(Shapiro 1999; Tehranian 2000). Shapiro argues that this "alleged cultural unity" is one way in which the modern state seeks legitimacy (1999, p. 112).

Conclusion

Egyptian cinema, as well as Algerian cinema, and Hollywood differ in their treatment of fundamentalists in several ways. First, the Arab cinemas' portrayal is more complex than that of Hollywood, as the Arab films portray various aspects of "being fundamentalist" as opposed to Hollywood's concentration on terrorism. Against this analysis, arguments like Armbrust's (2002), that Islamic fundamentalism in Egyptian cinema "stands for nothing but violence" (p. 928), seem untenable. Second, while Hollywood portrays these terrorists as ruthless, faceless killers, Egyptian cinema psychologizes fundamentalism. Third, Egyptian and Algerian cinemas praise religion but condemn extremism, while Hollywood blurs the two in the case of Islam. Fourth, while Hollywood essentializes fundamentalists as intrinsically "bad," Egyptian cinema's image of them is more complex and presents them as being misguided or traumatized. Fifth, Egyptian and Algerian cinemas do not blur Arabs (and some non-Arabs, like Iranians) into one primordial entity the way Hollywood does. Sixth, events relating to Islamic fundamentalism in Egyptian and Algerian cinemas often happen within the nations (versus outside the United States in Hollywood), which directs the focus to (inter)personal melodrama and away from naturalized images of deserts as the essential wild East. Thus, Hollywood still relies on an East/West divide, whereas Egyptian and Algerian cinemas portray differences within the "East." Finally, Egyptian cinema differs in how it includes the view of Islamic fundamentalism as a *reaction* to "Western . . . influences in Muslim lands" (Hyman 1985, p. 3). This is seen in *The Other*, where globalization is perceived by the fundamentalists as synonymous with Westernization (Tehranian 2000).

But the cinemas also converge in many ways. A distinct feature of the convergence between the portrayal of fundamentalists in Egyptian and American cinemas is that the two cinemas share the same "set of visual signifiers" (Karim 2000, p. 68) of Islamic fundamentalism: beards, white skullcaps and *gallabiyyas*, chador-wearing women. Thus, both sides use the same "sensationalist stereotypes" that are "meant to . . . reinforce a myopic vision of reality" (Esposito 1999, p. 220) about Islamic fundamentalists. The way Islamic fundamentalists are depicted to dress, in particular, serves to portray them "as 'medieval' in life-style and mentality" (Esposito 1999, p. 220), in contrast to the civilized "us." This constructs fundamentalism as being essentially anti-modern (O'Hagan 2000; Armbrust 2002), in contrast with both sides' portrayal of their respective nations as progressive and modern. This is interesting when you consider that fundamentalists, in addition to their reliance on traditional symbols, utilize modern weapons (computers, guns, etc.) in their fight against modernism (Agha 2000). However, in Algerian cinema, though fundamentalists are often charac- terized by their beards (and, in the case of Said in *Bab el-Oued City*, by his black eyeliner), they pose a bigger threat through blending in in society: in *Rachida*, the school pupil Sofiane, unbearded and dressed in Western clothing, turns out to be a terrorist. Egypt, Algeria, and the United States in the films are portrayed as being "defensive, responding with counterattacks" towards the Islamic fundamentalist "instigators" (Esposito 1999, p. 221). This serves to increase the legitimacy of the three states, despite their respective government criticism (*The Siege, Terrorism and Barbecue*, and *Bab el-Oued City*). Being instigators configures the cinematic images of fundamentalists as pathological in all three cases.

The cinemas seem to rely on clichés in their representations of "us" and "them." In this sense the cinemas can be said to be colonial towards Islamic fundamentalists, constructing the colonized (the fundamentalist) as a degenerate Other in order to justify their conquest of this figure. In their construction of the fundamentalist as an Other, the cinemas seem to project the fundamentalist image as "a fixed reality which is at once an 'other' and yet entirely knowable and visible" (Bhabha 1983, p. 21). The cinemas use similar techniques in their treatment of this Other. One is their reliance on the "cultural priority" factor in the "myth of historical origination" (Bhabha 1983, p. 26). They seem to present the fundamentalists as alien and inferior to their cultures. They also rely on the ideas of lack and difference in their portrayal of fundamentalists, the latter lacking "our" morals and being essentially different from "us." At the same time, the cinemas' represen- tations of fundamentalists are complex and paradoxical: the fundamentalist is "mystical, primitive, simple-minded and yet the most worldly and accomplished liar, and manipulator" (Bhabha 1983, p. 34).

The representation of Islamic fundamentalism in the cinemas suggests the difficulty of establishing any concept of a global identity. Although the cinemas and the three nations converge in their Othering of Islamic fundamentalists, in doing so they nevertheless resort to different, sometimes clashing, national experiences. This applies not only to the construction of Others, but also to the juxtaposition of Others with the national Self. While each side strives to strengthen its national identity, each refers to separate and exclusive memories and collective pasts. We can thus see that, despite the existence of a "global" enemy, the nation is not dead. In fact, the existence of this enemy has strengthened the plurality of national identity in a global world (Smith 1991). At the same time, seeing fundamentalism as an enemy suggests the limits in pluralism within the nation (Mouffe 1995). Moreover, we can see that the confrontation between Islamic fundamentalism and nationalism stresses how the former is a global force while the latter, though a global phenomenon, is a localization. Of course, even a global product like fundamentalism is localized when given interpretations that are different from those employed by the producers, and hence the need to look at fundamentalism in a historical context. In this sense, Islamic fundamentalism as seen in the films is contradictory: It is about both emergent and disappearing peripheries, hegemonization and fragmentation, expansion and contraction (Friedman 1994).

Having spoken about Islamic fundamentalists as defiled subalterns does not imply the necessity of reversing their status into a sanctified one. There is an equal danger in doing so; Chow argues that such a practice belongs to the same symbolic order as representing subalterns as defiled, in that it implies our own "self-deception as the non-duped" (1994, p. 146), a desire on our part to seize control. Only when the subaltern speaks can this situation change. But, as Spivak says, "If the subaltern can speak then, thank God, the subaltern is not a subaltern any more" (1990, p. 158).

Egyptian cinema, Algerian cinema, and Hollywood all use their Others to strengthen their respective national identities. In her analysis of the extremism of Pauline Hansen—the independent Australian federal MP for the seat of Oxley who is infamous for propagating a white, homogeneous

Australian identity—Ang warns that the danger lies in how any such argument is too essentializing. For Ang,

> the national . . . is not to be defined in terms of "identity" at all, but as a problematic process; the national is to be defined not in terms of the formulation of a positive, "common culture" or "cohesive community" but as the unending, day-to-day hard work of managing and negotiating differences.
>
> (2000, p. 9)

This is the climatic link between the Hollywood and the Arab films. In their strong national parade, both sides tend to construct communities devoid of Others. And this is where the two sides end up telling different versions of the same subjective Truth, and where the "East" and the "West" seem not to be divided that much after all. Thus, Said's discourse on Orientalism is complicated as the East tries to exclude a part of itself as an Other while the West excludes the East.

Epilogue: On Difference, Resistance, and Nationalism

Cinema is a powerful tool of cultural production. Whether in the United States or the Arab world, cinema functions within nationalist projects that narrate the American and the Arab nations, while also using their portrayal of Others in order to construct and strengthen their own identities. Looking at the different aspects of the representation of Middle Eastern politics in American and Arab films, three main threads can be drawn: the films' construction of the identities of the Self (as national identity) and the Other; the complication of notions of resistance; and the films' relationship with nationalism.

On difference

National identities in the films are defined in terms of difference. This difference relates both to external Others and to Others within. Hollywood's imagining of the American nation is one where the United States is contrasted with Arab terrorists who are associated with Islamic funda-mentalism and who pose an external threat to America. Hollywood's

202 FILMING THE MODERN MIDDLE EAST

construction of fundamentalism can be seen, in the words of Abaza and
Stauth, as a "new 'orientalism' . . . [which] attempts to reconstruct new
images of the East" as "native" (1990, p. 223). They argue that, following
the "old" Orientalism which used the harem to symbolize the Orient, this
"new" Orientalism has established the veil and the mosque as *religious*
symbols of the culture of the "native" Other. Abaza and Stauth (1990) add
that those notions of nativism are associated with irrationality, thereby
maintaining the divide between the civilized West and the barbaric East.
Abaza and Stauth's use of the terms "new" and "old" is an attempt to overcome Said's problematic construction of Orientalism as a fixed discourse
over time. Although Said's book *Orientalism* deals with a particular period in
history beginning in the eighteenth century, Said's discussion of Orientalism
also locates it within practices of the present; in his new introduction to the
book, published in August 2003, Said (2003) argues that he wrote the book
25 years ago and yet it is still relevant today. The film analysis has shown
that imaginings of the Arab Other do change with the political context, and
therefore complicates Said's discourse by reflecting on Orientalism as
process. The analysis has also drawn on parallels between the construction
of the Arab Others in Hollywood and that of the Americans and others in
Egyptian cinema in particular, and thus complicates the exclusionary
discourse employed by Hollywood by showing how the Other and the
dominant forces may embrace similar values, meanings, and practices.

Egypt in the Egyptian films is imagined in contrast to the portrayal of
the degeneracy of Israel and the United States. This again establishes the
Egyptian identity as different from external Others. However, the case of
Egypt is more complicated. The Othering of Israel and the United States in
the Egyptian films seems ironic considering Egypt's peace treaty with the
first and its reliance on the aid of the second. Therefore it can be argued that
Egypt's Othering of the two countries plays a role in bringing Egypt closer
to the rest of the Arab world that is feeling a degree of dismay towards the
role of the United States in Middle Eastern politics (namely in the context
of the cases of Palestine and Iraq), and also dismay about the strength of
Israel in the region vis-à-vis Palestinian resistance. At the same time, this
solidarity with the Arab world is an attempt at reviving a lost pan-Arabism
that glosses over what are seen as shameful divisions within the Arab world.
As Karr (1997) argues, "As nationalism was a way to divert the attention

from inner conflicts in the colonizing nations, so does nationalism in the struggling colonized countries divert attention from its inner problems and directs it towards fighting the outside imperialist enemy."

However, this is complicated by the Egyptian and Algerian cinemas' representation of Islamic fundamentalism as an enemy within. The cinemas converge in their construction of their nations in opposition to Islamic fundamentalism. This common Other complicates essentialist notions of East versus West. However, the representation of Islamic fundamentalism in the cinemas is not always convergent. The Arab cinemas' more nuanced portrayal of Islamic fundamentalism provides a challenge to Hollywood's essentialist equation of Arabs with fundamentalist terrorists. The Arab cinemas' Othering of fundamentalists is part of a nationalist agenda aiming at establishing a religious but not extremist myth of the nation. In this sense, Arab cinemas can be seen as offering resistant discourses to those of Hollywood through participating in the construction of alternative identities and perspectives.

On resistance

The analysis of films from the United States and the Arab world has emanated from the need to undo cultural barriers. The attention to Arab cinemas has been a step towards "unthinking Eurocentrism" (Shohat and Stam 1994), and shifting the focus of cinematic analysis from Hollywood and other Western cinemas. Even within the label "world cinema," a problematic title, Arab cinemas have not traditionally been given much attention. The analysis has thus attempted to give those cinemas a voice.

The analysis has also highlighted aesthetic differences between the American and the Arab films, especially in their representation of space. The use of camera shots and locations in Egyptian and Palestinian cinemas is different from that of Hollywood. This is due to economic factors, as the Egyptian and Palestinian films are not as well funded as the Hollywood ones, and also to generic factors, as the Egyptian films tend to be melodramas, focusing on interior spaces, the Palestinian films are dramas shot on location, while the American ones are mainly action films, focusing on exterior spaces. But the differences can also be related to the three sides' position

204 FILMING THE MODERN MIDDLE EAST

on the politics represented, with Hollywood's spatial use mirroring American mastery, and Egypt's and Palestine's in contrast assuming an insider view.

The analysis has stressed the importance of examining complex social and political issues not addressed in the mainstream. The analysis of the Arab films has shown how they address issues of local relevance and interest that are overlooked in a dominant cinema industry like Hollywood. Issues like everyday life aspects of the Israeli invasion of Lebanon, the Palestinian diaspora in refugee camps, and the way of life of Islamic fundamentalists are all represented in Arab cinemas while being absent in Hollywood. Those representations are a statement supporting the richness of socio-political experiences in the Middle East that play an important role in the construc-tions of the Self. This therefore goes beyond Hollywood's reductionism in its imagination of the Middle East; Arab cinemas have challenged dominant Hollywood discourses by providing a space for under-represented peoples to "speak." The depiction of the experiences of Palestinians under occupa-tion, for example, can be seen as an attempt to challenge their oppression and their under-representation in Hollywood. However, with processes of globalization, a number of those issues are no longer confined to a local realm. The Arab–Israeli conflict, the Gulf War, and Islamic fundamentalism are issues that go beyond the physical and political boundaries of the Middle East. Thus, the analysis presents a challenge to core–periphery models where certain political issues are relegated to the space of the Other.

Moreover, in presenting those issues, the analysis has shown how Arab cinemas can be a means of resistance. This parallels what Fanon (1994) calls the literature of combat. On one hand, the films can be seen as presenting an "oppositional form of 'reading practice'" that confronts dominant ideologies (Bahri 1996). In other words, the films form an alternative way of knowledge production that challenges the dominant narratives of Hollywood. In this sense, the films are resistant because they take a position against imperialism and Eurocentrism. However the Egyptian films' reversing of Otherness means that the films are engaging in polarization themselves. As Parry argues, "a simple inversion perpetuates the coloniser/colonised opposition within the terms defined by colonial discourse, remaining complicit with its assumptions by retaining undifferen-tiated identity categories, and failing to contest the conventions of that system of knowledge it supposedly challenges" (1994, p. 172).

On the other hand, resistance is not conceptualized only in the sense of mere reversal of dominant agendas or as being simply oppositional to them. The Arab films' resistance is threefold, presented as opposition, but also as subversion and as mimicry (Bhabha 1994), both in style and in content. Chahine for example, in *Destiny*, has taken a Hollywood genre, the epic, and made it his own, using it to depict a contemporary issue (the clash with the intolerance of Islamic fundamentalism). Subversion is also seen in how the Arab films illustrate the hybridity of Arab identities. The complexity of the Arab national identities has challenged essentialist notions of Self and Other.

The analysis has also challenged West-focused models of discourse generation. It challenges theories of cultural imperialism and neo-imperialism which focus on the West's active role in representation while denying the East that role by highlighting how the "East," through Arab cinemas, also engages in representation. At the same time, the analysis complicates theories on Orientalism. This presents a challenge to an East/West dichotomy not only by showing how the "East" represents the "West," but also how the "Orient" represents itself. Furthermore, by showing how the films reflect history from different perspectives, and also by showing how they play a role in reshaping national histories and traditions, the analysis poses a challenge to a uniform, unilateral writing of history that is projected from the West to the rest.

The analysis can be located within post-colonial theory, yet complicates notions of post-colonialism. The research is post-colonial in two main ways. First, Prakesh (1990) argues that post-colonialism sees "third world identities as relational rather than essential" (p. 399). The research has followed this by looking at the nation as position, rather than origin, which presents a challenge to Zionist constructions of Israel, for example, seen in the Hollywood films which construct Israel's relationship with Jews as a place embracing a people of common ancestry. Second, the analysis challenges the fixity of positions of heterogeneous circumstances and societies implied by terms like East/West or First/Third World. This research can thus be looked at as occupying a space "neither inside nor outside the history of Western domination, but in a tangential relation to it. This is what Homi Bhabha calls an 'in-between, hybrid position of practice and negotiation'" (Prakesh 1997, p. 491). The analysis therefore has not placed Arab cinemas in opposition to Hollywood, but rather has compared the different sides in order to complicate binaries of East and West, good and bad. Comparing Arab cinemas with Hollywood thus does not imply romanticizing the East vis-à-vis the West. The analysis has shown that notions of the Orient representing itself also mean that the Orient carries discourses of Otherness as demonstrated by the cases of Islamic fundamentalism, Israel, the United States, and gender divisions in the different Arab cinemas.

However, the research complicates notions of post-colonialism. Post-colonialism has been presented as a challenge to master narratives like nationalism. This is challenged by the zeal for nationalism seen in both Hollywood and the Egyptian and Palestinian films in particular. Nationalism has also been looked at as a Eurocentric model in post-colonial theory (Prakesh 1990). The advocacy of nationalism in Arab cinemas thus shows that the Arab world has not fully rejected Eurocentric models, but rather has adopted them and transformed them to fit in its political agendas.

Post-colonialism has also been alleged to exclude discourses on ethnic groups in conflict, instead focusing on relations between the East and the West (Dirlik 1997). While Islamic fundamentalism is not an ethnic entity, the conflict between the official government discourse and fundamentalist discourse in Egypt, as well as the representation of inter-Arab conflicts, draws attention to the importance of analyzing power struggles within the East. This relates to Dirlik's point that post-colonialism excludes radicals who believe they are still colonized. This point is an account of the position of Islamic fundamentalists in Egypt and Algeria who believe they are dominated by the West. Yet the films complicate this further by making connections between the imperialism of the West and the extremism of Islamic fundamentalism.

Finally, Dirlik points out how notions of hybridity within post-colonial discourse are always constructed as being between the First and Third Worlds, but never within the Third World. The Arab films illustrate both points. They do not construct "an Arab" identity that is stable and separate from that of the West. National identities in the Arab world are formed as hybrids of a multiplicity of affiliations. We cannot speak of "Arab culture" as carrying a separatist identity based on absolute disjuncture from the West. The films also focus on inter-Arab connections that illustrate the construction of a hybrid Arab identity. This refers to notions of pan-Arabism that are resurrected in the films. However, the films fail at adopting pan-Arabism wholesale, indicating how the past can be reclaimed but not reconstituted, and so it can only be revisited and realized in partial, fragmented ways.

Therefore, to argue that Arab identities are merely constructed as "different" risks the label of essentialism and the embrace of Orientalist discourse. The way the films embrace elements of Western culture (like popular music and attire) can be seen as marking them as hybrid, but also as an example of how the resistant carries traces of what it resists. In this way, the films rearticulate elements of the West, making the films themselves a kind of "liminal space" where dominant cultural ideals are unsettled (Young 1995). Yet the problem with hybridity as such is the risk of over-simplification. By that I mean that the films do not adopt Western culture wholesale or without discrimination. They seem to carefully select those components seen as salient to the establishment of a modern nation (such as education, democracy, technology) while at the same time adhering to more traditional values. It can therefore be said that the films articulate sameness (being democratic like the West) as well as difference (seeing the West as morally inferior).

On nationalism

The films' main focus is the strengthening of national identities. Scholars like Chatterjee (1992) have argued that national identity is fixed. Chatterjee adds that this perception of stability has led to violence that takes place "in the name of patriotic affirmation of identity in the Middle East" (1992, p. 215). However, this view on national identity is centered on the Third World, and therefore is misleading, as it implies that such violence cannot or does not happen in places like the United States. The films complicate this; *The Siege*'s depiction of the violent rejection of Arab-Americans is perhaps the best illustration of this point.

Chatterjee's argument is also implicated by the notions that the nation is inherently coercive, and that national identity is not only stable, but also fixed. This is challenged by the American films, which carry a strong nationalist stance that has moved on with the times. The American nation is, for example, now symbolized by caring yet still tough men (as in *Three Kings*), thereby replacing its symbolic representation by the action heroes of the Cold War era.

Chatterjee's argument is also challenged by the Arab films. First, the films complicate simple notions of the nation as coercive (Ahmad 1994) through their celebrated representation of issues like the Palestinian *intifada* and of Nasser's nationalization of the Suez Canal. Second, Arab cultural identities in the films are far from being fixed. As Stuart Hall (1994) argues, cultural identities are not essentialist and are forever transforming. The films' homage to the past is partially about finding a lost Arab identity, but also about negotiating the past to make sense of the present. For instance, the Egyptian national identity under Nasser seen in films like *Nasser 56* and *Nasser* is not the same one seen in films set at the present time. However, this "difference" does not imply that there are two national identities present; rather, looking at the films in a social/historical context reveals the way national identity transforms and develops. This transformation is also in response to changes in the political climate. For example, the rise of Islamic fundamentalism has meant that the Egyptian and Algerian national identities are also constructed in opposition to identities of internal Others.

In this way we can see that the representation of the Arab world as a collection of post-colonial nations is not just defined by its relation to colonizers. The reality of the Arab world in the films is thus not constituted by a "singular experience of colonialism and imperialism" (Ahmad 1995, p. 79). The films highlight not only the Arab world's relationship with an external enemy, but also the internal struggles in the Arab world itself. Ahmad (1995) argues against the assumption of a unitary colonial experience: In fact, looking at the films reveals that the experience of colonialism is different for different members of Arab society. The assumption of a unified Third World or Arab experience of colonialism risks homogenization under an Otherness label. However, the divide between the modern Egyptian or Palestinian identities and that of Islamic fundamentalist or patriarchal identity signals a battle over discourses of self-definition.

Following this argument on nationalism we can see that the American and Arab films present conflicting views on the nation. First, we have the representation of the nation as unifying, seen in Hollywood in films celebrating racial diversity (*Courage under Fire, Rules of Engagement, Three*

Kings), and in Arab cinemas in films about Nasser or films depicting harmony between different religious groups. Second, we encounter nationalism as separatist, demarcating the Self from the Other, seen in American films representing Arab terrorists like *The Delta Force* and *Hostage*, and in Egyptian films like the "anti-globalization" film *The Other*, which marks a distinct Egyptian identity that is oppositional to that of the United States. Third, nationalism as presented in the films can also be looked at as being totalitarian, advocating one coherent identity denied to Others (like Arab-Americans and Islamic fundamentalists). Finally, we have to pay attention to the employment of gender within national discourse. While the American nation presented in the films is based on masculine ideals, the Arab nations are feminine, yet are ultimately patriarchal.

Beyond the East/West divide

This study has juxtaposed Hollywood with Arab cinemas in their represen-tation of Middle Eastern politics in order to complicate an East/West dichotomy. Hollywood, or the West, has not been used as a reference point when analyzing the non-West; as Said (1988) warns, this trap means that "every opposition to the West only confirms its wicked power" (p. 70). But, at the same time, Fee (1995) also warns against implying absolute disjunction from Western discourse in works of resistance. She argues that it "is not possible simply to assume that a work written by an 'Other' (however defined), even a political Other, will have freed itself from the dominant ideology" (p. 244). She defines works of resistance as those which are "struggling, of necessity only partly successfully, to rewrite the dominant ideology from within, to produce a different version of reality" (pp. 244–245). Hence we can speak of the Arab films as works of resistance in the sense that they are on the margin but subvert the center. Thus they complicate any simple notion of the margin by "choosing" it as a space of resistance (hooks 1990), and hence break down the essentialist East/West divide.

Bibliography

Abaza, Mona and Stauth, Georg (1990). Occidental Reason, Orientalism, Islamic Fundamentalism: A Critique. In Martin Albrow and Elizabeth King (eds.), *Globalization, Knowledge and Society*, pp. 209–230. London: Sage.

Abdo, Nahla (1994). Nationalism and Feminism: Palestinian Women and the Intifada—No Going Back? In Valentine Moghadam (ed.), *Gender and National Identity*, pp. 148–173. London: Zed Books.

Afshar, Haleh (1996). Women and the Politics of Fundamentalism in Iran. In Haleh Afshar (ed.), *Women and Politics in the Third World*, pp. 121–141. London: Routledge.

Agha, Olfat Hassan (2000). Islamic Fundamentalism and its Image in the Western Media: Alternative Views. In Kai Hafez (ed.), *Islam and the West in the Mass Media*, pp. 219–234. Cresskill, NJ: Hampton Press.

Ahmad, Aijaz (1994). Orientalism and After. In Patrick Williams and Laura Chrisman (eds.), *Colonial Discourse and Post-Colonial Theory: A Reader*, pp. 162–171. London: Harvester Wheatsheaf.

Ahmad, Aijaz (1995). Jameson's Rhetoric of Otherness and the "National Allegory." In Bill Ashcroft, Gareth Griffiths and Helen Tiffin (eds.), *The Post-Colonial Studies Reader*, pp. 77–82. London: Routledge.

Al-Ahsan, Abdullah (1992). *Ummah or Nation? Identity Crisis in Contemporary Muslim Society*. Leicester: Islamic Foundation.

Allen, Roger (1994). Roger Allen Discusses Attack on Egypt's Nobel Laureate. *Compass* [Online]. Sept. 17. Available: http://www.upenn.edu/pennnews/current/features/1994/111794/mahfouz.html.

Alloula, Malek (1986). *The Colonial Harem*. Minneapolis: University of Minnesota Press.

Anderson, Benedict (1983). *Imagined Communities: Reflections on the Origin and Spread of Nationalism*. London: Verso.

Ang, Ien (2000). Identity Blues. In Paul Gilroy, Lawrence Grossberg and Angela McRobbie (eds.), *Without Guarantees: In Honour of Stuart Hall*, pp. 1–13. London: Verso.

Anthias, Floya and Yuval-Davis, Nira (1989). Introduction. In Nira Yuval-Davis and Floya Anthias (eds.), *Woman–Nation–State*, pp. 1–15. London: Macmillan.

Armbrust, Walter (2002). Islamists in Egyptian Cinema. *American Anthropologist*, 104 (3): 922–930.

Atef, Ahmed (1997). Le Destin by Youssef Chahine. *Ecrans d'Afrique*, 21–22 (3rd–4th quarter): 22–27.

Badran, Margot (1993). Independent Women: More than a Century of Feminism in Egypt. In Judith Tucker (ed.), *Arab Women: Old Boundaries, New Frontiers*, pp. 129–148. Bloomington: Indiana University Press.

Bahri, Deepika (1996). *Introduction to Postcolonial Studies* [Online]. Available: http://www.emory.edu/ENGLISH/Bahri/Intro.html.

Balibar, Etienne (1991). The Nation Form: History and Ideology. In Etienne Balibar and Immanuel Wallerstein, *Race, Nation, Class: Ambiguous Identities*, pp. 86–106. London: Verso.

Balibar, Etienne (1995). Culture and Identity (Working Notes). In John Rajchman (ed.), *The Identity in Question*, pp. 173–198. London: Routledge.

Baltazar, Ana Paula (2001). Architecture as Interface: Forming and Informing Spaces and Subjects. In A. Koivnen and S. Paasonen (eds.), Conference Proceedings for *Affective Encounters: Rethinking Embodiment in Feminist Media Studies* [E-book]. Available: http://www.utu.fi/hum/mediatutkimus/affective/proceedings.pdf.

Barthes, Roland (1993). *Mythologies*. London: Vintage.

Baudrillard, Jean (1983). *Simulations*. New York: Semiotext(e).

BBC News (2005). *Director Stone Making 9/11 Film* [Online]. July 10. Available: http://news.bbc.co.uk/1/hi/entertainment/film/4669467.stm.

Beauregard, Robert A. (1995). If Only the City Could Speak: The Politics of Representation. In Helen Liggett and David C. Perry (eds.), *Spatial Practices: Critical Explorations in Social/Spatial Theory*, pp. 59–80. London: Sage.

Beeley, Brian (1995). Global Options: Islamic Alternatives. In James Anderson, Chris Brook and Allan Cochrane (eds.), *A Global World? Re-Ordering Political Space*, pp. 167–208. Oxford: Oxford University Press.

Bennington, Geoffrey (1990). Postal Politics and the Institution of the Nation. In Homi K. Bhabha (ed.), *Nation and Narration*, pp. 121–137. London: Routledge.

Betterton, Rosemary (2001). Spaces of Memory: Photographic Practices of Home and Exile. In A. Koivnen and S. Paasonen (eds.), Conference Proceedings for *Affective Encounters: Rethinking Embodiment in Feminist Media Studies* [E-book]. Available: http://www.utu.fi/hum/mediatutkimus/affective/proceedings.pdf.

Bhabha, Homi (1983). The Other Question . . . Homi K Bhabha Reconsiders the Stereotype and Colonial Discourse. *Screen*, 24 (4): 18–36.

Bhabha, Homi (1986). Foreword: Remembering Fanon. In Franz Fanon, *Black Skin, White Masks*, pp. vii–xxvi. London: Pluto Press.

Bhabha, Homi (1990). The Third Space (Interview). In Jonathan Rutherford (ed.), *Identity, Community, Culture, Difference*, pp. 207–221. London: Lawrence & Wishart.

Bhabha, Homi (1994). Remembering Fanon: Self, Psyche and the Colonial Condition. In Patrick Williams and Laura Chrisman (eds.), *Colonial Discourse and Post-Colonial Theory: A Reader*, pp. 112–123. London: Harvester Wheatsheaf.

Bhabha, Homi (1995). Freedom's Basis in the Intermediate. In John Rajchman (ed.), *The Identity in Question*, pp. 47–62. London: Routledge.

Bhabha, Homi (1999). Preface: Arrivals and Departures. In Hamid Naficy (ed.), *Home, Exile, Homeland: Film, Media, and the Politics of Place*, pp. vii–xii. New York: Routledge.

Bingham, Dennis (1994). *Acting Male: Masculinities in the Films of James Stewart, Jack Nicholson, and Clint Eastwood*. Piscataway, NJ: Rutgers University Press.

Birch, Anthony H. (1989). *Nationalism and National Integration*. London: Unwin Hyman.

Bisharat, George E. (1997). Exile to Compatriot: Transformations in the Political Role and Social Identity of Palestinian Refugees in the West Bank. In Akhil Gupta and James Ferguson (eds.), *Culture, Power, Place: Explorations in Critical Anthropology*, pp. 203–233. Durham, NC: Duke University Press.

Bleiker, Roland (2000). The End of Modernity? In Greg Fry and Jacinta O'Hagan (eds.), *Contending Images of World Politics*, pp. 227–241. London: Macmillan Press.

Blunt, Alison (1994a). Mapping Authorship and Authority: Reading Mary Kingsley's Landscape Descriptions. In Alison Blunt and Gillian Rose (eds.), *Writing Women and Space: Colonial and Postcolonial Geographies*, pp. 51–72. London: Guilford Press.

Blunt, Alison (1994b). *Travel, Gender, and Imperialism: Mary Kingsley and West Africa*. London: Guilford Press.

Blythe, Martin (1993). "What's in a Name?": Film Culture and the Self/Other Question. In Hamid Naficy and Teshome H. Gabriel (eds.), *Otherness and the Media: The Ethnography of the Imagined and the Imaged*, pp. 221–231. Langhorne, PA: Harwood Academic Publishers.

Brah, Avtar (1996). *Cartographies of Diaspora: Contesting Identities*. London: Routledge.

Brennan, Timothy (1995). The National Longing for Form. In Bill Ashcroft, Gareth Griffiths and Helen Tiffin (eds.), *The Post-Colonial Studies Reader*, pp. 170–175. London: Routledge.

Brown, Michael (1997). Causes and Implications of Ethnic Conflict. In Montserrat Guibernau and John Rex (eds.), *The Ethnicity Reader: Nationalism, Multiculturalism and Migration*, pp. 80–99. Cambridge: Polity Press.

Budley, Mildred and Safran, Yehuda (1983). The Lay of the Land. *Undercut*, Spring, 7/8: 34–36.

Cabral, Amilcar (1994). National Liberation and Culture. In Patrick Williams and Laura Chrisman (eds.), *Colonial Discourse and Post-Colonial Theory: A Reader*, pp. 53–65. London: Harvester Wheatsheaf.

Carter, Paul (1995). Spatial History. In Bill Ashcroft, Gareth Griffiths and Helen Tiffen (eds.), *The Post-Colonial Studies Reader*, pp. 375–377. London: Routledge.

Castells, Manuel (1997). *The Power of Identity*. Oxford: Blackwell.

Chapman, Malcolm, McDonald, Maryon and Tonkin, Elizabeth (1989). Introduction —History and Social Anthropology. In Elizabeth Tonkin, Maryon McDonald and Malcolm Chapman (eds.), *History and Ethnicity*, pp. 1–21. London: Routledge.

Chatterjee, Partha (1992). Their Own Words? An Essay for Edward Said. In Michael Sprinker (ed.), *Edward Said: A Critical Reader*, pp. 194–220. Oxford: Blackwell.

Chow, Rey (1994). Where Have All the Natives Gone? In Angelika Bammer (ed.), *Displacements: Cultural Identities in Question*, pp. 125–151. Milwaukee: Regents of the University of Wisconsin System.

Clifford, James (1997a). Diasporas. In Montserrat Guibernau and John Rex (eds.), *The Ethnicity Reader: Nationalism, Multiculturalism and Migration*, pp. 283–290. Cambridge: Polity Press.

Clifford, James (1997b). *Routes: Travel and Translation in the Late Twentieth Century*. Cambridge, MA: Harvard University Press.

Collard, Anna (1989). Investigating Social Memory in a Greek Context. In Elizabeth Tonkin, Maryon McDonald and Malcolm Chapman (eds.), *History and Ethnicity*, pp. 89–103. London: Routledge.

Connolly, William E. (1989). Identity and Difference in Global Politics. In James Der Derian and Michael J. Shapiro (eds.), *International/Intertextual Relations: Postmodern Readings of World Politics*, pp. 323–334. Toronto: Lexington Books.

Conrad, Joseph (1925). *Notes on Life and Letters*. London: Gresham Publishing.

Crenshaw, Martha (1990). Is International Terrorism Primarily State-Sponsored? In Kegley, Charles W., Jr (ed.), *International Terrorism: Characteristics, Causes, Controls*, pp. 163–169. Columbia: University of South Carolina Press.

Dajani, Souad (1993). Palestinian Women under Israeli Occupation. In Judith Tucker (ed.), *Arab Women: Old Boundaries, New Frontiers*, pp. 102–126. Bloomington: Indiana University Press.

Davies, Jude and Smith, Carol R. (1997). *Gender, Ethnicity and Sexuality in Contemporary American Film*. Edinburgh: Keele University Press.

Delaney, Carol (1995). Father State, Motherland, and the Birth of Modern Turkey. In Sylvia Yanagisako and Carol Delaney (eds.), *Naturalizing Power: Essays in Feminist Cultural Analysis*, pp. 177–200. London: Routledge.

Dirlik, Arif (1997). The Postcolonial Aura: Third World Criticism in the Age of Global Capitalism. In Anne McClintock, Aamir Mufti and Ella Shohat (eds.), *Dangerous Liaisons: Gender, Nation, and Postcolonial Perspectives*, pp. 501–528. Minneapolis: University of Minnesota Press.

Doane, Mary Ann (1999). *Caught* and *Rebecca*: The Inscription of Femininity as Absence. In Sue Thornham (ed.), *Feminist Film Theory: A Reader*, pp. 70–82. Edinburgh: Edinburgh University Press.

Downing, John (1991). Review Essay, Cinema and Minority Hegemony: The Israeli Crisis in Israeli Film. *Quarterly Review of Film and Video*, 13 (1–3): 261–267.

Driver, Felix and Rose, Gillian (1992). Introduction: Towards New Histories of Geographical Knowledge. In Felix Driver and Gillian Rose, *Nature and Science: Essays in the History of Geographical Knowledge*, pp. 1–7. Cheltenham: Historical Geography Research Group Series, 28.

Dumm, Thomas (1996). *Michel Foucault and the Politics of Freedom.* London: Sage.

Durham Peters, John (1999). Exile, Nomadism, and Diaspora: The Stakes of Mobility in the Western Canon. In Hamid Naficy (ed.), *Home, Exile, Homeland: Film, Media, and the Politics of Place*, pp. 17–41. New York: Routledge.

Ehteshami, Anoushiravan (1997). Islamic Fundamentalism and Political Islam. In Brian White, Richard Little and Michael Smith (eds.), *Issues in World Politics*, pp. 179–199. London: Macmillan Press.

Eisenstadt, S.N. (1999). *Fundamentalism, Sectarianism, and Revolution: The Jacobin Dimension of Modernity.* Cambridge: Cambridge University Press.

Eisenstein, Zillah (2000). Writing Bodies on the Nation for the Globe. In Sita Ranchod-Nilsson and Mary Ann Tetreault (eds.), *Women, State, and Nationalism: At Home in the Nation?*, pp. 35–53. London: Routledge.

El Guindi, Fadwa (1999). *Veil: Modesty, Privacy and Resistance.* Oxford: Berg.

El Saadawi, Nawal (1997). *The Nawal El Saadawi Reader.* London: Zed Books.

Elsaddah, Hoda (2002). Gendering the Nation: Conflicting Masculinities in Selected Short Stories by Mustafa Sadiq al-Rafi'i (Abstract) [Online]. *Narrating and Imagining the Nation Workshop Three: Gender, Sexuality and the Nation*, SOAS. Available: http://www.soas.ac.uk/Literatures/Projects/Nation/nationthreeabstracts.pdf.

Enloe, Cynthia (1990). *Bananas, Beaches and Bases: Making Feminist Sense of International Politics.* Berkeley: University of California Press.

Eriksen, Thomas Hylland (1997). Ethnicity, Race and Nation. In Montserrat Guibernau and John Rex (eds.), *The Ethnicity Reader: Nationalism, Multi-culturalism and Migration*, pp. 33–42. Cambridge: Polity Press.

Esposito, John L. (1999). *The Islamic Threat: Myth or Reality?* Oxford: Oxford University Press.

Faksh, Mahmud A. (1997). *Fundamentalism in Egypt, Algeria and Saudi Arabia.* London: Praeger.

Fanon, Frantz (1994). On National Culture. In Patrick Williams and Laura Chrisman (eds.), *Colonial Discourse and Post-Colonial Theory: A Reader*, pp. 36–52. London: Harvester Wheatsheaf.

Fee, Margery (1995). Who Can Write as Other? In Bill Ashcroft, Gareth Griffiths and Helen Tiffin (eds.), *The Post-Colonial Studies Reader*, pp. 242–245. London: Routledge.

Fortin, Alfred J. (1989). Notes on a Terrorist Text: A Critical Use of Roland Barthes' Textual Analysis in the Interpretation of Political Meaning. In James Der

Derian and Michael J. Shapiro (eds.), *International/Intertextual Relations: Postmodern Readings of World Politics*, pp. 189–206. Toronto: Lexington Books.

Foucault, Michel (1970). *The Order of Things*. London: Routledge.

Foucault, Michel (1979). My Body, This Paper, This Fire. *Oxford Literary Review*, 4 (1): 9–28.

Franco, Jean (1994). Beyond Ethnocentrism: Gender, Power and the Third-World Intelligentsia. In Patrick Williams and Laura Chrisman (eds.), *Colonial Discourse and Post-Colonial Theory: A Reader*, pp. 359–369. London: Harvester Wheatsheaf.

Freeman, Nick (1999). See Europe with ITC: Stock Footage and the Construction of Geographical Identity. In Deborah Cartmell, I.Q. Hunter, Heidi Kaye and Imelda Whelehan (eds.), *Alien Identities: Exploring Difference in Film and Fiction*, pp. 49–65. London: Pluto Press.

Friedman, Jonathan (1994). *Cultural Identity and Global Process*. London: Sage.

Gottheim, Larry (1979). Sticking in/to the Landscape. *Millennium Film Journal*, Summer/Fall, no. 4/5, pp. 84–92.

Gregory, Derek (1997). Lacan and Geography: The Production of Space Revisited. In Georges Benko and Ulf Strohmayer (eds.), *Space and Social Theory: Interpreting Modernity and Postmodernity*, pp. 203–231. Oxford: Blackwell.

Gupta, Akhil and Ferguson, James (1992). Beyond "Culture": Space, Identity, and the Politics of Difference. *Cultural Anthropologist*, February, 7 (1): 6–23.

Haffner, Pierre (1997). Water and the Nation. *Ecrans d'Afrique*, 21–22 (3rd–4th quarter): 32–39.

Hall, Stuart (1989). Cultural Identity and Cinematic Representation. *Framework*, 36: 68–81.

Hall, Stuart (1994). Cultural Identity and Diaspora. In Patrick Williams and Laura Chrisman (eds.), *Colonial Discourse and Post-Colonial Theory: A Reader*, pp. 392–403. London: Harvester Wheatsheaf.

Halliday, Fred (1995). *Islam and the Myth of Confrontation: Religion and Politics in the Middle East*. London: I.B.Tauris.

Hamzeh, A. Nizar (1998). The Future of Islamic Movements in Lebanon. In Ahmad S. Moussalli (ed.), *Islamic Fundamentalism: Myths and Realities*, pp. 249–273. Ithaca, NY: Ithaca Press.

Hatem, Mervat (1993). Toward the Development of Post-Islamic and Post-Nationalist Feminist Discourses in the Middle East. In Judith Tucker (ed.), *Arab Women: Old Boundaries, New Frontiers*, pp. 3–29. Bloomington: Indiana University Press.

Hirsch, Eric (1995). Introduction: Landscape: Between Place and Space. In Eric Hirsch and Michael O'Hanlon, *The Anthropology of Landscape: Perspectives on Place and Space*, pp. 1–30. Oxford: Clarendon Press.

Hjarvard, Stig (2002). Mediated Encounters: An Essay on the Role of Communication Media in the Creation of Trust in the "Global Metropolis." In Gitte Stald and

Thomas Tufte (eds.), *Global Encounters: Media and Cultural Transformation*, pp. 69–84. Luton: University of Luton Press.

Hobsbawm, Eric (1990). *Nations and Nationalism since 1780*. Cambridge: Cambridge University Press.

Holmlund, Chris (1993). Masculinity as Multiple Masquerade: The "Mature" Stallone and the Stallone Clone. In Steven Cohan and Ina Rae Hark (eds.), *Screening the Male: Exploring Masculinities in Hollywood Cinema*, pp. 213–229. London: Routledge.

Holt, Maria (1996). Palestinian Women and the Intifada: An Exploration of Images and Realities. In Haleh Afshar (ed.), *Women and Politics in the Third World*, pp. 186–203. London: Routledge.

hooks, bell (1990). *Yearning: Race, Gender, and Cultural Politics*. Boston, MA: South End Press.

hooks, bell (1992). *Black Looks: Race and Representation*. London: Turnaround.

Huntington, Samuel P. (1996). *The Clash of Civilizations and the Remaking of World Order*. New York: Simon & Schuster.

Hyman, Anthony (1985). Muslim Fundamentalism. *Conflict Studies*, 174: 3–27.

Idris, Mohammad As-Said (1991). The American Vision of Israel. In Center for Arab Unity Studies, *American Policy and Arabs*, pp. 273–300 (Arabic). Beirut: CAUS.

Inness, Sherrie A. (1999). *Tough Girls: Women Warriors and Wonder Women in Popular Culture*. Philadelphia: University of Pennsylvania Press.

Jeffords, Susan (1993). Can Masculinity Be Terminated? In Steven Cohan and Ina Rae Hark (eds.), *Screening the Male: Exploring Masculinities in Hollywood Cinema*, pp. 245–262. London: Routledge.

Jeffords, Susan (1994). *Hard Bodies: Hollywood Masculinity in the Reagan Era*. Piscataway, NJ: Rutgers University Press.

Jenkins, Richard (1997). *Rethinking Ethnicity: Arguments and Explorations*. London: Sage.

Joseph, Suad (1999). Women between Nation and State in Lebanon. In Caren Kaplan, Norma Alarcon and Minoo Moallem (eds.), *Between Woman and Nation: Nationalisms, Transnational Feminisms, and the State*, pp. 162–181. London: Duke University Press.

Judd, Dennis R. (1995). The Rise of the New Walled Cities. In Helen Liggett and David C. Perry (eds.), *Spatial Practices: Critical Explorations in Social/Spatial Theory*, pp. 144–166. London: Sage.

Kallam, Mahmoud Abdullah (2001). *Naji al-Ali: The Whole of the Palestinian Soil; This is Why They Killed Me* (Arabic). Beirut: Baisan.

Kandiyoti, Deniz (1994). Identity and its Discontents: Women and the Nation. In Patrick Williams and Laura Chrisman (eds.), *Colonial Discourse and Post-Colonial Theory: A Reader*, pp. 376–391. London: Harvester Wheatsheaf.

Kaplan, E. Ann (1992). *Motherhood and Representation: The Mother in Popular Culture and Melodrama*. London: Routledge.

Karawan, Ibrahim A. (1997). *The Islamist Impasse.* New York: Oxford University Press.

Karim, Karim H. (2000). *Islamic Peril: Media and Global Violence.* Montreal: Black Rose Books.

Karr, Karolina M. (1997). *Nationalism vs. "Globalism": Are They Indeed Antagonistic Concepts?* [Online]. Available: http://www.mtholyoke.edu/~aamkpa/Karr. Nationalism.html.

Kedourie, Elie (1961). *Nationalism.* London: Hutchinson.

Keiller, Patrick (1982). The Poetic Experience of Townscape and Landscape and Some Ways of Depicting It. *Undercut,* March, no. 3/4: 43–51.

Keith, Michael and Pile, Steve (1993). Introduction Part I: The Politics of Place. In Michael Keith and Steve Pile (eds.), *Place and the Politics of Identity,* pp. 1–21. London: Routledge.

Kellas, James G. (1998). *The Politics of Nationalism and Ethnicity.* London: Macmillan Press.

Kepel, Gilles (1994). *The Revenge of God: The Resurgence of Islam, Christianity and Judaism in the Modern World,* translated by Alan Braley. Cambridge: Polity Press.

Kepel, Gilles (1997). *Allah in the West: Islamic Movements in America and Europe.* Cambridge: Polity Press.

Kerr, Malcolm (1980). Edward Said, Orientalism (review). *International Journal of Middle Eastern Studies,* December, vol. 12: 544–547.

Khan, Shahnaz (1998). Muslim Women: Negotiations in the Third Space. *Signs: Journal of Women in Culture and Society,* Winter, 23 (2): 463–494.

Kimmel, Michael S. and Kaufman, Michael (1994). Weekend Warriors: The New Men's Movement. In Harry Brod and Michael Kaufman (eds.), *Theorizing Masculinities,* pp. 259–288. London: Sage.

Kofman, Eleanore (1996). Feminism, Gender Relations and Geopolitics: Problematic Closures and Opening Strategies. In Eleanore Kofman and Gillian Youngs (eds.), *Globalization: Theory and Practice,* pp. 209–224. London: Pinter.

Landow, George P. (2002). Edward Said's Orientalism [Online]. *Political Discourse— Theories of Colonialism and Postcolonialism.* Available: http://www.scholars. nus.edu.sg/post/poldiscourse/said/orient14.html.

Lant, Anthony (1997). The Curse of the Pharaoh, or How Cinema Contracted Egyptomania. In Matthew Bernstein and Gaylyn Studlar (eds.), *Visions of the East: Orientalism in Film,* pp. 69–98. London: I.B.Tauris.

Lazarus, Neil (1994). National Consciousness and the Specificity of (Post) Colonial Intellectualism. In Francis Barker, Peter Hulme and Margaret Iversen (eds.), *Colonial Discourse/Postcolonial Theory,* pp. 197–220. Manchester: Manchester University Press.

Lazarus, Neil (1997). Transnationalism and the Alleged Death of the Nation-State. In Keith Ansell Pearson, Benita Parry and Judith Squires (eds.), *Cultural*

Readings of Imperialism: Edward Said and the Gravity of History, pp. 28–48. London: Lawrence & Wishart.

Lefebvre, Henri (1991). *The Production of Space*. Oxford: Oxford University Press.

Lehman, Peter (2001). James Bond's Penis. In Peter Lehman (ed.), *Masculinity: Bodies, Movies, Culture*, pp. 25–42. New York: Routledge.

Lehtonen, Mikko (2000). *The Cultural Analysis of Texts*. London: Sage.

Lentricchia, Frank (1989). Foucault's Legacy: A New Historicism? In H. Aram Veeser, *The New Historicism*, pp. 231–242. London: Routledge.

Lewis, Jon (1991). City/Cinema/Dream. In Mary Ann Caws (ed.), *City Images: Perspectives from Literature, Philosophy, and Film*, pp. 240–254. London: Gordon & Breach.

Liggett, Helen (1995). City Sights/Sites of Memories and Dreams. In Helen Liggett and David C. Perry (eds.), *Spatial Practices: Critical Explorations in Social/Spatial Theory*, pp. 243–273. London: Sage.

Little, Douglas (2003). *American Orientalism: The United States and the Middle East since 1945*. London: I.B.Tauris.

Lury, Karen and Massey, Doreen (1999). Making Connections. *Screen*, Autumn, 40 (3): 229–239.

McClintock, Anne (1994). The Angel of Progress: Pitfalls of the Term "Post-colonialism." In Patrick Williams and Laura Chrisman (eds.), *Colonial Discourse and Post-Colonial Theory: A Reader*, pp. 291–304. London: Harvester Wheatsheaf.

McClintock, Anne (1997). "No Longer in Future Heaven": Gender, Race and Nationalism. In Anne McClintock, Aamir Mufti and Ella Shohat (eds.), *Dangerous Liaisons: Gender, Nation, and Postcolonial Perspectives*, pp. 89–112. Minneapolis: University of Minnesota Press.

McEwan, Cheryl (1994). Encounters with West African Women: Textual Representations of Difference by White Women Abroad. In Alison Blunt and Gillian Rose (eds.), *Writing Women and Space: Colonial and Postcolonial Geographies*, pp. 73–100. London: Guilford Press.

McGrew, Anthony (1995). World Order and Political Space. In James Anderson, Chris Brook and Allan Cochrane (eds.), *A Global World? Re-Ordering Political Space*, pp. 11–64. Oxford: Oxford University Press.

McNeill, William H. (1982). The Care and Repair of Public Myth. *Foreign Affairs*, Fall, pp. 1–13.

McQuire, Scott (1998). *Visions of Modernity: Representations, Memory, Time and Space in the Age of the Camera*. London: Sage.

Majid, Anouar (1998). The Politics of Feminism in Islam. *Signs: Journal of Women in Culture and Society*, Winter, 23 (2): 321–361.

Mansour, Kamil (1991). American Policy and the Middle East: From Carter to Reagan. In Center for Arab Unity Studies, *American Policy and Arabs*, pp. 75–94 (Arabic). Beirut: CAUS.

Massey, Doreen (1993). Politics and Space/Time. In Michael Keith and Steve Pile (eds.), *Place and the Politics of Identity*, pp. 141–161. London: Routledge.

Massey, Doreen (1994). Double Articulation: A Place in the World. In Angelika Bammer (ed.), *Displacements: Cultural Identities in Question*, pp. 110–122. Milwaukee: Regents of the University of Wisconsin System.

Moallem, Minoo (1999). Transnationalism, Feminism, and Fundamentalism. In Caren Kaplan, Norma Alarcon and Minoo Moallem (eds.), *Between Woman and Nation: Nationalisms, Transnational Feminisms, and the State*, pp. 320–348. London: Duke University Press.

Moghadam, Valentine (1994). Introduction and Overview: Gender Dynamics of Nationalism, Revolution and Islamization. In Valentine Moghadam (ed.), *Gender and National Identity*, pp. 1–17. London: Zed Books.

Moghissi, Haideh (1999). *Feminism and Islamic Fundamentalism: The Limits of Postmodern Analysis*. London: Zed Books.

Mohamad, Husam A. (1999). Inter-Arab Politics and the Mainstream of the Palestinian Movement: Changes in Relations and Strategy and their Implications for the Peace Process [Online]. *JOUVERT*, 3 (3). Available: http://social.chass.ncsu.edu/jouvert/v3i3/moham.htm.

Mohanty, Chandra Talpade (1994). Under Western Eyes: Feminist Scholarship and Colonial Discourses. In Patrick Williams and Laura Chrisman (eds.), *Colonial Discourse and Post-Colonial Theory: A Reader*, pp. 196–220. London: Harvester Wheatsheaf.

Morley, David (1999). Bounded Realms: Household, Family, Community, and Nation. In Hamid Naficy (ed.), *Home, Exile, Homeland: Film, Media, and the Politics of Place*, pp. 151–168. New York: Routledge.

Morley, David and Robins, Kevin (1990). No Place like *Heimat*: Images of Home(land) in European Culture. *New Formations*, 12, pp. 1–23.

Morse, Margaret (1999). Home: Smell, Taste, Posture, Gleam. In Hamid Naficy (ed.), *Home, Exile, Homeland: Film, Media, and the Politics of Place*, pp. 63–74. New York: Routledge.

Moten, Rashid (1980). Palestinian Nationalism: Its Growth and Development. *International Studies*, 19: 198–219.

Mouffe, Chantal (1995). Democratic Politics and the Question of Identity. In John Rajchman (ed.), *The Identity in Question*, pp. 33–46. London: Routledge.

Moussalli, Ahmad S. (1998). Introduction to Islamic Fundamentalism: Realities, Ideologies and International Politics. In Ahmad S. Moussalli, *Islamic Fundamentalism: Myths and Realities*, pp. 3–40. Ithaca, NY: Ithaca Press.

Mowlana, Hamid (2000). The Renewal of the Global Media Debate: Implications for the Relationship between the West and the Islamic World. In Kai Hafez (ed.), *Islam and the West in the Mass Media*, pp. 105–118. Cresskill, NJ: Hampton Press.

Mulvey, Laura (1999). Visual Pleasure and Narrative Cinema. In Sue Thornham (ed.), *Feminist Film Theory: A Reader*, pp. 58–69. Edinburgh: Edinburgh University Press.

Mulvey, Laura and MacCabe, Colin (1989). Images of Women, Images of Sexuality: Some Films by J.L. Godard. In Laura Mulvey, *Visual and Other Pleasures: Language, Discourse, Society*, pp. 49–62. London: Macmillan.

Naficy, Hamid (1991). Exile Discourse and Televisual Fetishization. *Quarterly Review of Film and Video*, 13 (1–3): 85–116.

Naficy, Hamid (1996). Phobic Spaces and Liminal Panics: Independent Transnational Film Genre. In Rob Wilson and Wimal Dissanayake (eds.), *Global/ Local: Cultural Production and the Transnational Imaginary*, pp. 119–144. London: Duke University Press.

Naficy, Hamid (1999). Framing Exile: From Homeland to Homepage. In Hamid Naficy (ed.), *Home, Exile, Homeland: Film, Media, and the Politics of Place*, pp. 1–14. New York: Routledge.

Nash, Catherine (1994). Remapping the Body/Land: New Cartographies of Identity, Gender, and Landscape in Ireland. In Alison Blunt and Gillian Rose (eds.), *Writing Women and Space: Colonial and Postcolonial Geographies*, pp. 227–250. London: Guilford Press.

Nasr, Kameel B. (1997). *Arab and Israeli Terrorism*. Jefferson, NC: McFarland.

Natter, Wolfgang and Jones, John Paul (1997). Identity, Space, and Other Uncertainties. In Georges Benko and Ulf Strohmayer (eds.), *Space and Social Theory: Interpreting Modernity and Postmodernity*, pp. 141–161. Oxford: Blackwell.

Nietschmann, Bernard (1993). Authentic, State, and Virtual Geography in Film. *Wide Angle*, October, 15 (4): 4–12.

Niranjana, Tejaswini (1992). *Siting Translation: History, Post-structuralism, and the Colonial Context*. Berkeley: University of California Press.

O'Hagan, Jacinta (2000). A Clash of Civilizations? In Greg Fry and Jacinta O'Hagan (eds.), *Contending Images of World Politics*, pp. 135–149. London: Macmillan Press.

O'Healy, Aine (1999). Revisiting the Belly of Naples: The Body and the City in the Films of Mario Martone. *Screen*, Autumn, 40 (3): 239–256.

Paine, Robert (1989). Israel: Jewish Identity and Competition over "Tradition." In Elizabeth Tonkin, Maryon McDonald and Malcolm Chapman (eds.), *History and Ethnicity*, pp. 121–136. London: Routledge.

Parpart, Lee (2001). Male Nudity and Nation: Notes towards a Theory of Marginality, Colonialism and the Ever-Present Penis in Recent Canadian and Quebecois Cinema. In Peter Lehman (ed.), *Masculinity: Bodies, Movies, Culture*, pp. 167–192. New York: Routledge.

Parry, Benita (1994). Resistance Theory/Theorising Resistance, or Two Cheers for Nativism. In Francis Barker, Peter Hulme and Margaret Iversen (eds.), *Colonial Discourse/Postcolonial Theory*, pp. 172–196. Manchester: Manchester University Press.

Pecora, Vincent P. (1989). The Limits of Local Knowledge. In H. Aram Veeser, *The New Historicism*, pp. 243–276. London: Routledge.

Pettman, Jan Jindy (1992). *Women, Nationalism and the State: Towards an International Feminist Perspective.* Occasional Paper 4 in Gender and Development Studies. Bangkok: Asian Institute of Technology.

Pfeil, Fred (1995). *White Guys: Studies in Postmodern Domination and Difference.* London: Verso.

Phillips, Alastair (1999). Performing Paris: Myths of the City in Robert Siodmak's Emigre Musical La Vue Parisienne. *Screen*, Autumn, 40 (3): 257–277.

Pidduck, Julianne (1998). Of Windows and Country Walks: Frames of Space and Movement in 1990s Austen Adaptations. *Screen*, Winter, 39 (4): 381–400.

Porter, Dennis (1994). Orientalism and its Problems. In Patrick Williams and Laura Chrisman (eds.), *Colonial Discourse and Post-Colonial Theory: A Reader*, pp. 150–161. London: Harvester Wheatsheaf.

Prakesh, Gyan (1990). Writing Post-Orientalist Histories of the Third World: Perspectives from Indian Historiography. *Comparative Studies in Society and History*, 32 (2): 383–400.

Prakesh, Gyan (1997). Postcolonial Criticism and Indian Historiography. In Anne McClintock, Aamir Mufti and Ella Shohat (eds.), *Dangerous Liaisons: Gender, Nation, and Postcolonial Perspectives*, pp. 491–500. Minneapolis: University of Minnesota Press.

Preston, P.W. (1997). *Political/Cultural Identity: Citizens and Nations in a Global Era.* London: Sage.

Privett, Ray (1999). Letter from New York: The Apple and a Youssef Chahine Retrospective. *Film International*, Spring, 24.

Ranchod-Nilsson, Sita and Tetreault, Mary Ann (2000). Gender and Nationalism: Moving beyond Fragmented Conversations. In Sita Ranchod-Nilsson and Mary Ann Tetreault (eds.), *Women, State, and Nationalism: At Home in the Nation?*, pp. 1–17. London: Routledge.

Rex, John (1997a). The Concept of a Multicultural Society. In Montserrat Guibernau and John Rex (eds.), *The Ethnicity Reader: Nationalism, Multiculturalism and Migration*, pp. 205–219. Cambridge: Polity Press.

Rex, John (1997b). The Nature of Ethnicity in the Project of Migration. In Montserrat Guibernau and John Rex (eds.), *The Ethnicity Reader: Nationalism, Multiculturalism and Migration*, pp. 269–282. Cambridge: Polity Press.

Riggs, Larry W. (1993). Desire, Substitution, and Violence in the Contracting Space of Gender. In William Burgwinkle, Glenn Man and Valerie Wayne (eds.), *Significant Others: Gender and Culture in Film and Literature*, pp. 53–62. East and West: Selected Conference Papers. Honolulu: College of Languages, Linguistics and Literature, University of Hawaii and the East–West Center.

Rose, Gillian (1992). Geography as a Science of Observation: The Landscape, the Gaze and Masculinity. In Felix Driver and Gillian Rose, *Nature and Science:*

Essays in the History of Geographical Knowledge, pp. 8–18. Cheltenham: Historical Geography Research Group Series, 28.

Ryan, Michael and Kellner, Douglas (1990). *Camera Politica: The Politics and Ideology of Contemporary Hollywood Film*. Bloomington: Indiana University Press.

Sackur, Zina (1994). *Egypt: Islamic Fundamentalist Organisations: The Muslim Brotherhood and the Gama'a al-Islamiya (The Islamic Group)*. Writenet Country Papers.

Safty, Adel (1992). *From Camp David to the Gulf: Negotiations, Language and Propaganda, and War*. Montreal: Black Rose Books.

Said, Edward (1978). *Orientalism*. New York: Pantheon.

Said, Edward (1981). *Covering Islam: How the Media and the Experts Determine How We See the Rest of the World*. London: Routledge & Kegan Paul.

Said, Edward (1987). Orientalism and Zionism. In *Al-Majallah*, Dec. 2–8 (Arabic).

Said, Edward (1988). Through Gringo Eyes: With Conrad in Latin America. *Harper's Magazine*, April.

Said, Edward (1992). *The Question of Palestine*. London: Vintage.

Said, Edward (1993). *Culture and Imperialism*. London: Vintage.

Said, Edward (2003). *Orientalism*. New edition, Penguin Modern Classics. London: Penguin.

Saikal, Amin (2000). Islam and the West? In Greg Fry and Jacinta O'Hagan (eds.), *Contending Images of World Politics*, pp. 164–177. London: Macmillan Press.

Sardar, Ziauddin (1998). *Postmodernism and the Other: The New Imperialism of Western Culture*. London: Pluto Press.

Sardar, Ziauddin and Davies, Merryl Wyn (2003). *Why Do People Hate America?* Cambridge: Icon Books.

Sassen, Saskia (1999). Digital Networks and Power. In Mike Featherstone and Scott Lash (eds.), *Spaces of Culture: City, Nation, World*, pp. 49–63. London: Sage.

Saukko, Paula (2003). *Doing Research in Cultural Studies: An Introduction to Classical and New Methodological Approaches*. London: Sage.

Sayigh, Rosemary (1993). Palestinian Women and Politics in Lebanon. In Judith Tucker (ed.), *Arab Women: Old Boundaries, New Frontiers*, pp. 175–192. Bloomington: Indiana University Press.

Sayyid, Bobby S. (1997). *A Fundamental Fear: Eurocentrism and the Emergence of Islamism*. London: Zed Books.

Schaffer, Kay (1994). Colonizing Gender in Colonial Australia: The Eliza Fraser Story. In Alison Blunt and Gillian Rose (eds.), *Writing Women and Space: Colonial and Postcolonial Geographies*, pp. 101–120. London: Guilford Press.

Schiller, Herbert I. (1973). *The Mind Managers*. Boston, MA: Beacon Press.

Schlesinger, Philip (1991). *Media, State and Nation: Political Violence and Collective Identities*. London: Sage.

Schulze, Kirsten (1998). Communal Violence, Civil War and Foreign Occupation: Women in Lebanon. In Rick Wilford and Robert L. Miller (eds.), *Women, Ethnicity and Nationalism: The Politics of Transition*, pp. 150–169. London: Routledge.

Scott, Ian (2000). *American Politics in Hollywood Film*. Edinburgh: Edinburgh University Press.

Seed, Patricia (1999). The Key to the House. In Hamid Naficy (ed.), *Home, Exile, Homeland: Film, Media, and the Politics of Place*, pp. 85–94. New York: Routledge.

Selwyn, Tom (1995). Landscapes of Liberation and Imprisonment: Towards an Anthropology of the Israeli Landscape. In Eric Hirsch and Michael O'Hanlon, *The Anthropology of Landscape: Perspectives on Place and Space*, pp. 114–134. Oxford: Clarendon Press.

Shaheen, Jack (1984). *The TV Arab*. Bowling Green, OH: Bowling Green State University Popular Press.

Shaheen, Jack (1997). *Arab and Muslim Stereotyping in American Popular Culture*. Washington, DC: Center for Muslim–Christian Understanding, Georgetown University.

Shaheen, Jack (2001). *Reel Bad Arabs: How Hollywood Vilifies a People*. New York: Roundhouse Publishing.

Shapiro, Michael J. (1989). Representing World Politics: The Sport/War Intertext. In James Der Derian and Michael J. Shapiro (eds.), *International/Intertextual Relations: Postmodern Readings of World Politics*, pp. 69–96. Toronto: Lexington Books.

Shapiro, Michael J. (1999). *Cinematic Political Thought: Narrating Race, Nation and Gender*. Edinburgh: Edinburgh University Press.

Sharoni, Simona (1995). *Gender and the Israeli–Palestinian Conflict*. Syracuse, NY: Syracuse University Press.

Shields, Rob (1997). Spatial Stress and Resistance: Social Meanings of Spatialization. In Georges Benko and Ulf Strohmayer (eds.), *Space and Social Theory: Interpreting Modernity and Postmodernity*, pp. 186–202. Oxford: Blackwell.

Shohat, Ella (1989a). *Israeli Cinema: East/West and the Politics of Representation*. Austin: University of Texas Press.

Shohat, Ella (1989b). Anomalies of the National: Representing Israel/Palestine. *Wide Angle*, July, 11 (3): 33–41.

Shohat, Ella (1997a). Columbus, Palestine and Arab-Jews: Toward a Relational Approach to Community Identity. In Keith Ansell Pearson, Benita Parry and Judith Squires (eds.), *Cultural Readings of Imperialism: Edward Said and the Gravity of History*, pp. 88–105. London: Lawrence & Wishart.

Shohat, Ella (1997b). Gender and Culture of Empire: Toward a Feminist Ethnography of the Cinema. In Matthew Bernstein and Gaylyn Studlar (eds.), *Visions of the East: Orientalism in Film*, pp. 19–66. London: I.B.Tauris.

Shohat, Ella (1999a). By the Bitstream of Babylon: Cyberfrontiers and Diasporic Vistas. In Hamid Naficy (ed.), *Home, Exile, Homeland: Film, Media, and the Politics of Place*, pp. 213–232. New York: Routledge.

Shohat, Ella (1999b). The Invention of Mezrahim. *Journal of Palestine Studies*, Autumn, 29 (1): 5–20.

Shohat, Ella and Stam, Robert (1994). *Unthinking Eurocentrism: Multiculturalism and the Media*. London: Routledge.

Short, John Rennie (1991). *Imagined Country: Environment, Culture and Society*. London: Routledge.

Silence in the Nile: Egyptian Freedom of Speech under Peril (1998). Unauthored [Online]. Available: http://www.derechos.org/wi/2/egypt.html.

Slotkin, Richard (1998). *Gunfighter Nation: The Myth of the Frontier in Twentieth-Century America*. Norman: University of Oklahoma Press.

Smith, Anthony (1986). *The Ethnic Origins of Nations*. Oxford: Blackwell.

Smith, Anthony (1987). *The Geopolitics of Information: How Western Culture Dominates the World*. Oxford: Oxford University Press.

Smith, Anthony (1991). *National Identity*. London: Penguin Books.

Smith, Anthony (1999). *Myths and Memories of the Nation*. Oxford: Oxford University Press.

Smith, Anthony (2000). *The Nation in History: Historiographical Debates about Ethnicity and Nationalism*. Cambridge: Polity Press.

Smith, Michael (1997). Regions and Regionalism. In Brian White, Richard Little and Michael Smith (eds.), *Issues in World Politics*, pp. 69–89. London: Macmillan Press.

Sobchack, Thomas (1988). The Adventure Film. In Wes D. Gehring (ed.), *Handbook of American Film Genres*, pp. 9–24. New York: Greenwood Press.

Soja, Edward (1989). *Postmodern Geographies: The Reassertion of Space in Critical Social Theory*. London: Verso.

Soja, Edward (1996). *Thirdspace: Journeys to Los Angeles and Other Real-and-Imagined Places*. Oxford: Blackwell.

Soja, Edward and Hooper, Barbara (1993). The Spaces that Difference Makes: Some Notes on the Geographical Margins of the New Cultural Politics. In Michael Keith and Steve Pile (eds.), *Place and the Politics of Identity*, pp. 183–205. London: Routledge.

Spike Peterson, V. (1999). Sexing Political Identities/Nationalism as Heterosexism. *International Feminist Journal of Politics*, 1 (1): 34–65.

Spivak, Gayatri Chakravorty (1988). *In Other Worlds: Essays in Cultural Politics*. London: Routledge.

Spivak, Gayatri Chakravorty (1990). *The Post-Colonial Critic: Interviews, Strategies, Dialogues*, edited by Sarah Harasym. London: Routledge.

Stacey, Jackie (1999). Feminine Fascinations: Forms of Identification in Star–Audience Relations. In Sue Thornham (ed.), *Feminist Film Theory: A Reader*, pp. 196–209. Edinburgh: Edinburgh University Press.

Stubbs, Richard and Underhill, Geoffrey R.D. (1994). Introduction: Global Trends, Regional Patterns. In Richard Stubbs and Geoffrey R.D. Underhill, *Political*

Economy and the Changing Global Order, pp. 331–335. New York: St. Martin's Press.

Suleri, Sara (1995). Woman Skin Deep: Feminism and the Postcolonial Condition. In Bill Ashcroft, Gareth Griffiths and Helen Tiffin (eds.), *The Post-Colonial Studies Reader*, pp. 273–280. London: Routledge.

Taheri, Amir (1987). *Holy Terror: The Inside Story of Islamic Terrorism*. London: Sphere Books.

Tasker, Yvonne (1993). *Spectacular Bodies: Gender, Genre and the Action Cinema*. London: Routledge.

Tasker, Yvonne (1998). *Working Girls: Gender and Sexuality in Popular Cinema*. London: Routledge.

Tehranian, Majid (2000). Islam and the West: Hostage to History? In Kai Hafez (ed.), *Islam and the West in the Mass Media*, pp. 201–218. Cresskill, NJ: Hampton Press.

Tomlinson, John (1991). *Cultural Imperialism: A Critical Introduction*. London: Pinter Publishers.

Triandis, Harry C., McCusker, Christopher and Hui, C. Harry (2001). Multimethod Probes of Individualism and Collectivism. In Pat Chew (ed.), *The Conflict and Culture Reader*, pp. 52–55. New York: New York University Press.

Tseelon, Efrat (1995). *The Masque of Femininity: The Presentation of Woman in Everyday Life*. London: Sage.

Tucker, Judith E. (1993). The Arab Family in History: "Otherness" and the Study of the Family. In Judith Tucker (ed.), *Arab Women: Old Boundaries, New Frontiers*, pp. 195–207. Bloomington: Indiana University Press.

Tunstall, Jeremy (1977). *The Media are American: Anglo-American Media in the World*. London: Constable.

Turkle, Sherry (1996). *Life on the Screen: Identity in the Age of the Internet*. London: Weidenfeld & Nicolson.

Urry, John (1990). *The Tourist Gaze: Leisure and Travel in Contemporary Societies*. London: Sage.

Waylen, Georgina (1996). *Gender in Third World Politics*. Buckingham: Open University Press.

Welsch, Wolfgang (1999). Transculturality: The Puzzling Form of Cultures Today. In Mike Featherstone and Scott Lash (eds.), *Spaces of Culture: City, Nation, World*, pp. 194–213. London: Sage.

West, Cornel (1995). The New Cultural Politics of Difference. In John Rajchman (ed.), *The Identity in Question*, pp. 147–172. London: Routledge.

White, Brian, Little, Richard and Smith, Michael (1997). Issues in World Politics. In Brian White, Richard Little and Michael Smith (eds.), *Issues in World Politics*, pp. 1–23. London: Macmillan Press.

Wilford, Rick (1998). Women, Ethnicity and Nationalism: Surveying the Ground. In Rick Wilford and Robert L. Miller (eds.), *Women, Ethnicity and Nationalism: The Politics of Transition*, pp. 1–22. London: Routledge.

Williams, Patrick and Chrisman, Laura (1994). Colonial Discourse and Post-Colonial Theory: An Introduction. In Patrick Williams and Laura Chrisman (eds.), *Colonial Discourse and Post-Colonial Theory: A Reader*, pp. 23–26. London: Harvester Wheatsheaf.

Williams, W.A. (ed.) (1972). *From Colony to Empire*. London: John Wiley.

Willis, Sharon (1997). *High Contrast: Race and Gender in Contemporary Hollywood Film*. London: Duke University Press.

Wilmer, Franke (1997). First Nations in the USA. In Montserrat Guibernau and John Rex (eds.), *The Ethnicity Reader: Nationalism, Multiculturalism and Migration*, pp. 186–204. Cambridge: Polity Press.

Windschuttle, Keith (1999). Edward Said's "Orientalism Revisited": On the Writings of the Literary Critic and Academic Celebrity [Online]. *New Criterion*, 17 (5), January. Available: http://www.newcriterion.com/archive/17/jan99/said.htm.

Worsley, Peter (1990). Models of the Modern World-System. In Mike Featherstone (ed.), *Global Culture: Nationalism, Globalization and Modernity*, pp. 83–95. London: Sage.

Yegenoglu, Meyda (1998). *Colonial Fantasies: Towards a Feminist Reading of Orientalism*. Cambridge: Cambridge University Press.

Yoshimoto, Mitsuhiro (1996). Real Virtuality. In Rob Wilson and Wimal Dissanayake (eds.), *Global/Local: Cultural Production and the Transnational Imaginary*, pp. 107–118. London: Duke University Press.

Young, Robert (1995). *Colonial Desire: Hybridity in Theory, Culture and Race*. London: Routledge.

Filmography

11'09"01—September 11 (Youssef Chahine [segment], Egypt; Sean Penn [segment], USA, 2002)

48 Hours in Israel [48 Sa'aa fi Israel] (Nader Galal, Egypt, 1998)

The Ambassador (J. Lee Thompson, USA, 1984)

Bab el-Oued City (Merzak Allouache, Algeria, 1994)

Birds of Darkness [Touyour ez-Zalam] (Sherif Arafa, Egypt, 1995)

Black Rain (Ridley Scott, USA, 1989)

Borders (Duraid Lahham, Syria, 1987)

Bowling for Columbine (Michael Moore, USA, 2002)

Canticle of the Stones [Nashid al-hajar] (Michel Khleifi, Palestine, 1990)

Chronicle of a Disappearance [Sijil ikhtifa'] (Elia Suleiman, Palestine, 1996)

The Closed Doors [Al-Abwab al-Moghlaka] (Atef Hetata, Egypt, 1999)

Collateral Damage (Andrew Davis, USA, 2001)

Coming to America (John Landis, USA, 1988)

Courage under Fire (Edward Zwick, USA, 1996)

Curfew [Hatta ish'ar akhar] (Rashid Masharawi, Palestine, 1994)

Days of Sadat [Ayyam as-Sadat] (Mohammed Khan, Egypt, 2001)

The Delta Force (Menahem Golan, USA, 1986)

Destiny [Al-Masseer] (Youssef Chahine, Egypt, 1997)

Die Hard (John McTiernan, USA, 1988)

Divine Intervention: Chronicle of Love and Pain [Yadon ilahiyya] (Elia Suleiman, Palestine, 2002)

Don Juan de Marco (Jeremy Leven, USA, 1995)

The Door to the Sun (Yousri Nasrallah, Egypt/Palestine, 2004)

The Emigrant [Al-Mouhager] (Youssef Chahine, Egypt, 1997)

Execution of a Dead Man [I'dam Mayyit] (Ali Abdel-Khaleq, Egypt, 1985)

Executive Decision (Stuart Baird, USA, 1996)

Fahrenheit 9/11 (Michael Moore, USA, 2004)

The Fertile Memory [A-thakira al-khasba] (Michel Khleifi, Palestine,1980)

Girl from Israel [Fatat min Israel] (Ehab Rady, Egypt, 1999)

The Gulf War . . . What Next? [Harb al-Khalij . . . wa baad?] (Borhane Alaouié, Lebanon; Néjia Ben Mabrouk, Tunisia; Nouri Bouzid, Tunisia; Mostafa Darkaoui, Morocco; Elia Suleiman, Palestine; 1993)

The Guys (Jim Simpson, USA, 2002)

Hello America (Nader Galal, Egypt, 2000)

Hero from the South . . . Apple of my Eye [Batal min al-Janoub . . . Aziz eini] (Mohamad Abu Seif, Egypt/Lebanon, 2000)

Hostage (Hanro Mohr, USA, 1987)

Hot Shots (Jim Abrahams, USA, 1991)

Hot Shots! Part Deux (Jim Abrahams, USA, 1993)

Hysteria (Adel Adib, Egypt, 1997)

The Insider (Michael Mann, USA, 1999)

In the Army Now (Daniel Petrie Jr, USA, 1994)

In the Ninth Month [Fi a-shahr at-tasi'] (Ali Nassar, Palestine/Israel, 2002)

Into the Sun (Fritz Kiersch, USA, 1992)

Iron Eagle (Sidney J. Furie, USA, 1986)

Jesus of Nazareth (Franco Zeffirelli, Italy/UK, 1977)

Killing Streets (Stephen Cornwell, USA, 1991)

Kite [Tayyara min Warak] (Randa Chahhal-Sabbagh, Lebanon, 2003)

The Little Drummer Girl (George Roy Hill, USA, 1984)

Love in Taba [Al-Hob fi Taba] (Hisham Abd el-Hamid, Egypt, 1992)

The Matrix (Andy Wachowski, Larry Wachowski, USA, 1999)

The Milky Way [Darb at-tabbanat] (Ali Nassar, Palestine/Israel, 1999)

Mission in Tel Aviv [Mohimma fi Tal Abib] (Nader Galal, Egypt, 1992)

The Mummy (Stephen Sommers, USA, 1999)

Naji al-Ali (Atef at-Tayyeb, Egypt, 1991)

Nasser 56 (Mohamed Fadel, Egypt, 1996)

Nasser: The Story of a Man, A Story of a Nation (Anwar Kawadri, Egypt, 1998)

Navy Seals (Lewis Teague, USA, 1990)

Nights of the Jackal [Layali ibn awa] (Abdellatif Abdelhamid, Syria, 1988)

October [Oktyabr] (Sergei Eisenstein and Grigori Aleksandrov, Soviet Union, 1927)

The Olive Harvest [Mawsam az-Zaitoun] (Hanna Elias, Palestine, 2004)

The Other [Al-Akhar] (Youssef Chahine, Egypt, 1999)

Power (Sidney Lumet, USA, 1986)

Programmed to Kill (Alan Holzman and Robert Short, USA, 1987)

Rachida (Yamina Bachir, Algeria, 2002)

Rambo: First Blood (Ted Kotcheff, USA, 1982)

Rana's Wedding [Al-Quds fi yawm akhar] (Hany Abu-Assad, Palestine, 2002)

Refuge [aka *Deportation*] [At-Tarhil] (Raymond Boutros, Syria, 1997)

Road to Eilat [At-Tarik ila Eilat] (Inaam Mohamed Ali, Egypt, 1986)

Rocky IV (Sylvester Stallone, USA, 1985)

Rules of Engagement (William Friedkin, USA, 2000)

The Sheik (George Melford, USA, 1921)
The Siege (Edward Zwick, USA, 1998)
South Park: Bigger, Longer and Uncut (animation) (Trey Parker, USA, 1999)
Spy Game (Tony Scott, USA, 2001)
A Summer in la Goulette [Halaq al-wad] (Farid Boughedir, Tunisia, 1996)
Tale of Three Jewels [Hikayat al-jawahir a-thalath] (Michel Khleifi, Palestine, 1995)
Team America: World Police (supermarionation) (Trey Parker, USA, 2005)
The Tempest [Al-Asifa] (Khaled Youssef, Egypt, 2000)
The Terminator (James Cameron, USA, 1984)
Terrorism and Barbecue [Al-Irhab wal-Kabab] (Sherif Arafa, Egypt, 1993)
The Terrorist [Al-Irhabi] (Nader Galal, Egypt, 1994)
Three Kings (David O. Russell, USA, 1999)
Ticket to Jerusalem [Tathkara ila al-Quds] (Rashid Masharawi, Palestine, 2002)
Trap of Spies [Fakh al-Jawasis] (Ashraf Fahmi, Egypt, 1992)
Triumph of the Will [Triumph des Willens] (Leni Riefenstahl, Germany, 1934)
True Lies (James Cameron, USA, 1994)
Wedding in Galilee ['Ors al-Jaleel] (Michel Khleifi, Palestine, 1988)

General Index

1948 47, 48, 85, 92, 124, 128, 137, 141, 148, 152, 153 (see also al-Nakba)

1967 43, 46, 58, 59, 69, 77, 92, 99, 114, 122, 135, 138, 139, 144, 149, 152, 153 (see also Six Day War)

1973 4, 69, 77, 98, 134, 135, 138, 149, 166 (see also Yom Kippur, October War)

accent 6, 73, 124

agenda 4, 10, 11, 13, 16, 22, 32, 63, 70, 73, 90, 103, 107, 159, 167, 173, 181, 203, 205, 206

airplane (see plane)

Al-Ali, Naji 46–49, 100, 101, 148–151, 162

Algeria 2, 4, 11–13, 17, 34, 37, 39, 63, 64, 95, 102, 166, 167, 170, 172, 173, 182–184, 192, 193, 195–199, 203, 206, 208

Algiers 17, 37–39, 95

Amal 3, 74

America 1, 3–12, 16, 17, 19–33, 40, 41, 43, 60, 61, 64–79, 85, 86, 102–108, 110, 112–115, 118–120, 128, 135, 136, 148, 149, 151, 152, 155, 157, 159, 162, 166–168, 171, 174–182, 184, 185, 197, 201–204, 207–209 (see also United States)

ambivalence 8, 43, 64, 89, 116, 120, 196

ambivalent 25, 33, 43, 82, 120, 153

Arab (Arabia, Arabian) 1–8, 10–13, 15–17, 20, 22–25, 28–33, 44–47, 54, 58, 60, 61, 63–70, 73–81, 83, 85, 91, 98, 99, 102–105, 107, 108, 114, 115, 117–124, 128, 131, 134–137, 139–162, 165–167, 169, 173–178, 180–183, 185, 195, 197, 200–209

Arabic 6, 25, 115, 121, 124, 127, 131, 146, 175, 180, 187, 196

Arabism 13, 44, 105, 107, 108, 121, 134, 136, 138, 140, 141, 144, 147, 148, 150, 152, 153, 157, 159, 160, 174, 202, 207

Arab–Israeli conflict 2–4, 12, 13, 27, 45, 77, 78, 83, 84, 102, 105, 106, 108, 115–117, 120, 121, 134, 137, 140, 144, 149, 153, 157, 160, 171, 174, 204

Arafat, Yasser 56, 76, 132, 133, 138

army 6, 27–29, 49, 55, 71, 72, 76, 117, 125, 137, 143, 144, 147, 148, 150, 153–155, 157, 174, 190

audience 11, 25, 49, 56, 65, 79, 87, 88, 100, 102, 112, 122, 129, 130, 139, 146

Baghdad 155

barbaric 4, 5, 75, 76, 115, 202

Beirut 3, 21, 24, 25, 26, 29, 47, 48, 66, 74, 118, 126, 139, 149–151, 154, 157, 182

Bin Laden, Osama 21, 180, 185
binary 4, 9, 12, 18, 22, 53, 54, 64, 85,
    151, 158, 165, 167, 170, 206
Black September 135
bomb (suicide bomb) 3, 21, 24, 37, 66,
    115, 118, 119, 130, 132, 135, 155,
    180, 185, 190
border 19, 26, 27–29, 54, 55, 72, 108,
    111, 112, 130, 132, 144–146, 157,
    182
boundary 12, 25, 29, 37, 41, 54, 61, 80,
    84, 102, 140, 162, 167, 182, 192,
    193, 195, 204

Cairo 17, 25, 33–35, 137, 147, 155,
    180, 190
Camp David 3, 83, 136, 139, 147
censor 11, 151,187
Christian 58, 59, 73, 86, 95, 139, 140,
    141, 168, 189, 192, 193
civilized 4, 5, 78, 114, 176, 180, 198,
    202
collective 24, 46, 59, 63, 80, 111, 112,
    116, 140, 148, 157–159, 175, 178,
    189, 194, 199
colonial (colonize) 9, 16, 18, 19, 27, 38,
    39, 42, 61, 63, 79, 83, 90, 117, 122,
    123, 136, 158, 161, 162, 167, 170,
    174, 183, 198, 203, 204, 206, 208
conquer 6, 8, 27, 42, 60, 64–66, 79, 80,
    110
contest 17, 43–45, 101, 150, 177, 182,
    204
control 3, 5–7, 21, 31–33, 37, 38, 40,
    41, 46, 71, 76, 78, 83, 84, 89, 99,
    102, 114, 130, 184, 199
culture (cultural) 1, 6, 7, 9, 10, 13,
    15–18, 26, 27, 29, 30, 32, 34, 42,
    43, 45, 47, 60, 61, 64, 72–74, 80, 85,
    101–103, 105, 106, 108–110, 112,
    113, 115–117, 120, 121, 123, 131,
    134, 140, 150–152, 158–163,

165–167, 169, 171, 174, 176, 177,
    182, 183, 187, 194, 196–198,
    200–203, 205–208

debate 1, 8, 11, 15, 100
defeat 23, 70, 76, 78, 99, 137, 144, 149,
    153, 155, 176
Der Yassin 48, 141
dialect 6
dialogue 41, 42, 120, 128
diaspora 44, 46, 47, 61, 106, 108–110,
    148–151, 158–160, 204
dichotomy 64, 167, 171, 173, 183, 205
difference (different) 4–6, 8, 10, 11, 13,
    15–17, 19, 22, 24–26, 29, 31, 33, 36,
    42, 44, 45, 52–54, 61, 63, 67, 68, 70,
    73, 79, 80, 84, 87, 90–92, 94, 97,
    104, 105, 108, 111, 115–117, 123,
    140, 146–148, 150, 151, 157–161,
    163, 167–169, 171, 175, 178, 190,
    192–209
discourse 3–5, 7, 8, 9, 17, 48, 54, 63,
    64, 66, 75, 79, 80, 90, 104, 105, 107,
    110, 112–115, 117, 126, 130, 134,
    157–162, 166, 168, 172–174, 182,
    200, 202–209
diversity (diverse) 108, 110, 116, 152,
    167, 168, 169, 208
divide (division) 3, 45, 47, 55, 56, 78,
    83, 108, 117, 120, 135, 146, 147,
    150, 151, 155, 156, 169, 172,194,
    202, 206, 208
dominance (dominant) 4, 5, 9, 32–34,
    37, 45, 65, 89, 91, 106–108, 117,
    126, 130, 151, 157, 162, 166, 170,
    182, 202, 204, 205, 207, 209
East/West divide/dichotomy 4, 8, 10,
    13, 167, 171, 173, 183, 197, 200,
    202, 203, 205, 209

Eastoxification 9
economic 10, 40, 41, 45, 60, 70, 80,

109, 120, 122, 149–151, 158, 160,
162, 168, 182, 183, 187, 203
Egypt (Egyptian) 2–6, 9, 11–13, 16, 17,
33, 34, 36, 37, 39–46, 60, 63, 64, 69,
70, 81–88, 90, 91, 98–100, 102,
104–108, 113, 121–123, 134–140,
144, 147, 148, 150–153, 155, 157,
159, 160, 167, 170, 172, 173,
183–185, 187–199, 202–204, 206,
208, 209
enemy 12, 13, 21, 22, 33, 43, 54, 64,
73, 81, 83, 84, 102, 104, 107, 119,
121, 137, 140, 165, 166, 176–178,
184, 193, 199, 203, 208
essential (-ist, -ism) 5, 13, 25, 26, 32,
33, 53, 60, 63, 65, 73, 74, 77, 78, 83,
86, 87, 90, 98, 102–104, 106, 107,
111, 115, 121, 122, 151, 161–163,
165, 166, 174, 177, 178, 180, 188,
192–194, 196–198, 200, 203, 205,
207–209
ethnic 13, 31, 34, 71, 80, 86, 106–111,
113, 115–117, 134, 151, 157, 160,
175, 191, 194, 195, 206
exclusion (exclude) 13, 29, 30, 36, 41,
42, 81, 102, 111, 112, 117, 160, 170,
175, 177, 188, 190, 192, 199, 200,
202, 206
exile 42, 44, 46–48, 96, 110, 125, 136,
150, 153

fear 6, 22, 23, 26, 95, 96, 100, 101
foreign policy 8, 27, 65, 182
Foucault, Michel 3, 16, 29, 53, 173
fundamentalism (see Islamic
fundamentalism)

gaze 9, 19, 33, 43, 56, 60, 79, 87–89,
98, 100, 102, 131
global 1, 2, 11, 13, 42, 43, 61, 103, 107,
158, 159, 167, 168, 174, 179, 182,
183, 199

globalization (globalize) 13, 39, 43,
152, 171, 179, 197, 204, 209
Gulf 8, 11, 69, 70, 76, 102, 148, 156,
177
Gulf War 2, 3, 8, 12, 13, 22, 23, 27, 65,
70, 71, 72, 76, 77, 97, 105, 108, 120,
134, 140, 147, 155–157, 171, 174,
176–178, 181, 204

Hamas 3, 78
hegemony (hegemonic) 6–8, 32, 45,
106, 161, 168, 170, 172, 193, 199,
heterogeneity (heterogeneous) 8, 111,
116, 150, 157, 159, 176, 193, 205,
hijack (hijacker, hijacking) 3, 5, 26, 28,
73, 112, 114, 115, 118, 158, 174,
179, 182, 183
history (historical) 2–4, 8, 9, 12, 13,
15, 16, 18, 32, 36, 43–45, 48, 53,
60, 64, 72, 74, 80, 81, 90, 103, 107,
109–111, 113, 114, 116–118, 119,
126, 128, 130, 135, 138–140, 147,
150, 151, 153, 158–163, 168, 175,
177, 179, 181, 182, 191, 198, 199,
202, 205, 208
Hizbullah 3, 26, 74, 140
Hollywood 1, 2, 4–13, 15, 16, 18, 19,
31–33, 60, 64, 76, 78, 102–104, 106,
108, 110, 112, 115, 120, 122, 158,
159, 161, 162, 166, 173–181, 184,
188–190, 193, 196, 197, 199,
200–206, 208, 209
homogeneity (homogenous,
homogenize) 32, 61, 104, 108, 111,
112, 114–116, 121, 158, 159, 166,
188, 193, 199, 208,

ideal (idealize) 32, 37, 43, 46, 56, 67,
80, 81, 102, 174, 175
identity 3, 5, 11, 15–18, 27, 29, 32, 37,
41, 44, 46, 64, 69, 71, 76, 83–85, 91,
102, 111, 114–116, 121, 140, 148,

158, 159, 162, 163, 167, 168, 170, 172–174, 175, 177, 178, 188, 189, 192–196, 199–202, 204, 206–209 (see also national identity)

ideology (ideological) 3, 7, 8, 19, 22, 24, 26, 29, 31, 32, 37, 44, 80, 108, 110, 111, 112, 117, 119, 151, 153, 160, 168, 170, 171, 173–175, 177–179, 193, 194, 204, 209

image (imagination) 1, 2, 6, 7, 12, 15–20, 22, 27, 29, 30, 31–34, 41, 42, 44–47, 50, 52–54, 57, 60, 61, 63, 64, 67, 68, 70, 74, 78, 81, 90, 97, 98, 100, 102, 106, 107, 112, 113, 114, 116, 122, 127, 128, 143, 147, 150, 151, 154, 155, 157, 162, 167, 174, 175, 180–182, 184, 189, 191, 193, 194, 197, 198, 201, 202, 204

imperial 9, 16, 33, 40–42, 73, 86, 121, 122, 146, 152, 158, 161, 166, 195, 203, 204–206, 208

individual 24, 39, 41, 42, 48, 60, 71, 79, 103, 111, 126, 130, 158, 159, 178, 188, 194

inferiority (inferior) 5, 8, 102, 117, 119, 162, 198, 207

innocence (innocent) 9, 55–57, 66, 72, 87, 88, 119, 146, 148, 150, 179, 186–188, 190, 192,

intifada 3, 50, 51, 109, 126, 147, 151, 162, 208

Islam (Islamic, Muslim) 3, 4, 10, 13, 37, 58, 82, 83, 86, 89, 90, 139–141, 165, 166, 168–175, 178–180, 182–184, 186, 187, 191, 192, 195–197

Islamic fundamentalism (Islamism) 2–4, 6, 12, 13, 17, 20, 26, 33, 34, 36, 37, 39–42, 61, 64, 81, 86, 87–91, 95, 96, 102, 104, 151, 165, 166–175, 177–186, 190–199, 201, 203–206, 208, 209

Iran 3, 27, 72, 140, 157, 168, 175–177, 193, 197

Iraq (Iraqi) 1, 5, 22, 23, 26–28, 70–72, 75, 77, 120, 147, 148, 155–157, 165, 177, 178, 180, 181, 202

Israel (Israeli) 1–4, 12, 13, 17, 26, 27, 33, 43–47, 49–52, 54–56, 58, 63, 69, 70, 73, 74, 77–81, 83–85, 92–95, 97–102, 105–145, 147–153, 156–162, 171, 174, 185, 193, 202, 204, 206

Jew 52, 58, 59, 73, 107, 108, 109, 110, 112–119, 123, 131, 132, 137–139, 156, 158–160, 174, 180, 182, 205

Jihad 170, 178, 180,

Jordan 99, 135, 138, 141, 150, 157,

knowledge 3, 7, 16, 31, 32, 53, 204

Kuwait 70, 120, 147, 148, 151, 155, 156

lack 5, 12, 21, 40, 49, 65, 73, 78, 82, 99, 110, 126, 152, 153, 169, 174, 198

language (linguistic) 77, 108, 110, 113, 140, 152, 157, 179, 180, 194

Lebanon (Lebanese) 2, 3, 11, 21, 24, 26, 27, 30, 46–49, 54, 55, 61, 74, 100, 105, 114, 115, 124, 125, 134, 139, 140, 143, 145, 148, 150–156, 160, 204

local 12, 16, 37, 39, 43, 55, 61, 71, 74, 110, 124, 141, 142, 153, 154, 158, 171, 179, 183, 199, 204

Libya 22, 23, 50, 176, 182

margin 18, 32, 39, 45, 47, 48, 52, 53, 61, 79, 113, 174, 195, 209 (see also periphery)

Middle East (Middle Eastern) 1–6, 8–13, 15, 16, 18, 19, 26, 32, 43, 58, 59, 64, 70, 74, 77, 78, 80, 83, 102, 105, 107, 114, 118, 119, 121, 145,

149, 156, 165, 175, 181, 185, 193, 195, 201, 202, 204, 207, 209

military (militant) 8, 21–23, 26, 27, 30, 49, 55, 64, 69–71, 73, 74, 76, 78, 80, 86, 98–101, 116–119, 124, 130, 135, 147, 166, 169–171, 180

modern 1, 3, 4, 12, 24, 57, 64, 81, 82, 91, 97, 102, 104, 115, 125, 162, 171–173, 191, 195, 197, 198, 207, 208

monolithic 6, 54, 80, 165, 175, 184, 188

moral (immoral, morality) 5, 8, 9, 12, 24, 65, 71, 80, 81, 83–88, 102, 103, 120, 136, 160, 166, 171, 172, 185–188, 195, 198, 207

Morocco (Moroccan) 2, 11, 105, 134, 156

Muslim (see Islam)

myth 9, 25, 30, 41, 44, 56, 63, 64, 106, 108–110, 115, 116, 117, 125, 134–136, 163, 165–167, 174–177, 179, 180, 198, 203

Al-Nakba 141 (see also 1948)

narrative 3, 11, 22, 63, 90, 103, 105, 128, 146, 148, 150, 158, 162, 163, 166, 175, 204, 206

Nasser, Gamal Abdel 45, 46, 69, 81, 82, 106, 107, 134–138, 141, 149, 170, 174, 184, 191, 208, 209

nation 6, 10–12, 15, 24, 26, 29, 33, 41, 42, 44, 45, 61, 63–66, 68, 69–73, 75, 77, 78, 80–86, 90, 93, 101–104, 106, 109, 110, 112, 113, 115–117, 122, 138, 146–149, 151, 156, 160, 162, 166–169, 174–178, 191, 194, 195, 197–199, 201, 203, 205, 207–209

national (nationalism) 11–13, 17, 33, 34, 37, 39, 41, 43, 45, 47, 48, 55, 60, 61, 63, 64, 69, 71, 72, 74, 76, 80, 81, 83, 85, 90, 91, 97–111, 113, 117, 121, 122, 134–136, 138, 140, 142,

144, 145, 147, 149, 150, 151, 153, 157–160, 162, 167, 170, 171, 173–175, 177, 179, 182, 184, 186–188, 191–196, 199–203, 205–209

national identity 37, 69, 71, 91, 102, 121, 177, 196, 199, 201, 207, 208

New World Order 8

nostalgia 26, 39, 43–48, 120, 121, 134, 141, 144, 160

object (objectify, objectivity) 6, 7, 9, 10, 17–19, 21, 26, 28, 33, 60, 78, 79, 87, 89, 98, 100, 102, 116

Occident (Occidental) 6, 7, 75, 114, 166

occupy (occupied) 23, 44, 47, 82–84, 92, 93, 99, 110, 111, 117, 126, 127, 129, 135, 139, 145, 156, 161, 204

October War 4, 98, 134, 135, 149 (see also Yom Kippur, 1973)

oil 4, 69, 70, 76, 102, 144, 147, 156

oppress (repress) 2, 12, 13, 27, 41, 42, 51–53, 64, 65, 81, 87, 90, 91, 95, 102, 104, 108, 113, 116, 124, 126, 130, 134, 158, 159, 161, 162, 184, 188, 189–191, 193, 195, 204

Orientalism (Orient, Oriental) 1, 4–10, 13, 26, 57, 63, 69, 73–75, 78, 79, 89, 90, 98, 102, 104, 114, 120, 124, 160, 161, 166, 171–173, 178, 180, 188, 192, 200, 202, 205–207

Orientalism (Edward Said) 5, 10, 18, 202

Other (Otherness) 2, 4, 5, 7–10, 12, 13, 16–21, 23–33, 37, 54, 55, 60, 63, 64, 65, 67, 68, 72, 73, 75–81, 83–87, 89, 90, 101, 102, 104, 107, 115, 150, 151, 161, 165–168, 171, 173, 174, 176, 177, 179, 180, 182–185, 188, 192, 195, 196, 198–206, 208, 209

Palestine (Palestinian) 1–4, 11–13, 17, 44–58, 60, 61, 63, 64, 77–79, 85,

91–95, 97–100, 102, 105–154, 156–162, 165, 185, 202–204, 206, 208

pan-Arab, pan-Arabism, pan-Arab nationalism (see Arabism)

past 2, 15, 39, 43, 46, 64, 110, 113, 116, 117, 141, 159, 160, 162, 163, 173, 194, 199, 207, 208

peace 3, 13, 43, 46, 56, 58, 65, 78, 79, 83, 84, 95, 107, 114, 115, 119–121, 123, 129, 135, 136, 138, 139, 141, 157, 159, 192, 193, 202

periphery 12, 17, 18, 29, 31, 117, 199, 204 (see also margin)

petrol (see oil)

plane 3, 5, 19, 20, 23, 26, 28, 29, 31, 73, 76, 112, 115, 118, 119, 138, 144, 174, 179, 183, 196

PLO (Palestine Liberation Organization) 3, 51, 99, 110, 111, 114, 115, 150, 151, 154, 155

possession 6, 7, 23, 84, 89, 173, 177, 194

post-colonial(-ism) 108, 117, 157, 158, 160, 161, 167, 170, 182, 205, 206

power 1–3, 5, 7, 10, 13, 15–18, 21, 27, 31, 32, 33, 36–38, 40, 41, 43, 44, 46, 47, 52–54, 65, 67, 69, 70, 72, 79, 80, 89, 91, 95, 100–103, 106, 112, 118–120, 122, 130, 131, 138, 145, 150, 155, 157–159, 161, 163, 166–171, 174, 177, 187, 201, 206, 209

psychology (psychological) 13, 91, 112, 125, 169, 184, 188, 189, 197

refuge (refugee) 37, 47, 48, 52–54, 61, 89, 95, 99, 110, 127, 141–143, 146, 148, 149, 153, 154, 159, 160, 188, 190, 204

region (regional) 1, 2, 4, 5, 9, 11, 13, 16, 71, 110, 117, 120, 134, 140, 152, 153, 157, 159, 175, 181, 202

religion (religious) 6, 24, 37, 44, 58, 73, 74, 89, 90, 93, 107–109, 113, 116, 120, 138, 140, 152, 157, 168–171, 173, 175, 179, 186, 187, 190–194, 197, 202, 203, 209

repress (see oppress)

rescue 5, 8, 21, 23, 24, 26–28, 46, 65, 66, 69, 72, 75, 98, 115, 118, 120, 122, 153, 154

resist (resistance, resistant) 4, 6, 8–10, 18, 33, 36, 42, 44, 45, 48–50, 52, 53, 91–93, 95, 97–100, 104, 108, 111, 117, 118, 120, 121, 126–129, 131, 139, 143, 147, 148, 150, 151, 153, 154, 158, 161, 162, 170, 172, 201–205, 207, 209

revolution 3, 4, 79, 82, 83, 97, 99, 111, 118, 136–138, 193

Sadat, Anwar 3, 69, 83, 107, 136, 138, 139, 147, 187, 193

Said, Edward 3, 5–10, 18, 152, 166, 169, 172, 173, 200, 202, 209

Saudi Arabia 20, 21, 168, 170, 180

secular 91, 116, 168–171, 177, 183, 186, 192

self 4, 9, 27, 28, 30, 32, 37, 41, 54, 55, 60, 76, 83, 84, 86, 102, 103, 107, 108, 159, 160, 170, 174, 178, 187, 193, 199, 204, 205, 208, 2–9

September 11 1, 3, 31,

sexuality (sexual) 7, 12, 35, 36, 41, 63, 65, 71, 77–81, 83–86, 88, 89, 91, 98, 102, 104, 122, 184, 186, 190

silence (silent) 7, 12, 36, 81, 90, 91, 102, 115, 124, 129, 130, 150, 155, 156, 160, 181, 191, 195

Six Day War 69, 138, 144, 149 (see also 1967)

society (social) 2, 4, 6–8, 10, 13, 15, 17, 18, 23, 24, 29, 32, 33, 34, 37, 41, 42, 47, 53, 58, 61, 65, 76, 80, 82, 83, 91, 93, 97, 99, 100, 103, 109, 111, 112, 114–116, 120, 140, 144, 150, 153, 158, 160, 162, 165, 168, 169, 170, 171, 173, 175, 177, 178, 182, 186, 192, 194–196, 198, 204, 205, 208

status quo 7

stereotype (stereotyping) 10, 78, 79, 101, 166, 198

subjectivity (subjective) 4, 7, 17, 19, 34, 36, 105, 158, 159, 200

subordinate 81, 91, 108, 161, 177

Suez 136, 147, 208

suicide bomb (see bomb)

superiority (superior) 5, 6, 13, 21, 25, 72, 77, 107, 117, 119, 120, 166, 168, 178, 195

symbol 6, 12, 22, 25, 33, 34, 37, 41, 44, 52, 56, 63, 64, 67, 69, 70, 72, 74, 76–78, 80, 81, 83–86, 90–93, 98, 104, 116, 123, 126, 127, 142, 147–149, 162, 167, 176, 177, 193, 195, 198, 199, 202, 208

Syria (Syrian) 2, 11, 13, 100, 105, 107, 108, 114, 121, 134, 138, 141–144, 154, 159, 160

Tehran 182

terror (terrorism, -ist) 4, 5, 7, 8, 13, 19, 20, 24–26, 28–32, 40, 66–69, 73, 74, 78, 79, 86, 87, 90, 95–97, 107, 113–115, 118, 119, 122, 126, 165, 166, 169, 173–186, 189, 190, 193, 196–198, 201, 203, 209

tradition 23, 24, 26, 27, 30, 33, 54, 57, 63, 64, 69, 70, 90, 97–99, 101, 106, 110, 123, 130, 131, 167, 168, 172, 173, 176, 180, 192, 198, 203, 205, 207

trauma 47, 65, 99, 141, 151, 188, 197

treaty 13, 46, 107, 121–123, 135, 147, 202

truth 2, 4, 6, 71, 125, 143, 148, 167, 168, 171–173, 200

Tunisia (Tunisian) 2, 11, 58, 59, 105, 121, 135, 155, 157

United Nations (UN) 23, 146

unified 33, 52, 80, 108, 112, 115, 135, 136, 152, 161, 174, 175, 177, 178, 208

uniformity (uniform) 6, 8, 17, 49, 50, 76, 99–101, 150, 161, 180, 181, 183, 205

United States (USA) 3, 4, 7–9, 12, 13, 16, 20, 23, 29, 30, 32, 39, 42, 61, 63–66, 69–78, 86, 97, 102, 107, 108, 112, 117–120, 136, 138, 147, 151, 152, 157, 159, 161,166, 168, 171, 175, 177, 178, 180, 182, 185, 193, 197, 198, 201–203, 206, 207, 209 (see also America)

unity 8, 32, 45, 55, 73, 108, 116, 118, 135, 138, 144, 152, 155, 157, 159, 193, 197

veil 7, 12, 24, 25, 81, 88, 90, 91, 94–96, 102, 142, 172, 202

victim 5, 10, 28, 32, 45, 55, 86, 110, 113, 114, 121, 122, 126, 147, 152, 156, 160, 161, 179,

war 1–4, 8, 12, 13, 21–23, 26, 27, 43, 46–48, 54, 58, 59, 65, 69–72, 74, 76, 77, 97, 98, 100, 105–108, 118, 120, 122, 134–140, 144, 147, 149, 152–157, 160, 165, 170, 171, 174, 176–178, 180, 181, 204, 208

World Trade Center 3, 179, 180, 185,

Yemen 19, 20, 22, 68, 69
Yom Kippur 63 (see also October War, 1973)

Zion 73, 107, 110, 112, 115, 117, 131, 138, 141, 147, 153, 159, 160, 193, 205

Index of Films

11'09"01 – September 11 177, 185
48 Hours in Israel 98, 101, 135,
The Ambassador 77–79, 110, 112, 114,
   115, 118, 119, 162
Bab el-Oued City 37, 38, 184, 187, 192,
   193, 196, 198
Birds of Darkness 90, 184, 186, 187,
   190, 191, 195, 196
Black Rain 69
Borders 144–146
Bowling for Columbine 9
Canticle of the Stones 123, 153
Chronicle of a Disappearance 126–131
The Closed Doors 186, 188, 189,
   191
Coming to America 180
Courage Under Fire 22, 26, 70, 77, 103,
   208
Curfew 51
Days of Sadat 138, 139, 187, 193
The Delta Force 24–26, 28, 66, 73, 110,
   112–114, 118, 119, 174, 175, 178,
   179, 182, 183, 209
Destiny 36, 189, 191, 196, 205
Die Hard 64
Divine Intervention 126, 129, 130, 131,
   133, 134
Don Juan de Marco 7
The Door to the Sun 92, 99, 123, 153
The Emigrant 191
Execution of a Dead Man 84, 135

Executive Decision 28, 66, 73, 115, 175,
   176, 178, 179, 182, 183, 196
Fahrenheit 9/11 9
The Fertile Memory 50, 92, 93, 139
Girl from Israel 43, 84, 85, 102, 122
The Gulf War. . . What Next? 11, 105,
   155
The Guys 177
Hello America 9, 148, 151, 159, 184
Hero from the South 139
Hostage 5, 28, 66, 73, 175, 178–183,
   209
Hot Shots 181
Hot Shots! Part Deux 181
Hysteria 190
In the Army Now 8, 22, 26, 31, 75,
   182
In the Ninth Month 97, 124
Iron Eagle 20, 66, 180, 181
The Insider 24, 25
Into the Sun 23, 66, 76, 178
Jesus of Nazareth 157
Killing Streets 24, 26, 66, 73
Kite 54
The Little Drummer Girl 77–79, 107,
   111–113, 117, 118, 162
Love in Taba 84, 85, 122
The Matrix 132
The Milky Way 149, 158
Mission in Tel-Aviv 98, 135
The Mummy 5, 6

Naji Al-Ali 44, 45, 47, 48, 98, 100, 101, 148–151, 158–160, 162

Nasser 56 44, 45, 106, 136, 138, 208

Nasser 44, 45, 82, 136, 137, 184, 208

Navy Seals 8, 21, 24–26, 66, 74, 182, 196

The Nights of the Jackal 144, 145

October 49

The Olive Harvest 54, 55

The Other 33, 34, 39, 40, 42, 86, 89, 90,185, 188–190, 191, 193, 196, 197, 209

Power 23, 24, 69, 70, 76

Programmed to Kill 24–26, 66, 119, 175, 178, 179

Rachida 37, 95, 96, 186, 192, 195, 196, 198

Rambo: First Blood 69

Rana's Wedding 93, 94, 126

Refuge 141

Rocky IV 64

Road to Eilat 44, 45, 98, 99, 122, 135

Rules of Engagement 20, 22, 24, 25, 66, 68, 103, 208

The Sheik 8

The Siege 6, 20, 21, 24, 28, 29, 30, 31, 33, 77–79, 119, 174, 175, 177, 179, 180, 196, 198, 207

South Park 76

Spy Game 24, 25, 66, 73, 74

A Summer in la Goulette 58, 59

Tale of Three Jewels 126–128

Team America: World Police 180

The Tempest 105, 147, 155

The Terminator 69

Terrorism and Barbecue 87, 88, 184, 186, 188, 191, 194, 196, 198

The Terrorist 33–35, 89, 90, 172, 184, 186, 189–193, 195, 196

Three Kings 5, 8, 23, 26, 27, 31, 69, 71, 75, 103, 178, 180

Ticket to Jerusalem 52, 53

Trap of Spies 84, 122, 135, 136

Triumph of the Will 19

True Lies 6, 28, 29, 66, 67, 73

Wedding in Galilee 49, 51, 95, 126